Laptop & Tablet Basics

Windows 8 Edition

Joli Ballew

Use your laptop or tablet with confidence

Get to grips with practical tasks with minimal time, fuss and bother.

In *Simple Steps guides* guarantee immediate results. They tell you everything you need to know on a specific application; from the most essential tasks to master, to every activity you'll want to accomplish, through to solving the most common problems you'll encounter.

Helpful features

To build your confidence and help you to get the most out of your laptop or tablet, practical hints, tips and shortcuts feature on every page:

ALERT: Explains and provides practical solutions to the most commonly encountered problems

HOT TIP: Time and effort saving shortcuts

SEE ALSO: Points you to other related tasks and information

DID YOU KNOW? Additional features to explore

WHAT DOES THIS MEAN?
Jargon and technical terms explained in plain English

Practical. Simple. Fast.

Dedication:

For Neil Salkind, Ph.D., friend, mentor, literary agent. Enjoy your retirement!

Author acknowledgments:

I love writing books for Pearson. Steve Temblett, Rob Cottee, Viv Church and the rest of the gang are great to work with. They take my simple Word documents and meticulously edit, place and replace my text and images to produce a beautiful book complete with four-colour photos and easy-to-read pages. We've had a great run of titles and I hope to work again with them in the future. I am thankful to everyone at Pearson and for the opportunities they've given me, and I am thankful to you, gentle reader, for putting your faith in me and my abilities to teach you something about your new laptop or tablet (and hopefully whet your appetite for more).

I am thankful for many other things, too, and I am fully aware of all of the blessings in my life. My 92-year-old father is still alive, although he now lives in a memory care facility. This is endurable because he is always happy, he eats anything they feed him, and he is still quite independent. I myself have been blessed with good health and a great doctor, and even though I'm nearing 50, show no signs of slowing down. I have a wonderful family, including Jennifer, Andrew, Dad and Cosmo, and a brand new granddaughter, Allison. We look out for each other and manage life day by day. We celebrate the good things that happen to us and gloss over the bad.

I am also thankful to my agent, Neil Salkind, from Studio B and the Salkind Literary Agency. He always looks out for me, provides new opportunities, and forces me to think out of the box when it comes to new projects. There's always a new technology or gadget, a new publisher, or a new book series to discover. Neil has my back, and offers unconditional support. Even when I'm wrong, I'm right, at least in his eyes. I doubt many people have someone like that in their lives.

Publisher acknowledgments:

The publishers are grateful to the following for permission to reproduce copyright material:

Adobe product screenshots reprinted with permission from Adobe Systems Incorporated. Microsoft screenshots reprinted by permission of Microsoft Corporation. Satellite Signals Ltd (www.satsig.net) for permission to reproduce the screenshot on page 75.

Contents at a glance

9 Configure and use Mail

10 Personalise Windows 8

11 Explore Media apps

12 Stay in touch with others

13 Access and use online stores

14 Manage, protect, secure and restore your device

15 Tips for tablet users

Top 10 Laptop & Tablet Problems Solved

Contents

Top 10 Laptop & Tablet Tips

1 Explore your laptop and tablet

2 Learn Windows 8 essentials

3 Explore Start screen apps and personalise their tiles

4 Use the Internet Explorer Start screen app

5 Get an always-available Internet connection

6 Perform computer basics on the Desktop

7 Explore Desktop apps

8 Use the Internet Explorer Desktop app

9 Configure and use Mail

10 Personalise Windows 8

11 Explore Media apps

12 Stay in touch with others

13 Access and use online stores

14 Manage, protect, secure and restore your device

Top 10 Laptop & Tablet Problems Solved

Top 10 Laptop & Tablet Tips

Tip 1: Connect to a Wi-Fi network

You may have connected your laptop to your home Wi-Fi network during set-up, but if you didn't it's easy to do. You'll use this same technique to access a free, Wi-Fi hotspot at a café, library, hotel or pub.

1. Press the Windows key + C to access the charms. Click Settings.
2. Click Available.

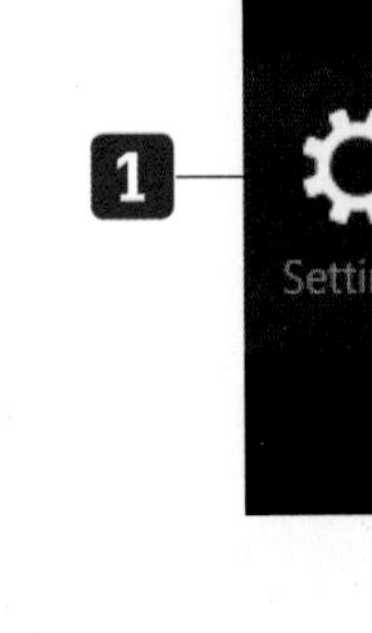

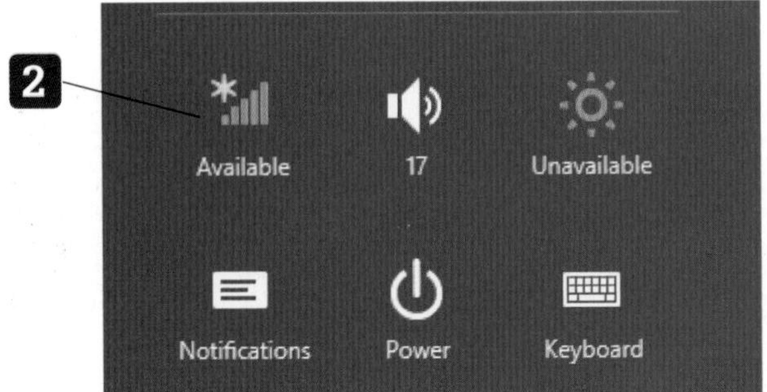

3. Click the desired network from the list and click Connect.
4. Place a tick by Connect automatically and if applicable type the required password. Click Next.
5. Choose your sharing option. For a home or other trusted network, click Yes, turn on sharing and connect to devices. For any other network, choose No, do not turn on sharing and connect to devices.

SEE ALSO: Chapter 14: Manage, protect, secure and restore your laptop for more information on network sharing options.

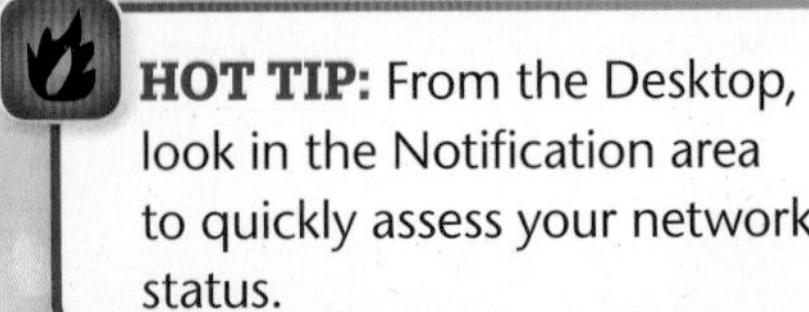

HOT TIP: From the Desktop, look in the Notification area to quickly assess your network status.

Tip 2: Move among open apps

You may have lots of Start screen apps open at any given time. That's okay because open apps don't use any system resources when you aren't using them. However, you do need to know how to get back to those apps when you are ready to use them again. Although you can always return to the Start screen and tap the app icon, there are better ways.

If you have a keyboard and mouse, try these techniques while on any screen or in any app:

- Hold down the Alt key and press the Tab key to show a row of open apps. Press Tab repeatedly until you get to the app you want to use, then let go.

- Position your mouse in the top left corner of the screen to view and click the last used app, or drag the mouse downwards slowly to view the other available apps to access those.

HOT TIP: If you have a touch screen, flick inwards with your thumb from the left side of the screen to move to a previously used app.

? DID YOU KNOW?

You can use the Alt + Tab and Windows + Tab combinations on older computers, too (like Windows 7). You won't move through apps, but you will move through open windows.

Tip 3: Pin your favourite Desktop apps to the taskbar

If there is a Desktop app you use often and you don't want to have to access the Start screen to find it each time you need it, you can pin the app's icon to the taskbar on the Desktop.

1. Locate the app's icon on the Start screen or the All apps screen.
2. Right-click the icon.
3. Click Pin to taskbar.

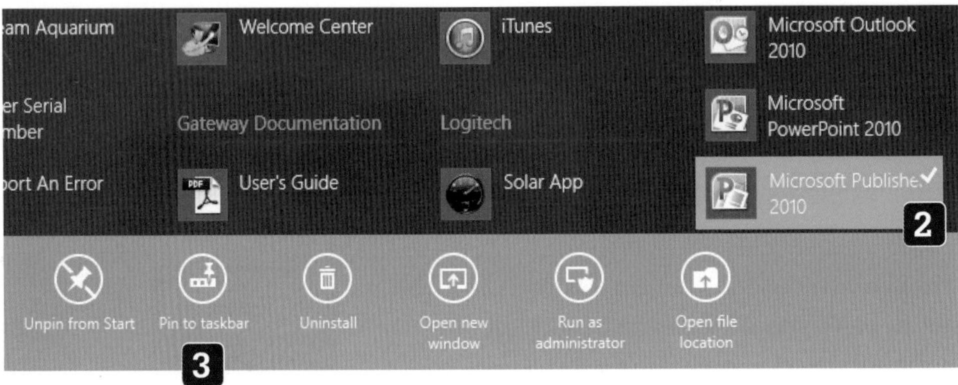

4. Return to the Desktop to see the item on the taskbar.

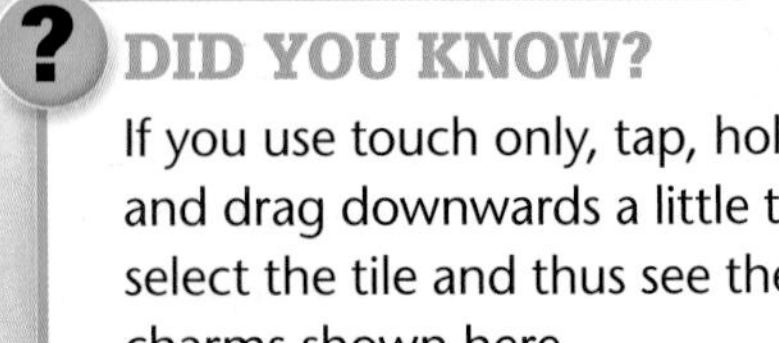

Tip 4: Format email text

Formatting options are hidden away in the Mail toolbar. You access those options with a right-click of a mouse or track pad, or a flick upwards with your finger on a touch screen. Once the options are available, you apply them as you would any formatting tools in any word-processing program.

1. Compose a new email, then click in the body pane.
2. Right-click to see the formatting options. (Note that you can click More to see additional options.)

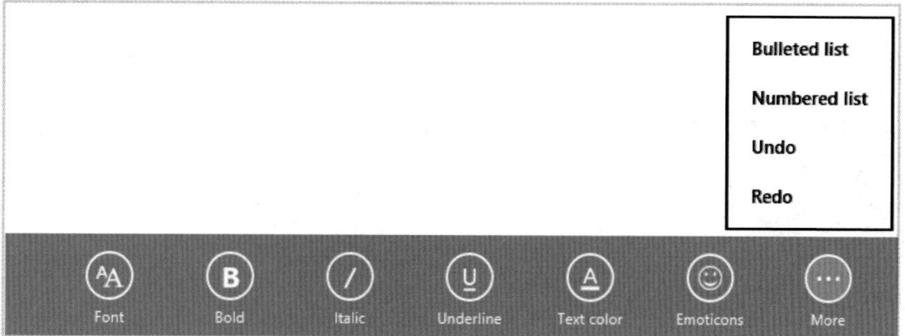

3. Click any formatting option (perhaps Bold) and then click another (perhaps Italic).
4. Click Font and choose a new font and font size.
5. Type a few words in the body of the email.

DID YOU KNOW?
If you apply formatting options without any text selected, those options will be applied to all future text until you change it. If you select text and then apply formatting, the formatting is applied to the selected text only.

ALERT: If the new font choices aren't applied when you type, try clicking in a new line, pressing Enter to go to a new line, or click under the signature. Sometimes this type of application of the formatting tools is a little tricky.

Tip 5: Log on faster: create a PIN

When you log in to your Windows 8 device, you have to type a password. This can become tiring after a while, especially if you don't have a physical keyboard. Even if you do have a keyboard, typing a complex password still takes time. You can change your login requirements so that you need only enter a numeric personal identification number (PIN) instead.

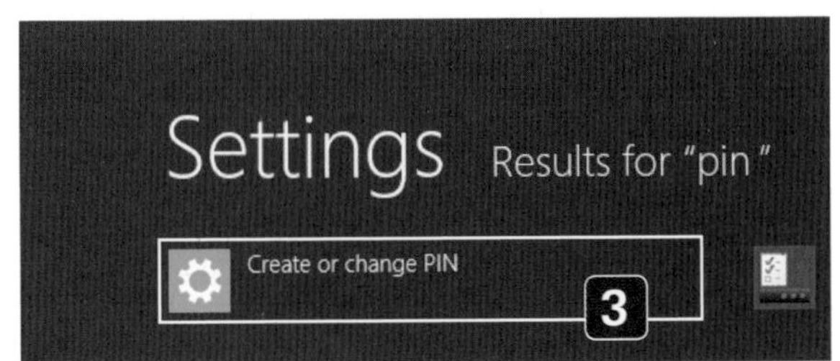

1. At the Start screen, type PIN. (If you don't have access to a physical keyboard, from the Settings charm, tap Keyboard and select a keyboard option.)
2. On the right side of the screen, click Settings.
3. Click Create or change PIN.
4. Click Create a PIN.
5. Type your current password, click OK, then enter the desired PIN twice.
6. Click Finish.

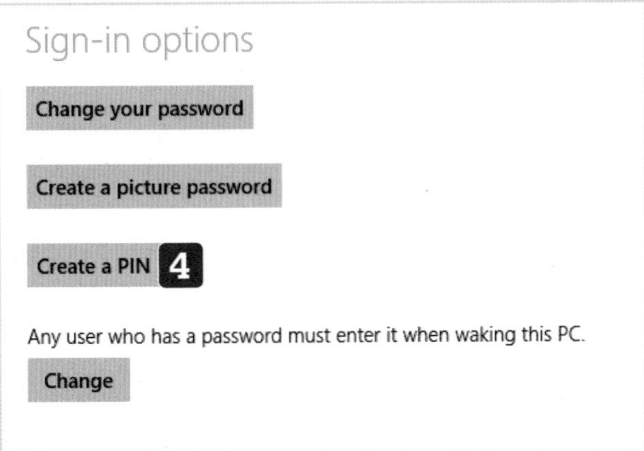

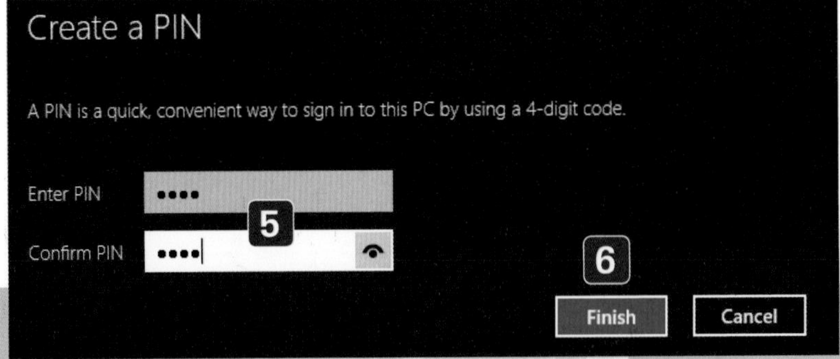

HOT TIP: When creating a PIN, try to avoid things like 12345 or 9876. Avoid using your birthday, too. (Make it at least a little difficult to guess!)

HOT TIP: You create a PIN in PC Settings. You can use this same interface to configure many of the other available personalisation options.

Tip 6: Share with the Public folder

Windows 8 comes with Public folders you can use to share data easily with others on your network or others who share your computer. The Public folders are located on your local disk, generally C:, under Users.

1. From the Desktop, open File Explorer.
2. Click Computer, double-click the disk that contains your data and double-click Users.
3. Double-click the Public folder.
4. Now save, move or copy data to these folders as desired.

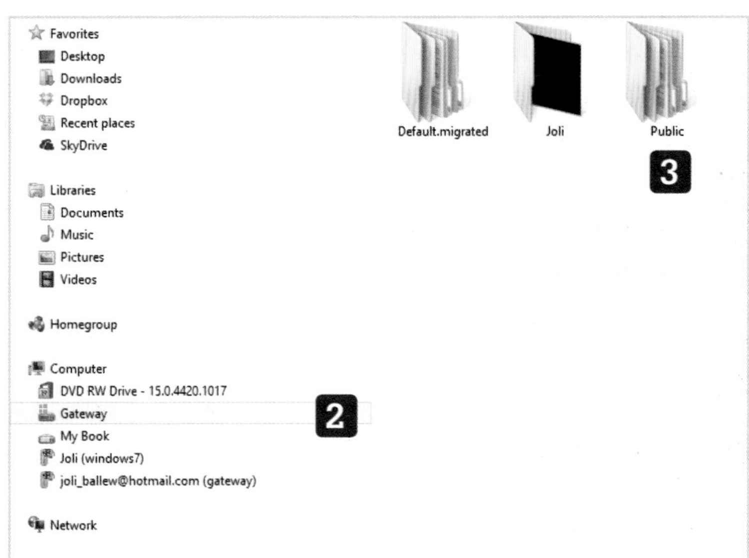

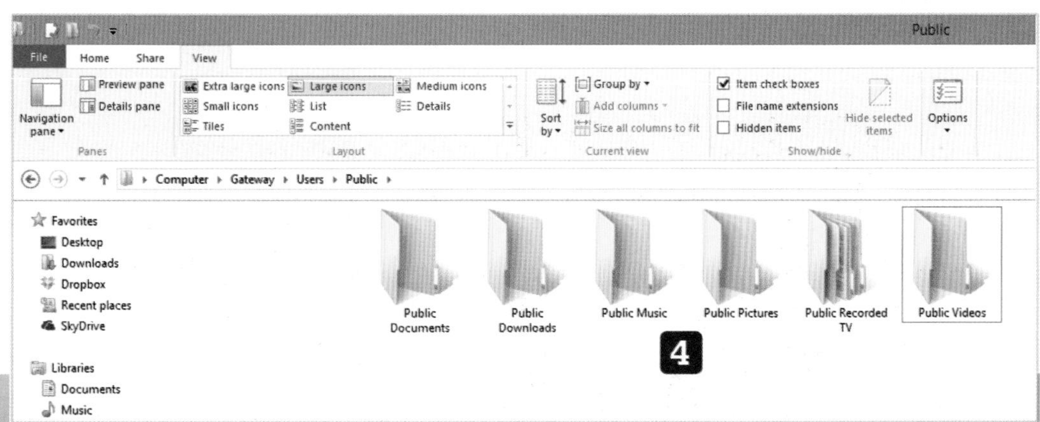

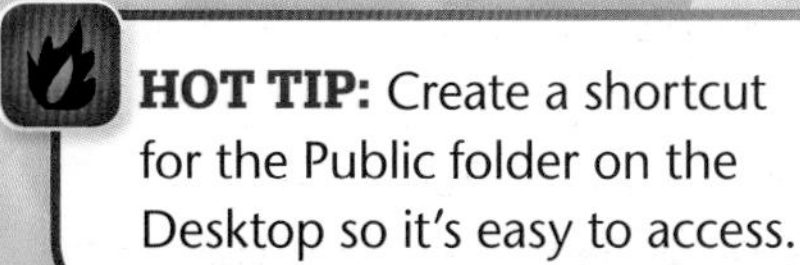

HOT TIP: Create a shortcut for the Public folder on the Desktop so it's easy to access.

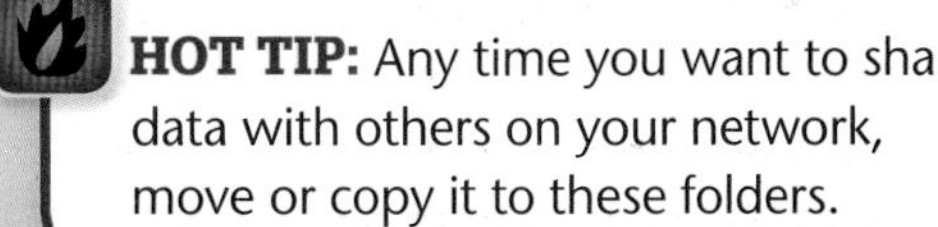

HOT TIP: Any time you want to share data with others on your network, move or copy it to these folders.

Tip 7: Add a social network to the People app

You can add information about the social networks you belong to while inside the People app. When you do, you can see their status updates, access their contact information, send them email and messages, and more. It's a great way to populate a new laptop with contacts.

1. While inside the People app, access the default charms (Windows key + C or flick inwards).
2. Click the Settings charm and then click Accounts.
3. Click Add an account.
4. Choose the account from the resulting list.
5. Click Connect and input the required information.

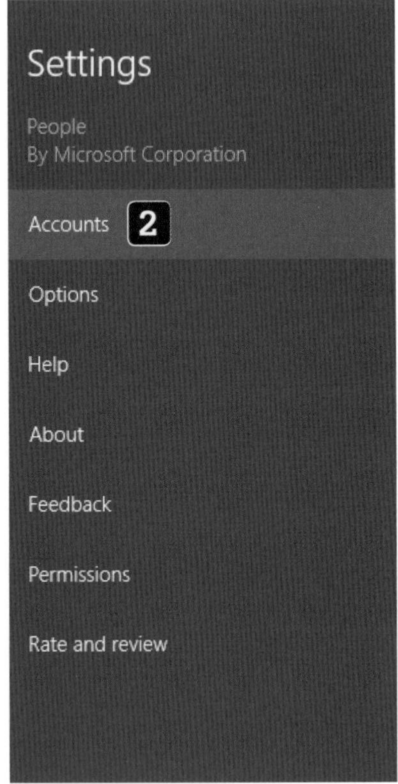

HOT TIP: You may not have to input this information if you've already input it for other apps. Once you tell Windows 8 something, it remembers it!

DID YOU KNOW?
If you position your mouse in the bottom right corner of the People app and click the – sign that appears, the screen will change from the large tiles you currently see for your contacts to small, alphabetic tiles you can use to go directly to groups of contacts.

Tip 8: Choose the proper power plan

All Windows 8 computers are set to use a specific power plan. This means that after a predetermined period of time, the display will dim and the hard drive will sleep. (There are two sets of settings: one for when the device is plugged in and one for when it is running on batteries.) In addition, some power plans restrict specific resources more than others to lengthen battery life. If you aren't happy with your computer's performance or you feel your battery is being drained too quickly, you can change this behaviour.

1. From the Start screen, type Power.
2. Click Settings and click Power Options.
3. Next to the selected plan (or any other), click Change plan settings.

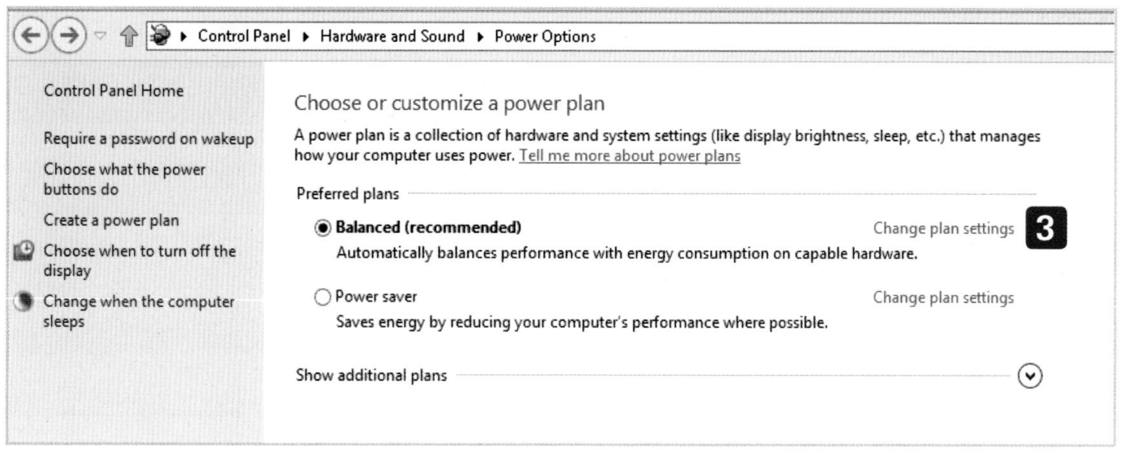

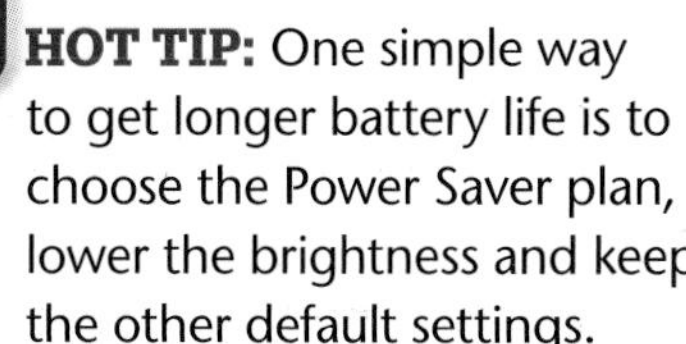

HOT TIP: One simple way to get longer battery life is to choose the Power Saver plan, lower the brightness and keep the other default settings.

DID YOU KNOW?

You can restore any power plan's defaults by clicking Restore default settings for this plan.

4 Use the drop-down lists to make changes you wish to make.

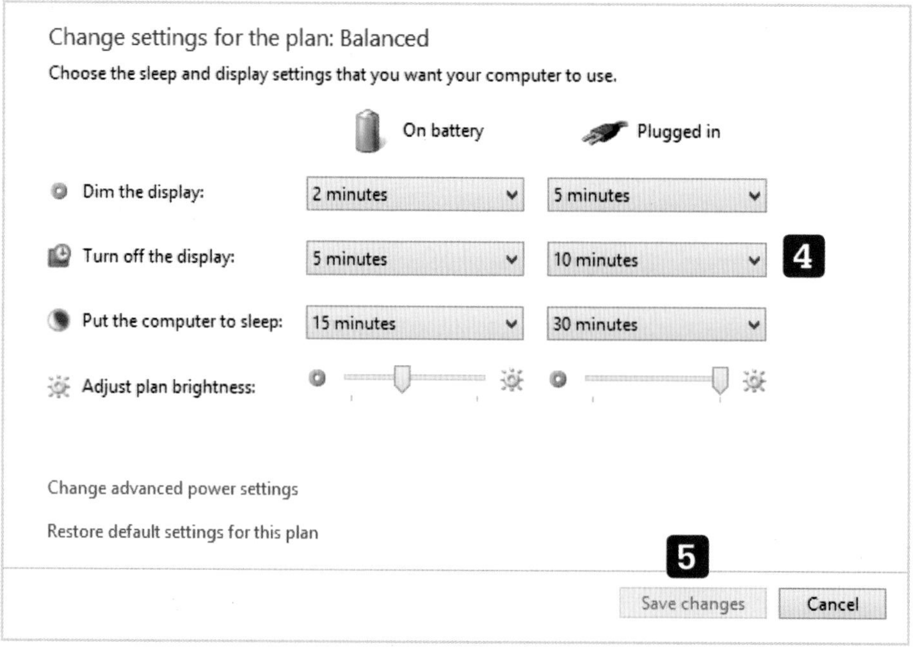

5 Click Save changes.

Tip 9: Store data in SkyDrive

When you set up a Microsoft account you are given some free space on Microsoft's Internet servers to store some of your files, pictures and other data. This space is called SkyDrive. If you save your data to SkyDrive when you work from your laptop or tablet, when you get back home or to the office you can use that copy of the file to work with (and then resave it to SkyDrive when you are finished there). When you do this, you always have access to the most up-to-date version of the file, no matter where you are or how you work.

1. From the Start screen, click SkyDrive. If applicable, type your Microsoft account and password.
2. If you've used SkyDrive before, it will already be personalised, as shown here (if not, you'll see only the default folders).
3. Click any category to see what's inside. If subfolders exist, explore those too.

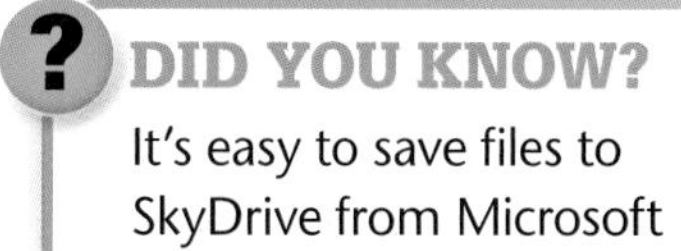

DID YOU KNOW?
It's easy to save files to SkyDrive from Microsoft Office 2013 applications on tablets: it is the default!

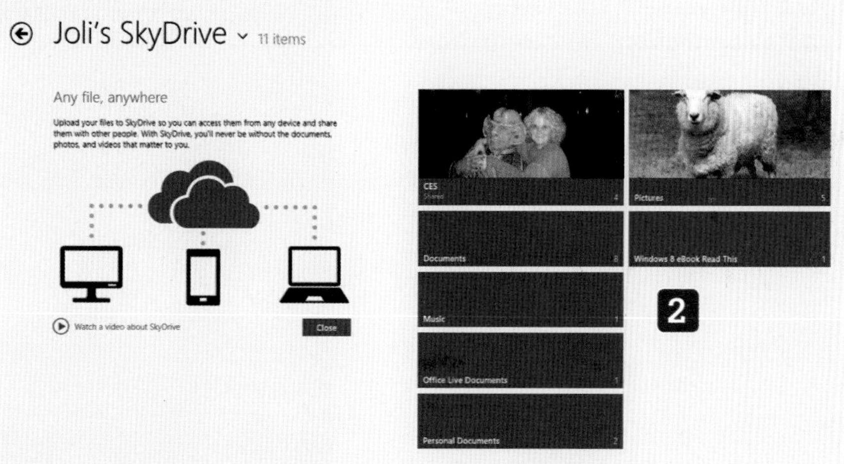

DID YOU KNOW?
You can access data you've saved to SkyDrive from any Internet-enabled computer. It does not have to be a Windows 8 computer.

HOT TIP: When you save a file in any program, in the Save as dialogue box, look for SkyDrive in the left pane, under Favorites.

WHAT DOES THIS MEAN?

SkyDrive: means that you have access to a *drive* (like a hard drive) in the *sky* (which is actually the Internet). Because the Internet is often represented in technical documentation as a cloud, the word sky kind of fits here.

Tip 10: Know when you're on Wi-Fi and when on a metered data plan

It's okay to watch movies on Netflix, videos on YouTube and other large online data when you are connected to a Wi-Fi network. But if you do this while connected to a mobile data network, one with a data limit, you'll use up your weekly or monthly data quota very quickly. It's important to be able to tell quickly what kind of network you're connected to.

1. From the Settings charm, tap the Network icon.
2. Select the network you are currently connected to.
3. If you notice that you are connected to a metered data connection, be careful how much data you use.
4. To make sure you always know when you connect to your mobile data plan or device, deselect Connect automatically.

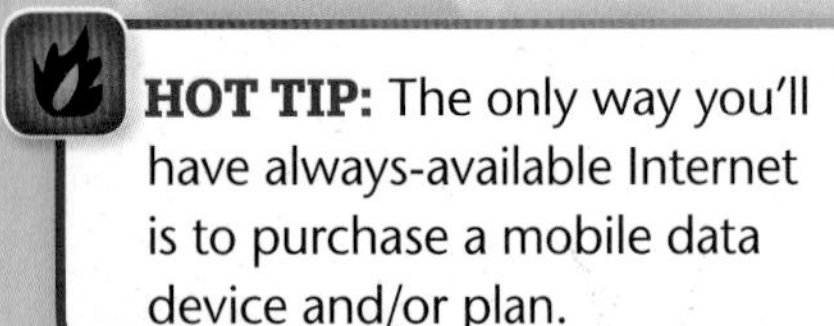

HOT TIP: The only way you'll have always-available Internet is to purchase a mobile data device and/or plan.

DID YOU KNOW?
Even if your device isn't supported by default by a mobile data provider, you can purchase an external USB device to connect with (provided your tablet offers this kind of port).

1 Explore your laptop and tablet

Introduction

A laptop computer is designed to be portable; thus, your laptop differs from a traditional desktop computer in many ways. It probably has a chargeable, removable battery and battery bay, a touch pad or track pad, an on-screen keyboard (thanks to Windows 8) and maybe even a touch screen. If you're new to laptops, you may not have any experience with these features.

Most mobile devices (laptops and some tablet computers) do have features desktop computers offer, though. Almost all come with USB ports, some with an HDMI and/or DVI port, an Ethernet port, a CD/DVD drive and an old-fashioned keyboard, among other things. And, of course, all devices run an operating system, in our case some version of Windows 8.

In this chapter you'll learn what kind of device you have and what features are available on it. After that, you'll power up your laptop or tablet, work through any setup processes and learn to use a few of the features unique to Windows 8, including the functionality associated with the Windows key.

HOT TIP: You don't have to have a laptop to use this book, you can have a tablet.

ALERT: By the time you get this book, Microsoft might have updated Windows 8. If this happens, some of the explanations in this book won't match exactly with what you see on your screen.

Know your device

There are many different types of mobile devices that can run Windows 8, including tablets, netbooks and various types of laptops. It's important to establish what kind of device you own and what edition of Windows 8 is installed on it, so that you'll know which features of the Windows 8 operating system and what kind of hardware are available to you. You can learn more about your computer from Control Panel. The laptop below runs Windows 8 Pro with Media Center and has limited touch support.

- Laptop (or netbook) – laptop computers run a full version of Windows 8 and you'll have access to all of the features available in the operating system. Laptops come with a keyboard and some type of pointing device (track pad, track ball, touch pad and so on). A good laptop can replace a desktop computer.
- High-end tablet – high-end tablets almost always run a full version of Windows 8, but you may not have access to a physical keyboard, speciality ports and other laptop hardware. Some tablets can be attached to a dock that contains these features though; docks are often sold separately. Likewise, you can generally connect Bluetooth devices such as keyboards and mice, if you wish.
- Simple tablet – simple tablets often come with Windows 8 RT installed. This is not the full version of Windows 8 that is installed on laptop computers. You can access the Start screen and the various apps, and you can get more apps from the Store. You can connect to wireless networks, access and play media and games, and use other tablet-specific features. You can access the traditional Desktop. However, there are limitations: you can't install software from CDs or DVDs, among other things.

HOT TIP: If you have a tablet with no keyboard, you'll have to rely on touch techniques to navigate it. You'll see tips for doing so throughout this book.

Plug in the power cable

A power cable is the cable that you will use to connect the laptop to the wall outlet (power outlet). When you connect the power cable to both the laptop and the power outlet, the laptop will use the power from the outlet and charge the battery at the same time. When you unplug the laptop from the power outlet, the laptop will run on stored battery power.

1 Locate the power cord. It may consist of two pieces that need to be connected.

2 Connect the power cord to the back or side of the laptop as shown in the documentation.

3 Plug the power cord into the wall outlet.

HOT TIP: If your new laptop did not come with documentation, visit the manufacturer's website and search for a user's guide.

DID YOU KNOW?

You can connect and disconnect the power cable at any time, even when the computer is running.

Access and use USB ports

USB ports, or universal serial bus ports, offer a place to connect USB devices. USB devices include mice, external keyboards, mobile phones, digital cameras and other devices, including USB flash drives.

1. Locate a USB cable. The length and shape depend on the device, although one end is always small and rectangular.

2. Plug the rectangular end of the USB cable into an empty USB port on your laptop.

3. Connect the other end to the USB device.

4. Often, you'll need to turn on the USB device to get Windows 8 to recognise it, but not always.

HOT TIP: When you connect a device via USB, Windows 8 will search for the required software (called device drivers) to make it run.

DID YOU KNOW?
You do not generally have to 'turn on' USB storage units, such as flash drives.

HOT TIP: FireWire, also called IEEE 1394, is often used to connect digital video cameras, professional audio hardware and external hard drives to a computer. FireWire ports are larger than USB ports and move data more quickly.

Locate and use the Ethernet port

Ethernet, also called RJ-45, is used to physically connect a laptop to a local network. If you have a cable modem, router or other high-speed Internet device at home, you can use Ethernet to connect to it. Ethernet connections are often faster than wireless ones.

1. Locate an Ethernet cable. They are often blue, although they can be grey, white or some other colour.
2. Connect the cable to both the PC and the Ethernet outlet on a router or cable modem.

HOT TIP: An Ethernet cable looks like a telephone cable, except both ends are slightly larger.

DID YOU KNOW?

When looking for an Ethernet port on your laptop, look for an almost square port. The Ethernet cable will snap in.

Connect headphones

Most laptops come with built-in speakers, cameras and microphones. However, you may want to connect headphones for privacy. These are easy to install.

1. If necessary, turn on the headphones. This is generally not necessary.
2. Connect the headphones to the applicable port. You'll see a picture of headphones on it.

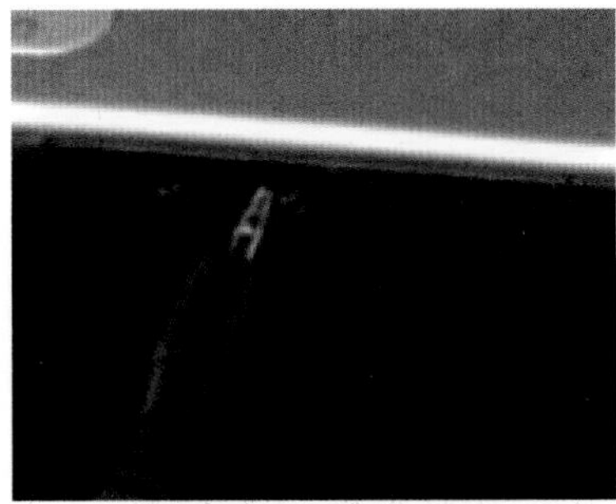

3. If prompted, work through any setup processes.

DID YOU KNOW?

Line-in jacks bring data into the laptop; line-out jacks port data out to external devices such as speakers or headphones.

WHAT DOES THIS MEAN?

Line-in jack: accepts audio from external devices, such as CD players.

Microphone-in jack: accepts input from external microphones.

Headphone or speaker jack: lets you connect your laptop to an external source for output, including, but not limited to, speakers and headphones.

Locate additional ports

You'll see other ports not mentioned here depending on the make and model of your laptop. You may see ports for a modem (doubtful in this day and age), external monitor, FireWire, serial, DVI, mini-USB and media card slots. You'll probably also see a CD/DVD drive bay on a laptop, though probably not on a tablet.

1. Turn the laptop and view all sides of it.
2. View all the available ports.
3. Refer to your user's guide to explore these ports. Here is a serial port.

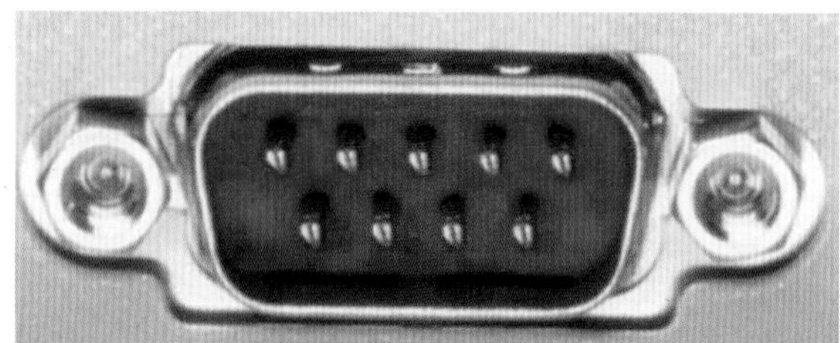

DID YOU KNOW?

A serial port can be used to connect your laptop to an external monitor.

WHAT DOES THIS MEAN?

Kensington lock slot: used to connect the laptop to a lock (and the lock to something unmovable) to prevent it from being stolen.

DVI port: used to connect the laptop to a television set or other DVI device. DVI stands for Digital Video Interface.

S-video: used to connect the laptop to a television or other display that also offers s-video connectivity.

SD card slots or card readers: used to accept digital memory cards found in digital cameras and similar technologies.

AV-in: accepts input from various audio/video devices.

RF-in: accepts input signal from digital TV tuners.

Locate, insert or remove the battery

There are several items that have to do with the battery and they're probably all located on the underside or back of your laptop. Before you turn the laptop upside down to look at them, make sure you switch it off and unplug it.

1. If the computer is turned off, skip to step 3.
2. If the computer is turned on, tap the Power button on the laptop. The laptop should shut down safely.
3. Unplug the laptop from the wall outlet and remove the power cable. Set the power cable aside.
4. Close the laptop's lid and carefully turn the laptop upside down and place it on a desk or table.
5. Locate the battery bay and open it, if applicable.
6. Unlatch the battery latch.
7. Remove or install the battery.
8. Lock the battery into place, if applicable.
9. Secure the latch and close the battery bay door, if applicable.

HOT TIP: Use the key combination Windows + I to access Settings, where you can choose to shut down the computer from the Power options there.

DID YOU KNOW?
Tablets may not have a battery bay and the battery may not be removable.

WHAT DOES THIS MEAN?

Battery bay: holds the computer's battery. Sometimes you have to use a screwdriver to get inside the battery bay, but most of the time you simply need to slide out the compartment door.

Battery release latch: holds the battery in place, even after the battery bay's door has been opened. You'll need to release this latch to get to the battery.

Battery lock: locks the battery in position.

Locate the power button and start Windows 8

Before you can use your laptop you have to press the power button. The first time you turn on a new laptop, you'll have to work through the Windows 8 setup process.

1. If applicable, open the laptop's lid.
2. Press the power button to turn on the computer.
3. If applicable, work through the setup process.
4. Setup is complete when you see the Start screen. Part of a Start screen is shown here.

? DID YOU KNOW?
Starting a computer is also called 'booting' it. If a computer won't boot there are various troubleshooting tools built in to Windows 8 that can help resolve the problem.

! ALERT: Although it isn't mandatory, during the setup process, create or input a Microsoft account. This enables you to use all the features built into Windows 8.

Use the Windows key

All keyboards offer a Windows key. It is on the left side, at the bottom, between the Ctrl key and the Alt key. Most touch-only tablets have a button with the Windows logo on it that serves the same purpose.

The Windows key plays a significant role in Windows 8. Here are a few things you'll use this key for:

- Press the Windows key to return to the Start screen from anywhere.
- Press Windows (the Windows key) + I to access the command to shut down the computer. You'll choose from the available Power choices, as shown here.
- Press Windows + F to search for a file.
- Press Windows + X to open a shortcut menu similar to the old Start button.

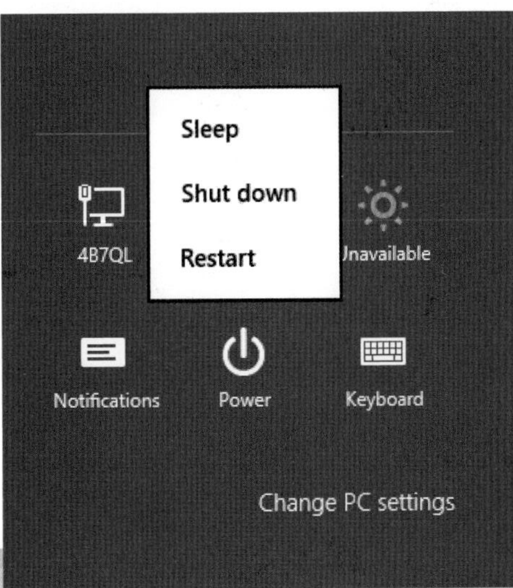

? DID YOU KNOW?
If you have a tablet without a keyboard, there will be a Windows button on the outside of the tablet.

HOT TIP: There are many more keyboard shortcuts that involve the Windows key than those shown here.

Use the touch pad/track pad

When you open your laptop for the first time, you'll probably see a device for moving the mouse, usually a touch pad. You'll use this to move the mouse around the screen.

1. Place your finger on the touch pad and move it around. Notice the cursor moves.
2. If there are buttons, for the most part the left button functions in the same way as the left button on a mouse.
3. The right button functions the same way as the right button on a mouse.
4. If there is a centre button, often this is used to scroll through pages. Try clicking and holding it to move up, down, left or right on a page.

HOT TIP: Double-click the left touch pad button to execute a command. Click once to select something.

HOT TIP: Click the right touch pad button to open contextual menus to access Copy, Select All and similar commands.

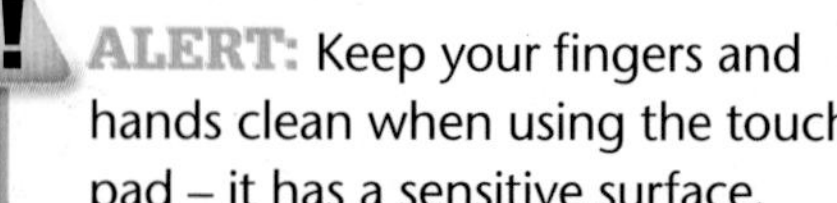

ALERT: Keep your fingers and hands clean when using the touch pad – it has a sensitive surface.

2 Learn Windows 8 essentials

Introduction

The first time you press the power button on a new Windows 8 laptop or tablet, you are prompted to complete a few setup tasks. These tasks require you to select a background colour for the Start screen, create a user account, connect to a home network if you have one and configure other personalisation options. Once these tasks are complete, Windows 8 is ready to use. In this chapter, we'll assume you've done these things and are ready to get started.

Before you really dive in though, you'll need to understand a few terms that are new to Windows 8 (and probably new to you, too). These include words such as Microsoft Account, Charms, Start screen apps and Desktop apps. With that out of the way, you'll learn some Windows 8 basics like bypassing the Lock screen, logging on, browsing the Start screen and accessing the traditional Desktop.

Understand new Windows 8 terms

There are a few terms to understand before you jump into Windows 8. You'll see these terms throughout the book.

- Lock screen – you must bypass the Lock screen before you can unlock the computer. To unlock your computer you input your unique password, password picture pattern or PIN in the resulting screen. This is a Lock screen.

- Start screen – the Start screen appears after you unlock the computer. It holds tiles that you use to open apps, programs, folders and so on. The charms are also shown.

- Start screen app – a simple program that enables you to do something quickly and easily, such as check email, send a message, check the weather or surf the Internet. *Apps*, as they are known, offer less functionality than fully fledged programs (*Desktop apps*) and are more like what you'd see on a smartphone. Here is the Internet Explorer app.

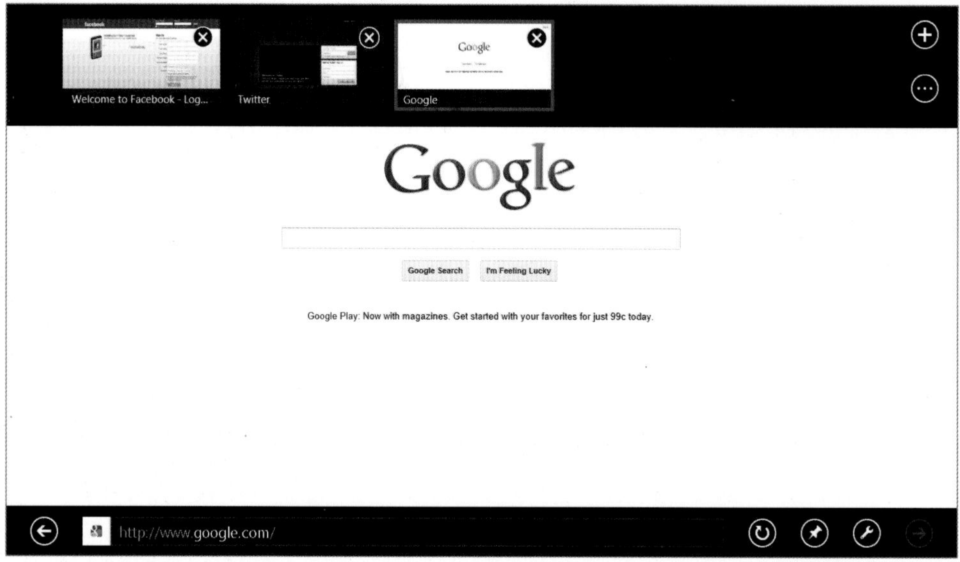

- Desktop app – this type of app represents the traditional programs you may already be familiar with. Desktop apps are complete programs like Paint, Notepad, Windows Media Player, Internet Explorer and similar third-party programs such as Adobe Reader. They open on the Desktop. Here is the Internet Explorer Desktop app – you can see the traditional Desktop behind it.

- Desktop – the Desktop is the traditional computing environment complete with the taskbar, Desktop background, shortcuts to programs and so on. If you've ever used a computer, you've used the Desktop. This is what my Desktop looks like.

HOT TIP: We believe the majority of Desktop apps are on their way out and that new, more streamlined Start screen-type apps will eventually take their place. Thus, when there are two versions of an app available (such as is the case with Internet Explorer), use the app available from the Start screen whenever possible.

DID YOU KNOW?

You can right-click an empty area of the Start screen to view all the available apps. If you use a touch screen, flick upwards from the bottom instead.

DID YOU KNOW?

Some applications have two versions. For instance, there is an Internet Explorer app that is available from the Start screen and an Internet Explorer Desktop app available from the Desktop.

Understand your account options

When you set up your Windows 8 laptop or tablet, you were prompted to create and/or log in with a Microsoft account. In most instances, this is an email account you already have that ends in live.com or hotmail.com, but it can be something else. If you opted not to do this, then you created a local account instead. We suggest you use a Microsoft account, like the one shown here.

Your account

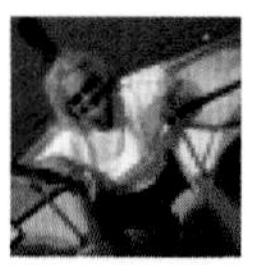

Joli Ballew

joli_ballew@hotmail.com

- Local account – a personal account you create and use to log on to your Windows 8 computer that is associated with that computer only. Your account settings and preferences don't follow you from one Windows 8 computer to another like a Microsoft account can.
- Microsoft account – a personal but global account you use to log in to your Windows 8 computer. When you use this kind of account, Windows 8 will automatically configure certain apps with personalised information and your preferences and settings will be available no matter what Internet-enabled Windows 8 computer you log on to.

HOT TIP: It's never too late to switch from a local account to a Microsoft account. You do this from PC Settings. Refer to Chapter 10: Personalise Windows 8 to learn how.

Log in to Windows 8

The Lock screen appears when you turn on or wake up your Windows 8 computer. You must bypass the Lock screen before you can use your computer.

1. If you have a touchscreen, use your finger to swipe upwards from the bottom or touch the screen. If you have a physical mouse and keyboard, do any of the following:
   a. Swipe upwards with the mouse.
   b. Tap the space bar.
   c. Click anywhere on the screen.
2. Type your password or PIN and tap Enter or the keyboard, or type your password and tap or click the right-facing arrow.

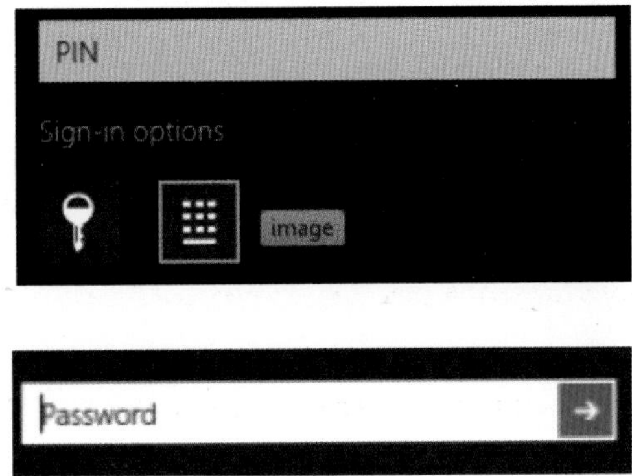

3. The Start screen appears.

DID YOU KNOW?
You can tap or click the icon that looks like an eye which appears in the Password window after you've entered a letter or two to see the actual characters (instead of the dots that appear by default).

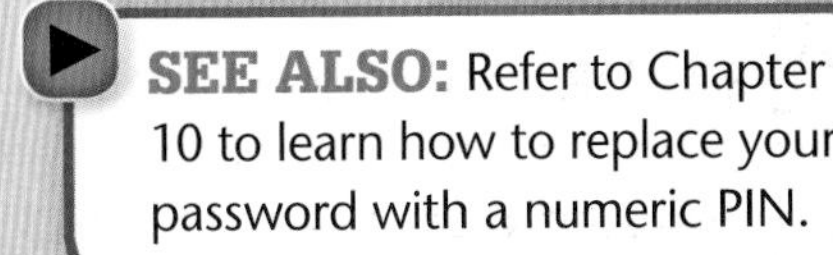

SEE ALSO: Refer to Chapter 10 to learn how to replace your password with a numeric PIN.

Explore the Start screen

Once you gain access to the Start screen, your computer is ready to use. Note the items available there and understand that your Start screen will look different from ours.

1. Position your mouse at the bottom of the screen. A scroll bar appears that allows access to apps that run off the screen on the right. (You can tap and drag from right to left on a touch screen.)
2. If you click or tap a tile, the related app opens.

3. To return to the Start screen from any app:
   a. Move the cursor to the bottom left corner of the screen and click the Start screen thumbnail that appears.

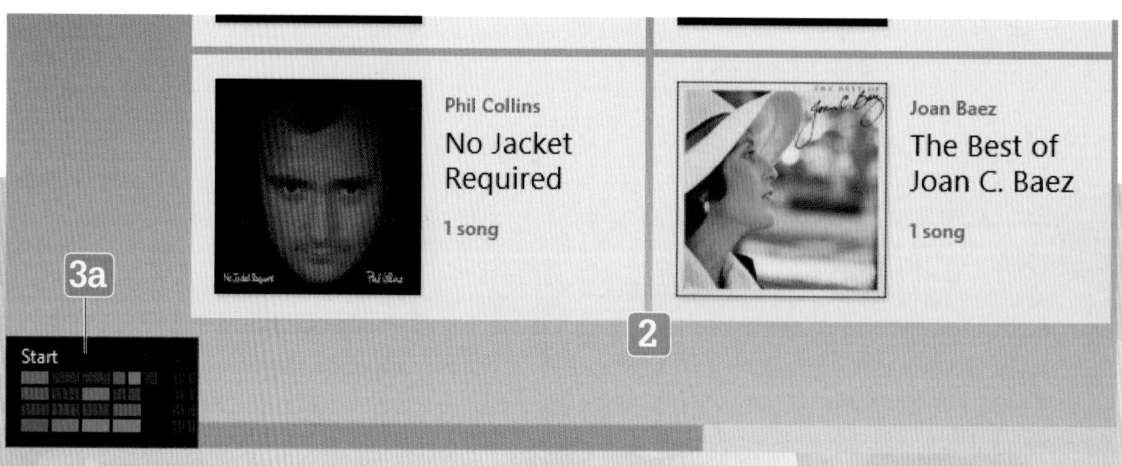

b. Tap the Windows key on the keyboard or on the laptop or tablet itself.
c. On a touch screen, from the middle of the right side of the screen, flick inwards with your right thumb. Tap the Start charm that appears.

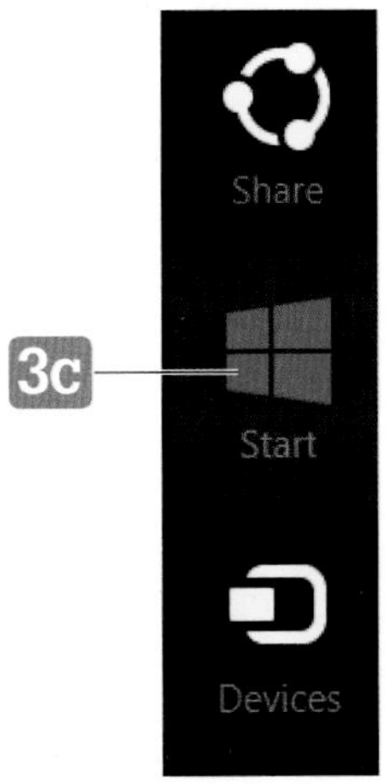

HOT TIP: If you use a tablet that runs Windows 8 RT, you'll also see some Microsoft Office apps on the Start screen.

HOT TIP: To view all your apps, right-click an empty area of the screen and click All Apps. On a touch screen, flick up from the bottom.

ALERT: If you have a tablet that does not have a physical keyboard, you'll have to rely on touch to navigate the device. We'll offer tips and techniques for doing so throughout this book.

Access charms

Charms enable you to configure settings, share information, view devices, search for data and, as you've just learned, access the Start screen. You can access the charms in many ways.

- Using touch, place your thumb in the middle of the right side of the screen and flick left (inwards).
- On a keyboard, use the key combination Windows key + C.
- Using a mouse or touchpad, move the cursor to the bottom or top right corner of the screen and when the transparent charms appear, move the cursor upwards or downwards.

HOT TIP: If you're using a touch screen on a tablet, use your thumb and flick inwards from the right edge of the screen to bring up the charms. On a touch screen monitor (such as one you might connect to a small laptop), try your right index finger instead.

DID YOU KNOW?

The Shut Down command is available from the Settings charm, from the Power icon that appears there.

Explore charms

There are five charms. What you see when you click each may differ depending on what you're doing when you click them. For instance, if you click the Share charm while on the Start screen, you'll be notified there's nothing available to share there. If you click the Share charm while in Maps, you can share the location or directions you've looked up with others via email or other options.

- Search – to open the Search window where you can type what you're looking for. Note the categories: Apps, Settings, Files. What's shown on the left side of the screen changes when you start typing your search term.

? DID YOU KNOW?

You can access charms from anywhere in Windows 8, even from the Desktop or while in an app.

- Share – to share something with others, such as a map to a location.

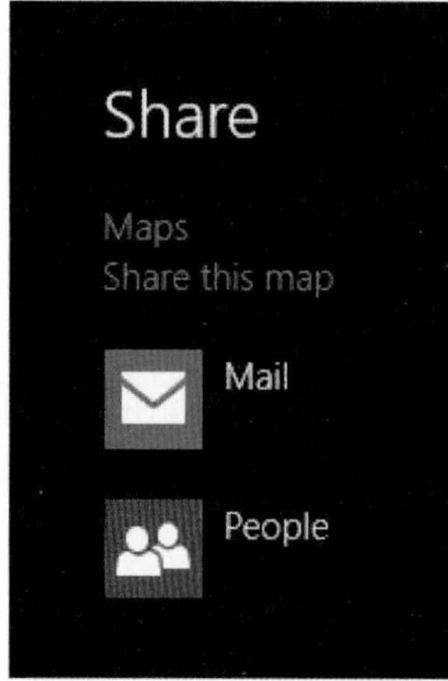

- Start – to access the Start screen.
- Devices – to access devices that can be used with the open app, window or program.
- Settings – to access settings available with the open screen, app, program and so on. You'll use this charm to join networks, change the volume, shut down the computer and more.

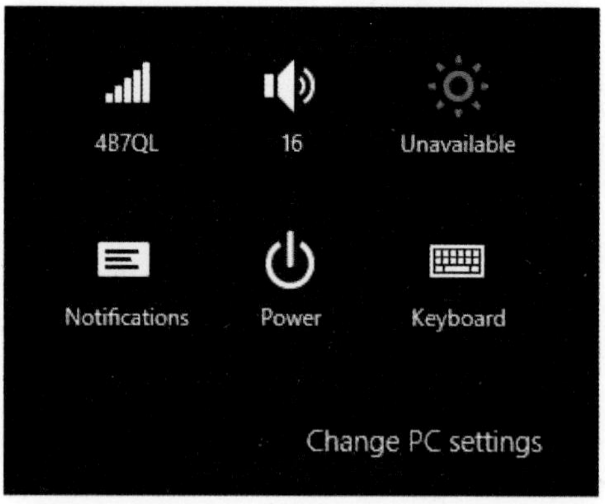

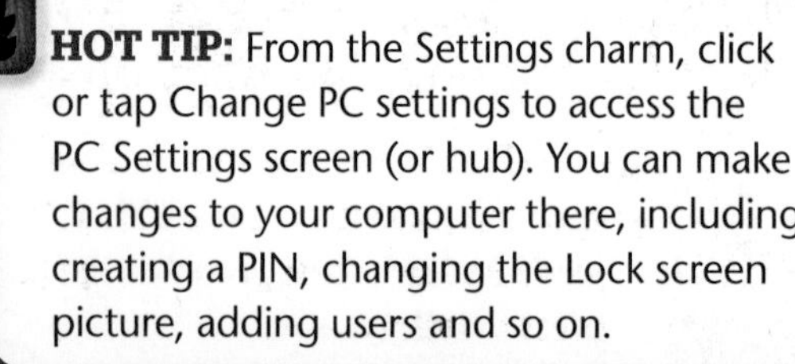

HOT TIP: From the Settings charm, click or tap Change PC settings to access the PC Settings screen (or hub). You can make changes to your computer there, including creating a PIN, changing the Lock screen picture, adding users and so on.

Access the traditional Desktop

If you've ever used a computer, you've worked at the Desktop, the traditional computing environment. Your Windows 8 laptop or tablet also offers a Desktop – which you access from the Desktop tile.

1. Use any method to access the Start screen if you aren't already on it. (You can tap the Windows key on a keyboard.)
2. From the Start screen, click or tap Desktop.
3. Note the Desktop features:
   a. The Recycle Bin.
   b. The Taskbar (with icons for open files and programs).
   c. The Internet Explorer icon (the program is open here).
   d. The File Explorer icon (we've opened File Explorer here).
   e. The Notification area.
   f. Various items stored on the Desktop itself.

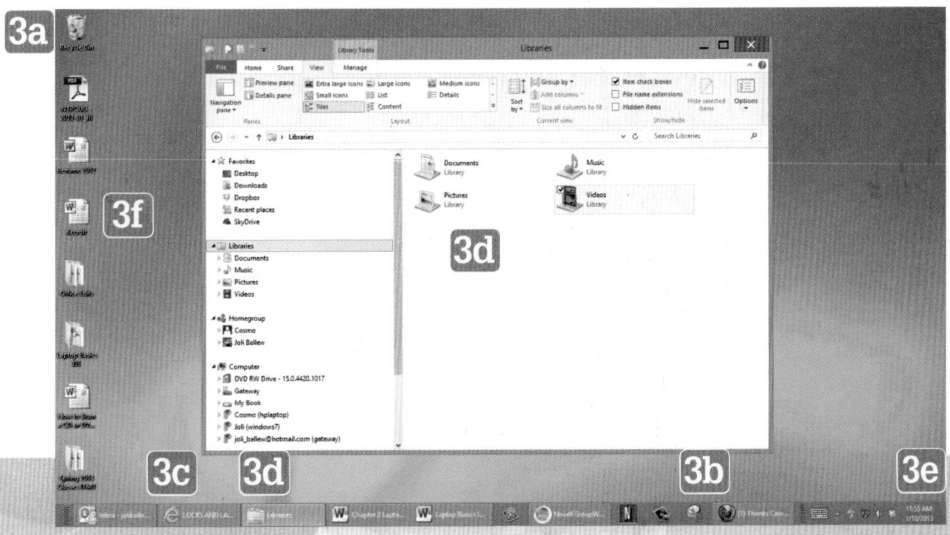

? DID YOU KNOW?
You can use the keyboard icon in the Notification area to access an on-screen keyboard.

! ALERT: The Start button is no longer available on the taskbar. If you'd like to access something like it, press Windows + X.

Connect to a Wi-Fi network

You may have connected your laptop to your home Wi-Fi network during setup, but if you didn't it's easy to do. You'll use this same technique to access a free Wi-Fi hotspot at a café, library, hotel or pub.

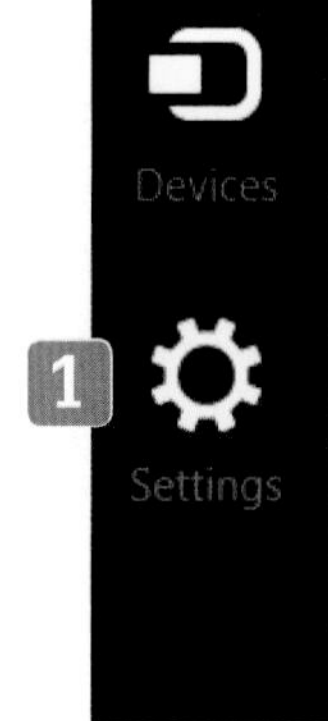

1. Press the Windows key + C to access the charms. Click Settings.
2. Click Available. (If you're connected already, you'll see the network name instead.)

3. Click the desired network from the list and click Connect.
4. Place a tick in Connect automatically and if applicable type the required password. Click Next.
5. Choose your sharing option. For a home or other trusted network, click Yes, turn on sharing and connect to devices. For any other network, choose No, do not turn on sharing and connect to devices.

SEE ALSO: Chapter 14: Manage, protect, secure and restore your laptop for more information on network sharing options.

HOT TIP: From the Desktop, look in the Notification area to quickly assess your network status.

Connect to an Ethernet network

If a Wi-Fi network isn't available but an Ethernet network is, and if your device has an Ethernet port, you can connect to the network using the proper cable.

1. Locate the Ethernet port on your laptop and on the network device (switch, hub, modem or router).
2. Connect these two devices using an Ethernet cable.
3. Follow prompts as applicable to connect to the network. There may not be any.
4. Use the Notification area on the Desktop's taskbar to verify that the network is connected.

SEE ALSO: Chapter 10 and Chapter 14.

Flick, tap, double-tap and scroll for touch

If your device does not have a physical keyboard, you'll rely on touch techniques to perform tasks, access data, type and so on. Although you'll learn more techniques as you work through this book, here are the more common ones.

- Flick up from the bottom to access additional commands and features specific to the open app or window. Here's what you see when you flick upwards in Maps.

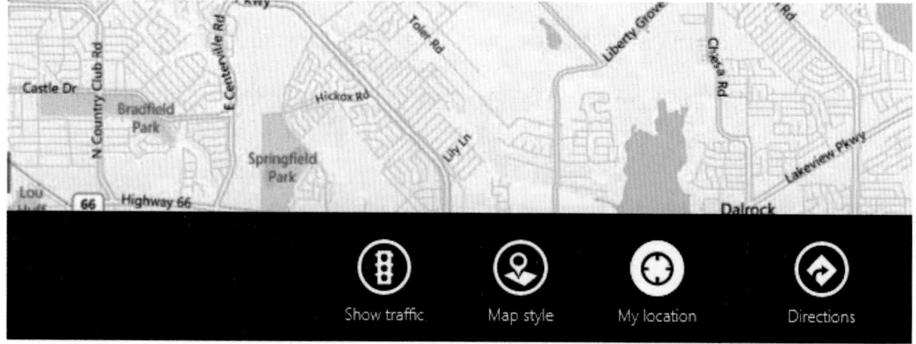

- Flick inwards from the middle of the left side of the screen to move from one open app to another. One app slides in and the other slides out.

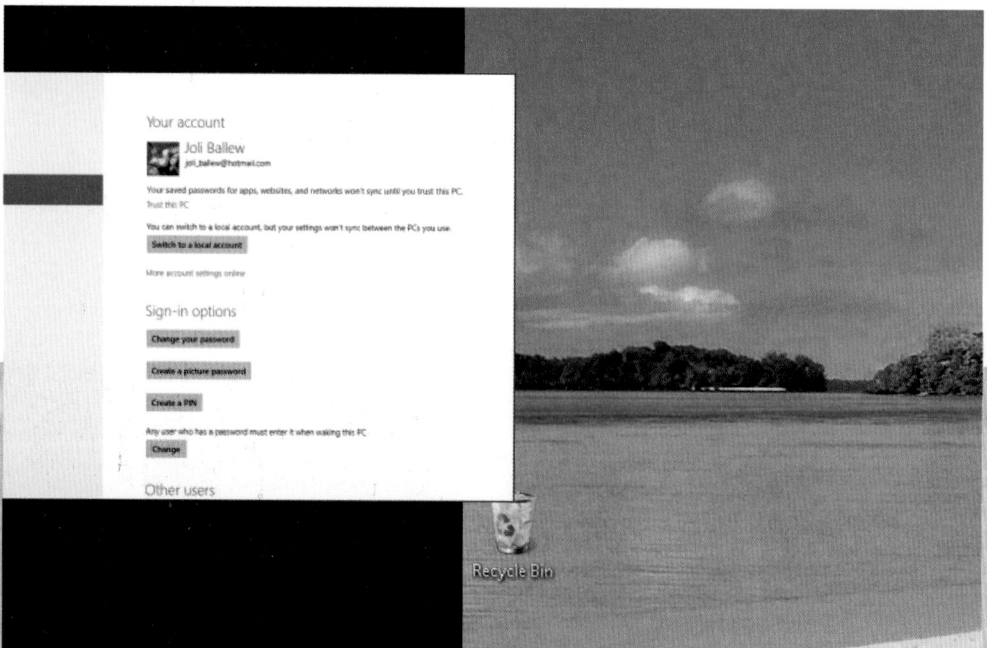

- Flick inwards from the middle of the right side of the screen to access charms.
- Tap any item to open it; tap and hold any item to select it; tap, hold and drag downwards a little to perform other tasks (such as to move an item).

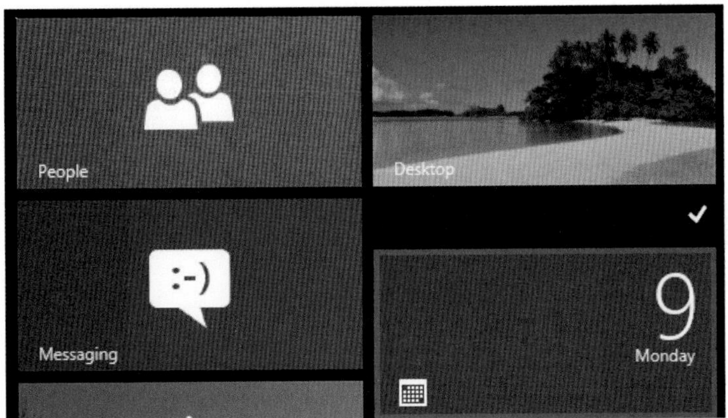

- Double-tap an item on the Desktop to open it.
- Tap and hold an icon on the Desktop to access the contextual menu.

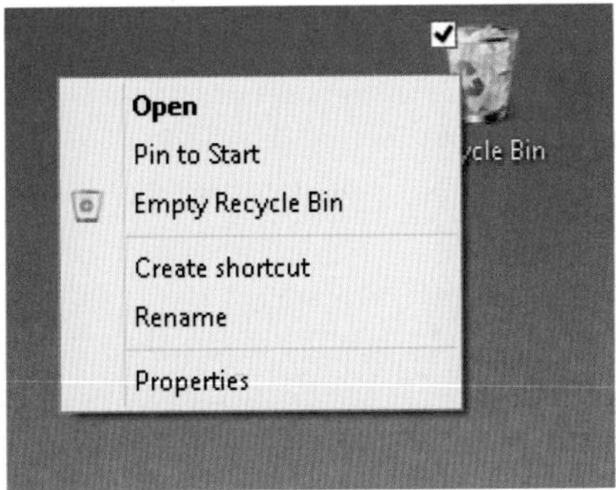

- While on the Desktop, tap the keyboard icon on the taskbar to bring up the on-screen keyboard.

DID YOU KNOW?

The tap-and-hold technique often produces what a traditional right-click does. A double-tap is like a double-click using a mouse. Likewise, tap-hold-and-drag is similar to holding down the mouse button and dragging an item.

3 Explore Start screen apps and personalise their tiles

Introduction

If you've ever used a high-end smartphone, i-device, Android tablet or Windows phone, you've used apps. Apps are programs that enable you to do something quickly and without much effort, and they don't offer menus, drop-down lists and other distractions to slow you down. Almost all apps use the Internet to obtain their information, so if you aren't connected, you'll want to connect now. Remember, Start screen apps open in their own unique way and do not open on the traditional Desktop.

After you've explored a few of the more basic Start screen apps and reviewed their available charms, you'll learn how to personalise their related tiles. All tiles that appear on the Start screen can be moved or hidden, and some can be made smaller and then larger again. App tiles can also be configured to show up-to-date information, such as the current weather.

View your local weather

You can easily view information about the current weather and access your local weather forecast from the Weather app. Its tile is located on the Start screen by default.

1. From the Start screen, click the Weather tile.

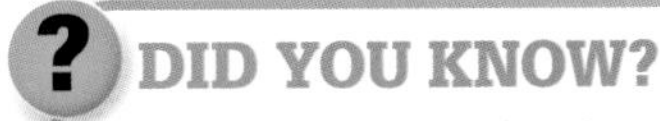

DID YOU KNOW?
If you use a Microsoft account and configure the Weather app on one computer, when you log on to another Windows 8 computer using that account, your app settings will be synced.

2. If prompted, click Allow to let the Weather app learn your location.
3. Review the information on offer.
4. Use the scroll bar to view additional information including but not limited to various regional maps, historical weather information and the hourly forecast for your area.

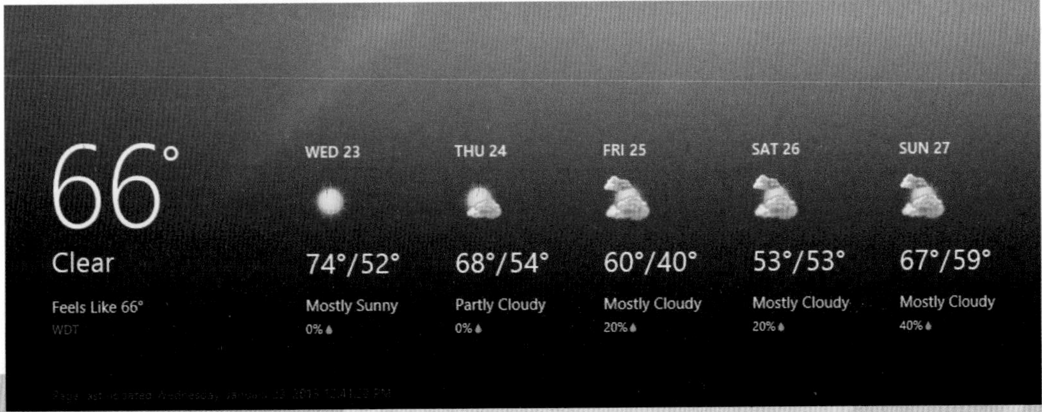

HOT TIP: If you have a touch screen, use your finger to flick left and right to access other areas of the Weather app.

DID YOU KNOW?
You can right-click or flick upwards from the bottom to access the Weather app's personalised charms. You can use these to manipulate the information shown in it, such as changing from Celsius to Fahrenheit.

Explore the Travel app

The Travel app is one of the easiest to use and is packed with information about places you may want to visit or read about. One of the most outstanding features is the ability to explore cities in 360-degree views. As with other apps, you can right-click or flick upwards to access the app's charms.

1. From the Start screen, click Travel.
2. Use the scroll bar on the screen or the wheel on your mouse to move through the information.
3. Click any item to view it; click the resulting 'back' button to return.
4. Locate the Panoramas section, specifically any item with 360 degrees on it. Click the item.
5. Use your finger or mouse to drag on the image to move it around on the screen.

HOT TIP: When you access a city from the Featured Destinations section, you'll have access to an overview of the city, photos, a list of attractions and more.

DID YOU KNOW?
While in any app (in this case, Travel) you can access the previously used app (in this case, Weather) by moving the mouse cursor to the top left corner and clicking. If you use touch only, flick inwards from the left middle edge.

Search for a location with Maps

You can use the Maps app to locate a place or get directions from one place to another. By default, Maps will use your current location as the starting point, provided you allow it to access your position when prompted.

ALERT: You will not be able to view traffic conditions if the traffic where you are is not monitored.

1. From the Start screen, click Maps.
2. Right-click or swipe upwards from the bottom to access the available Maps charms.

3. Explore the following, then click Directions:
   a. Show Traffic – to view the current flow of traffic as green, yellow or red. Green means traffic is moving; red means it's extremely slow.
   b. Map Style – to switch from the default Road view to Aerial view.
   c. My location – to have Maps place a diamond on the map to indicate where you are or to recalculate your location.
   d. Directions – to get directions from one place to another.
4. Leave your starting address as your current location and type an ending address.
5. Press Enter on the keyboard.
6. Right-click to access the option to clear the map of the directions on it.

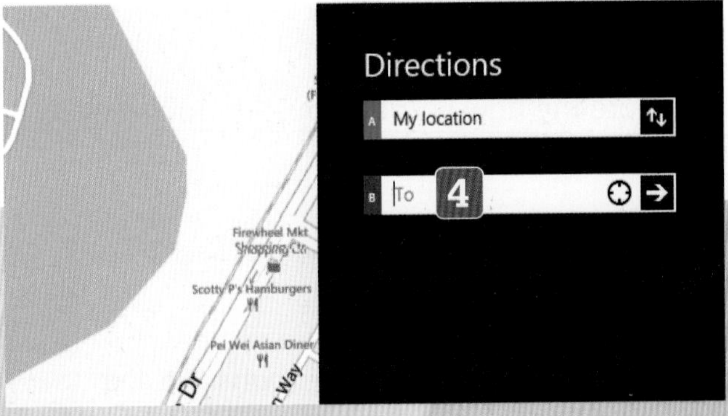

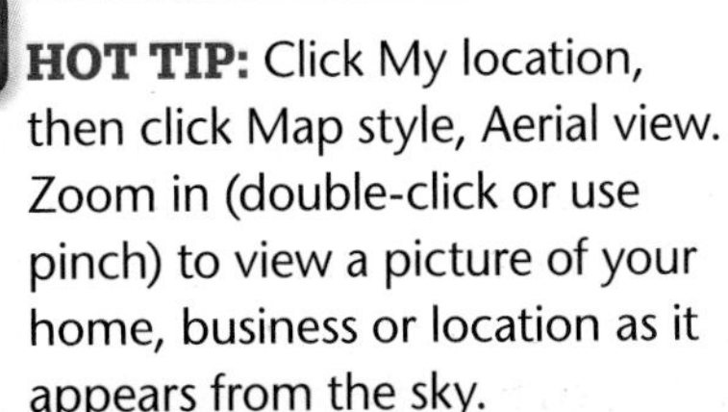

HOT TIP: Click My location, then click Map style, Aerial view. Zoom in (double-click or use pinch) to view a picture of your home, business or location as it appears from the sky.

Get the latest sports news and follow a team

Like most apps, the Sports app also offers a host of information. There are articles, photos and the ability to add your favourite teams so you can follow them easily through the app.

1. From the Start screen, click Sports.
2. Scroll through the available articles, news, schedules and photos.
3. On the far right, locate the Favorite Teams section. Click the + sign.

HOT TIP: To remove a team from your list of favourite teams, click Favorite Teams, then right-click the team to remove. Click Remove.

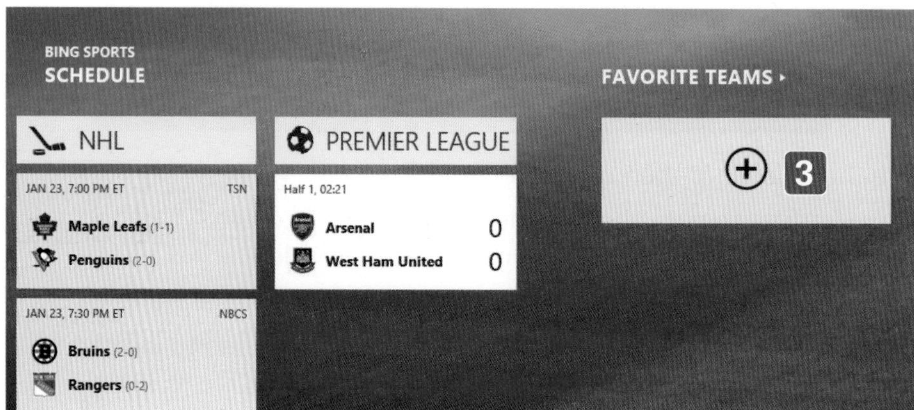

4. Type the team to follow and repeat as desired. Click Add if applicable.
5. Click Cancel when finished.
6. Note the new entries. You can now click any of these to learn more.

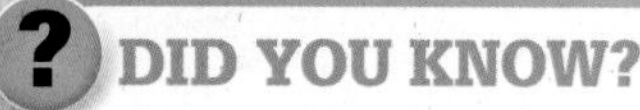

You can position your mouse in the bottom right corner of the Sports app and click the dash that appears to access a list of available categories (such as Top Stories, News, Schedule and Favorite Teams).

Use an app's charms

When you right-click inside an app or flick upwards with your finger, the app's available charms appear. The charms differ depending on which app you're using. To use a charm, you click or tap it. What you see after you click the charm differs from app to app and from charm to charm as well.

- News app charms include Bing Daily, My News and Sources.

- The Finance apps offer multiple charms, including World markets.

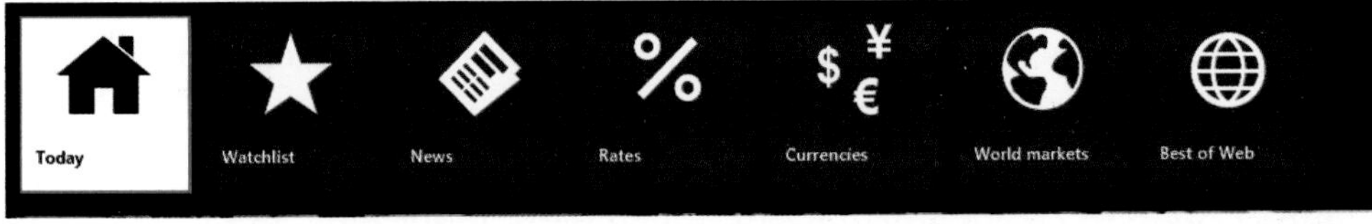

- The Messaging app offers charms that let you invite people to become a 'friend', change your online/offline status and delete conversations.

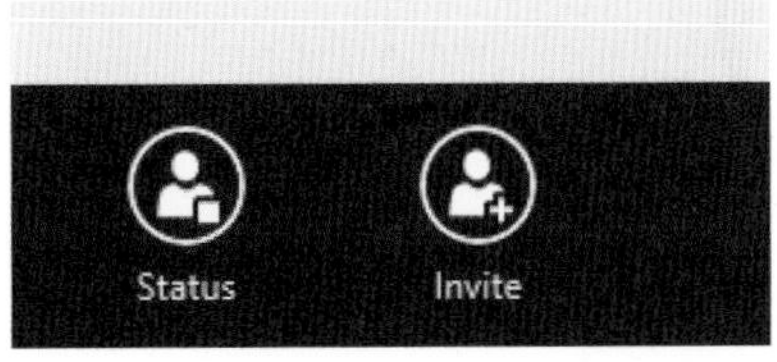

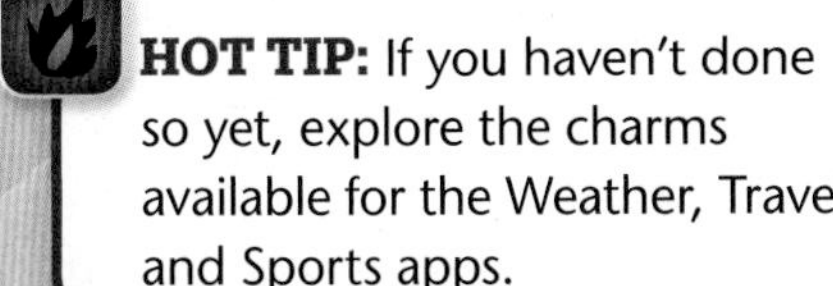

HOT TIP: If you haven't done so yet, explore the charms available for the Weather, Travel and Sports apps.

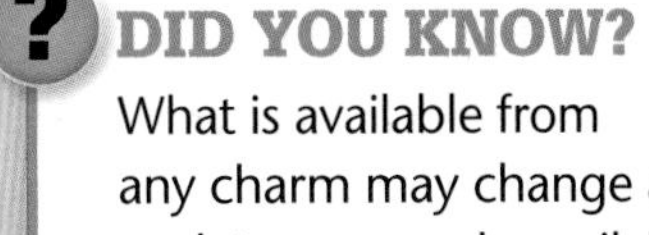

DID YOU KNOW?
What is available from any charm may change as updates are made available to the specific app or to Windows 8.

View your personal calendar

The Calendar app lets you input calendar data including major events, goals, birthdays, appointments and so on, which are ultimately synced with your Microsoft account *in the cloud*. Because the data is synced to third-party computers that are connected to the Internet, any changes you make to the calendar from other compatible devices are automatically synced, too. This also means calendar data will be up-to-date no matter how many devices you use, and you can access the calendar data from anywhere.

1. From the Start screen, click Calendar.
2. Right-click with a mouse or flick upwards with your finger from the bottom of the screen to access the Calendar's charms.

3. Explore Day, Week and Month by clicking them each once. Click Today.
4. Click New.
5. Note the option to create a new event. If you wish, input data and information and click the Save icon.

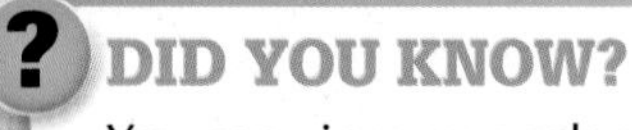

DID YOU KNOW?

You can view your calendar from almost anywhere. It's on the web at https://calendar.live.com/.

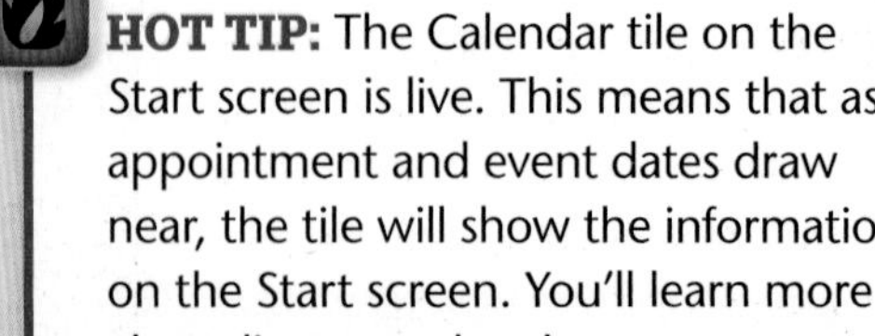

HOT TIP: The Calendar tile on the Start screen is live. This means that as appointment and event dates draw near, the tile will show the information on the Start screen. You'll learn more about live apps shortly.

Move among open apps

If you've been following along, you probably have lots of open apps. That's okay, because open apps don't use any system resources when you aren't using them. However, you do need to know how to get back to those apps when you are ready to use them again. Although you can always return to the Start screen and tap the app's tile, there are better ways.

If you have a keyboard and mouse, try these techniques while on any screen or in any app:

- Hold down the Alt key and press the Tab key to show a row of open apps. Press Tab repeatedly until you get to the app you want to use, then let go.

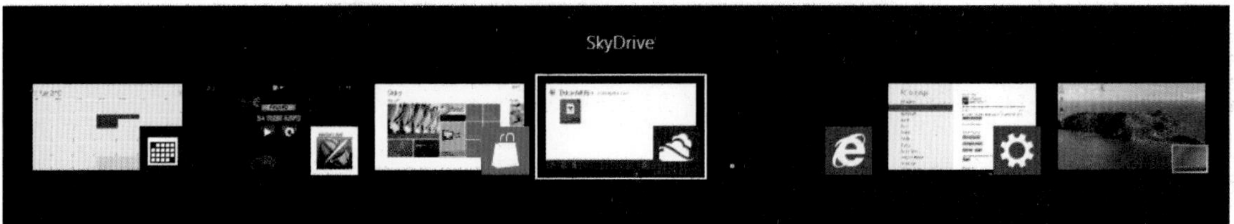

- Position your mouse in the top left corner of the screen to view and click the last used app, or drag the mouse downwards slowly to view the other available apps to access those.

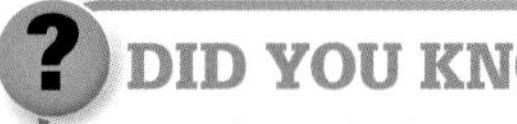

DID YOU KNOW?
Try the Windows + Tab key combination. You may be able to move through apps that way as well.

HOT TIP: If you have a touch screen, flick inwards with your thumb from the left side of the screen to move through apps you've used previously.

Move tiles on the Start screen

As you become more familiar with apps, you may find you use some quite often and others rarely, if ever. It's easy to move the tiles for the apps you use often to the left side of the Start screen for easier access and move others further away (or remove them completely).

1 At the Start screen, click and hold on a tile to move.

2 Drag the tile to a new area of the screen and drop it there.

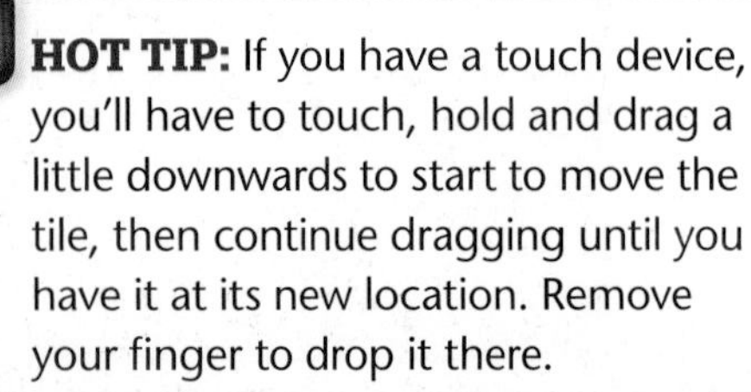

HOT TIP: If you have a touch device, you'll have to touch, hold and drag a little downwards to start to move the tile, then continue dragging until you have it at its new location. Remove your finger to drop it there.

3 Repeat as desired.

4 To remove a tile from the Start screen:
   a. Right-click the tile. (Touch users tap, hold and drag a little downwards.)
   b. Click Unpin from Start.

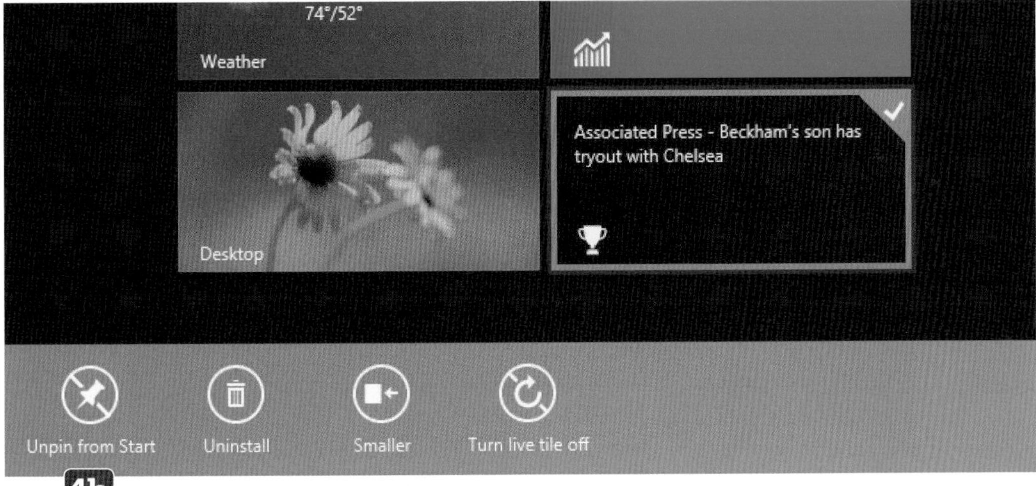

HOT TIP: If you decide you want to put an app tile back on the Start screen after removing it, right-click the Start screen, click All Apps, right-click the app to add and click Pin to Start.

Turn live tiles on or off

You may have started to notice that most of the apps you've explored so far in the chapter become 'live' after you use them. That means they show up-to-date information on the Start screen. Here Weather, Sports and Finance are live. If this bothers you, you can disable the live feature.

1 Note the tiles that are currently live. (Three of the four tiles shown here are live.)

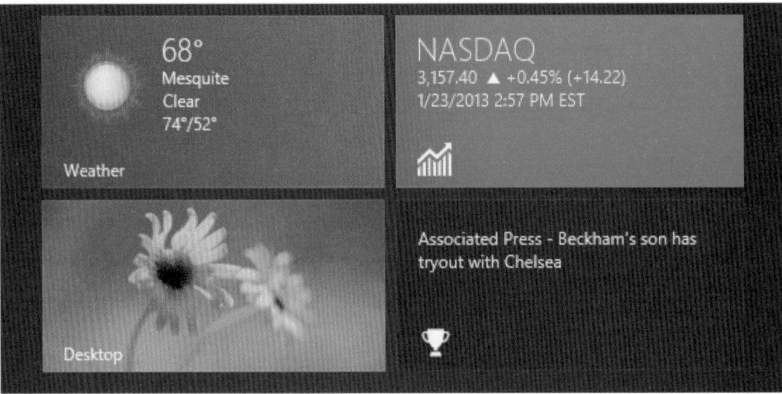

2 Right-click the live tile you want to turn off.

3 Click Turn live tile off.

4 Repeat these steps but click Turn live tile on to undo this.

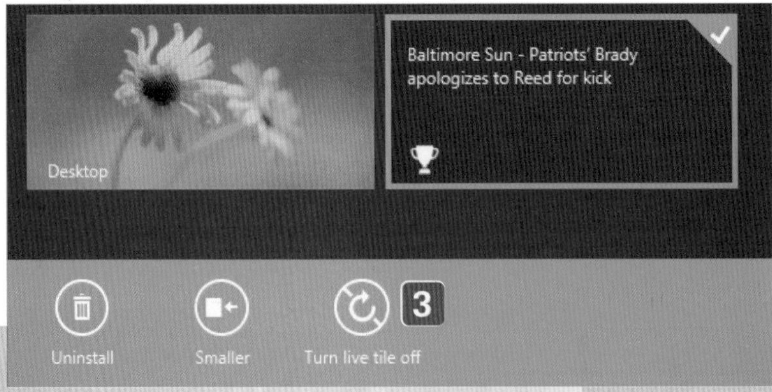

DID YOU KNOW?
Not all tiles are live. Maps is not a live tile, for instance.

HOT TIP: To select a tile with touch only, tap, hold and drag downwards a little. You'll know a tile has been selected when a tick appears on it.

Make app tiles larger or smaller

You can make large, rectangular tiles smaller and square. You cannot make tiles that are small and square by default larger and rectangular though. You may want to make larger tiles smaller so that you can fit more tiles in the Start screen viewing area (so that you don't have to scroll so much).

1. Right-click a rectangular tile.
2. Click Smaller.
3. To undo this, repeat and click Larger.
4. Repeat as you wish. Here most of the tiles are small.

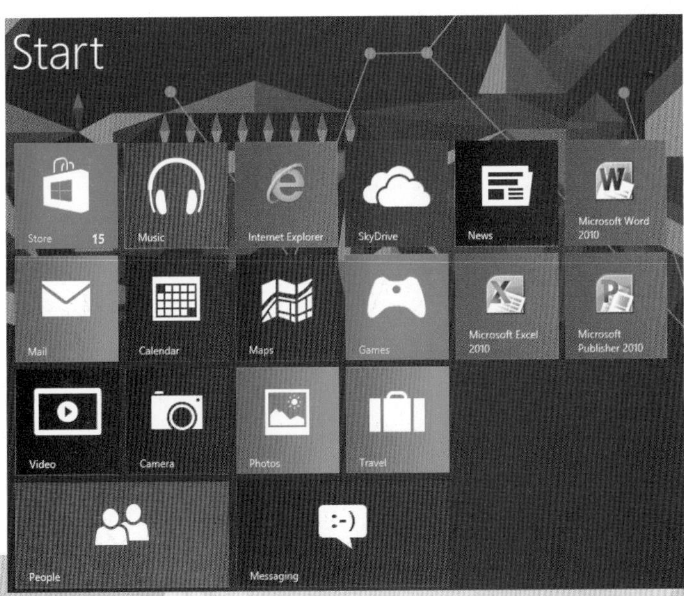

DID YOU KNOW?

Although you can select multiple tiles at once in some instances, if you select multiple tiles to make smaller, the option 'Smaller' disappears. You must make tiles smaller one at a time.

SEE ALSO: Chapter 10: Personalise Windows 8 for more information on personalising the Start screen.

4 Use the Internet Explorer Start screen app

Introduction

There are two versions of the Internet Explorer (IE) application available in Windows 8. The Internet Explorer Start screen app is one of them. That's the version you'll learn about in this chapter. You'll learn about the other (the traditional Internet Explorer Desktop app) in Chapter 8. The IE app's tile is on the Start screen.

The IE Start screen app (from here on referred to as the IE app) is great for laptop and tablet users because it is clean and streamlined, and is not cluttered with title bars, menus and menu options, dialogue boxes, drop-down lists, status bars and so on. With this app, you are able to use your entire screen to view webpages. Unfortunately, this means the app offers fewer features compared with its Desktop counterpart. However, the features you'll use most often are available – there's a hidden toolbar that holds charms, offers access to sites you visit often, and enables you to pin a tile for a website on the Start screen, among other things. There are also settings to explore.

Understand the versions of IE

You learned in the introduction that there are two versions of Internet Explorer. One is an app on the Start screen and one is a Desktop app. Here are some of the major differences between them:

- Whenever you click a link in an email, message, document and so on, the IE app will open. It is the default.
- The IE app is available from the Start screen (its tile is shown here), but the Desktop version is not, although you can add it if you want.
- The IE app is a better option on tablets, laptops and computers with small screens than its full-version counterpart because it was built to offer a full-screen browsing experience in a limited space.
- The IE Desktop app is a traditional application that looks and acts much like its predecessor. It opens on the Desktop.
- Sometimes you will have to switch from the IE app to the Desktop if a web page won't function properly, such as when unsupported technologies are required.

HOT TIP: Even if you are uncomfortable at first, get to know the IE app. Once you are used to it, you'll find it's a much better fit for your laptop than the traditional version.

DID YOU KNOW?

View on the desktop is an option in the IE app. This means you can use the app until you need the other version and then switch to it easily.

Explore the Internet Explorer app

You open the IE app by clicking or tapping its tile on the Start screen. When the app opens, look for the features listed here. You must right-click or flick upwards from the bottom of a touch screen to access these features. By default, nothing shows on the screen but the website itself.

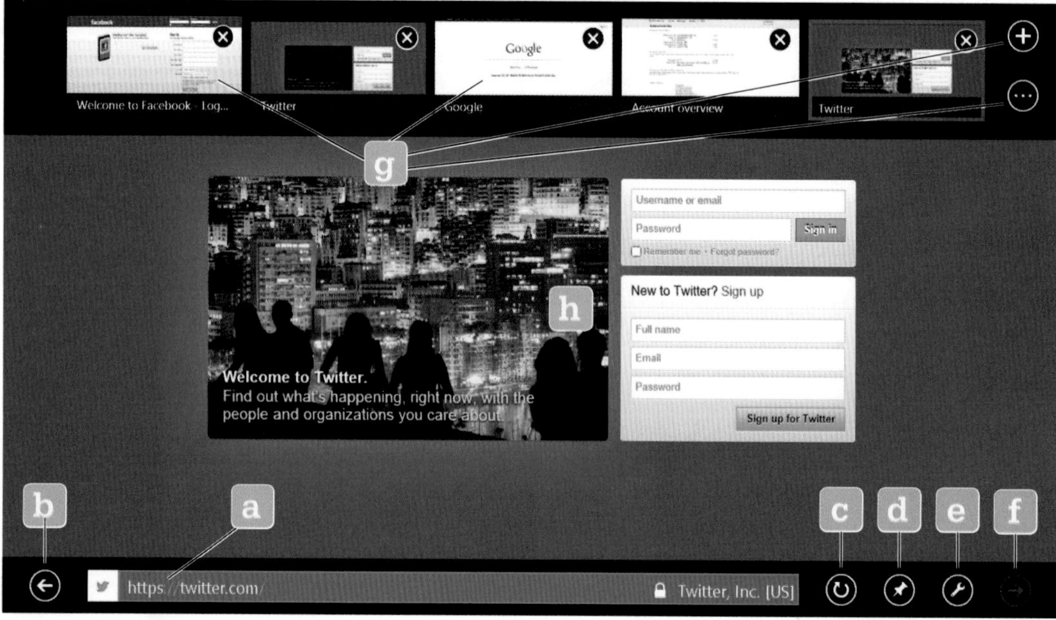

a. Address bar. Here we've navigated to https://twitter.com.
b. Back. Use this to return to the previously visited webpage.
c. Refresh. Use to reload the webpage.
d. Pin to Start. Click to create a tile for the webpage on the Start screen.
e. Page Tools. Click to find something on a page, view the website in the Desktop app, and more.

HOT TIP: Click anywhere on the webpage to hide the features shown.

f. Forward. Click to move to a previously visited page. This is available only after clicking the Back button.
g. Tabs. Click any thumbnail to return to a previously tabbed website. Note the option to remove the thumbnail (X) and the options to open and close tabs (+ and . . .).
h. Content. This is the webpage content.

DID YOU KNOW?

If you position your cursor in the middle of the left or right side of the page, transparent Back and Forward arrows appear.

Visit a website

There are several ways to visit a website, including clicking links on other web pages, in emails and in messages. You can also navigate to a website by typing its name in the Address bar.

1. From the Start screen, click the Internet Explorer tile.
2. Click once in the Address bar. (Right-click if it's not visible.)
3. Type the desired web address.
4. If you've visited the page before, it will appear above the Address bar and you can click it. If not, simply press Enter on the keyboard or click the right-facing arrow.

HOT TIP: Navigate to a second and third website using the Address bar, then practise using the Back and Forward buttons and arrows.

DID YOU KNOW?

After you've used the IE app for a while, the app will determine which websites you visit most. Then, when you click inside the Address bar, thumbnails will be available to quickly access those sites.

Manage tabs with the hidden toolbar

You saw the tabs on the hidden toolbar on the previous page. You use these features to manage open websites and to open and close tabs. Before you work through this page, navigate to several websites from the Address bar or using any other method.

1 Right-click the screen.

2 Click the X by any tab to close it.

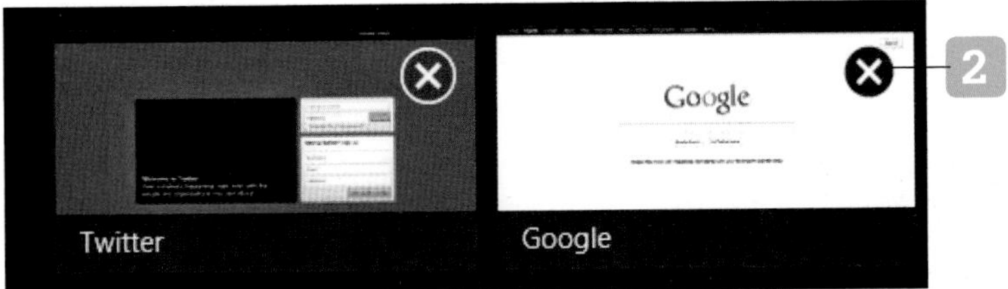

3 Click the + sign to open a new, blank page and type the desired address or choose from the thumbnails that appear.

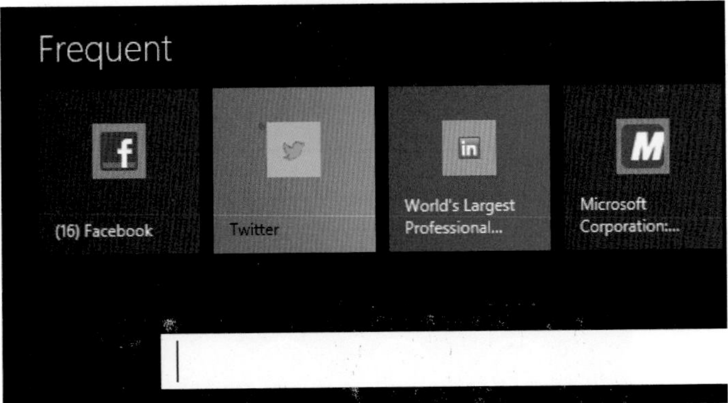

4 Right-click again, and click the three dots (...). Note the options and explore as desired.

? DID YOU KNOW?
If you opt to open a new tab using the InPrivate option (available from the ellipses from Tab tools), IE won't remember the website in its History list and won't save anything else related to your visit either.

HOT TIP: To close all your open tabs quickly, right-click, click the Tab tools icon (...) and click Close Tabs.

Pin a website to the Start screen

If there's a website you visit often you can pin it to the Start screen. Then you can simply click the tile to open the IE app and go directly to it.

1. Use the IE app to navigate to a website.
2. Right-click if applicable to show the toolbars.
3. Click the Pin to Start charm and click Pin to Start.
4. If you wish, type a new name for the website.
5. Click Pin to Start again.

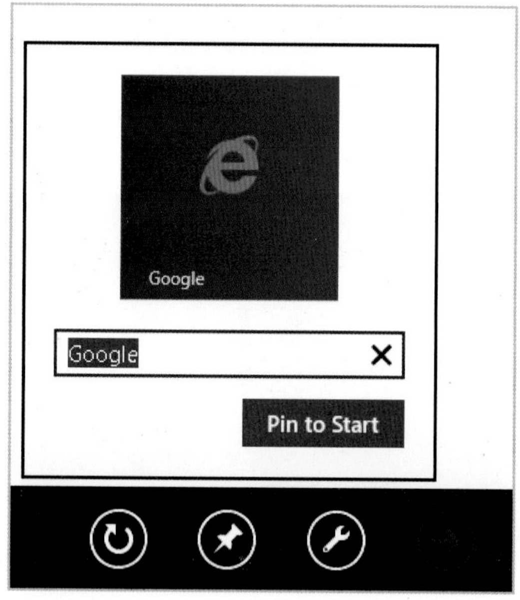

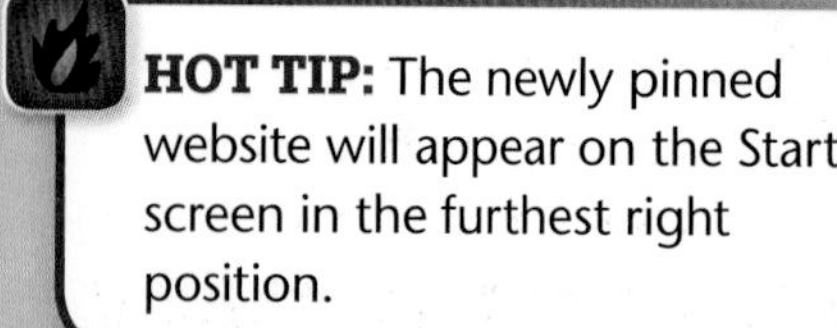

HOT TIP: The newly pinned website will appear on the Start screen in the furthest right position.

DID YOU KNOW?

If you use a Microsoft account to log in to Windows 8, when you log in to another Windows 8 machine your Start screen configuration will be available there, too.

Explore Settings

You can configure settings for the IE app from the Settings charm. These include the ability to delete your browsing history, enable or disable the ability for websites to ask for your physical location, and more.

1. Open the IE app and using any method, bring up the charms.
2. Click Settings.
3. Click Internet Options.

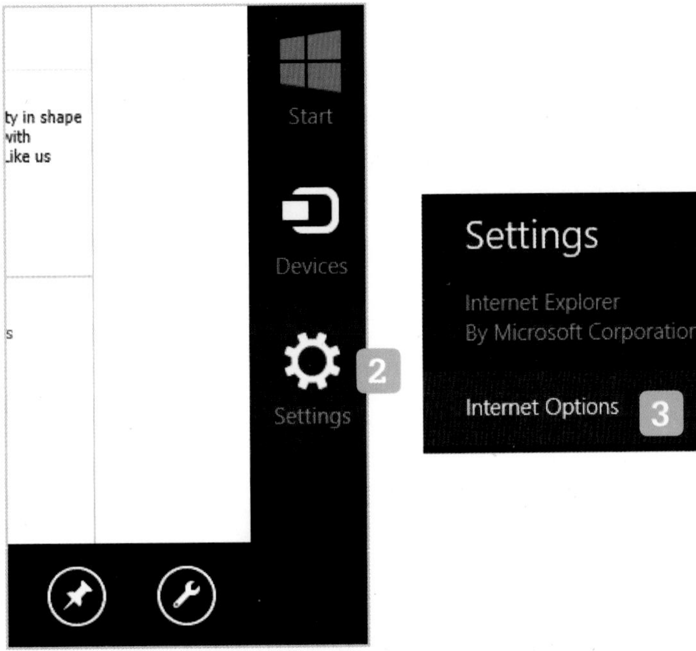

DID YOU KNOW?
Permissions is another option from the Settings charm while in the IE app. Here you can enable or disable notifications.

HOT TIP: You can zoom in and out from the Internet Explorer Settings area.

4 Explore the options.

Delete Browsing History

Deletes temporary files, history, cookies, and saved passwords from Internet Explorer.

Delete

Permissions

Sites can ask for your physical location.

Ask for location

On

If you've already allowed specific sites to locate you, you can clear all existing permissions and start over.

Clear

5 Get an always-available Internet connection

Introduction

You can get online for free at no-cost Wi-Fi hotspots, such as those you find in coffee houses, hotels, libraries and pubs. You can get online through your home network using a router and your ISP's Internet connection. However, if you want to get online from anywhere and at any time, even when there is no free Wi-Fi to connect to, you'll need to sign up with a compatible provider and pay some sort of fee on a weekly, monthly or an as-you-use basis.

There are lots of options available for making a connection to the Internet from your laptop or tablet, including using hardware that is compatible with or provided by mobile phone providers, connecting through personal hotspots you create using a mobile phone you already own, connecting in various ways through numerous Internet service providers (ISPs), and using hardware acquired from satellite providers. In this chapter you'll learn how to choose the option that's best for you and how to get connected.

Set up Wi-Fi settings appropriately

Most companies that provide an Internet connection for a fee limit how much time you can spend on the Internet through their service. 'Time' is really measured in terms of data, though; you're often given a certain amount of data you can use per billing cycle, and if you go over that limit, you have to pay more. Therefore, before you do anything else, you need to verify your Wi-Fi settings are configured to kick in any time a free Wi-Fi network is available.

1. Use the keyboard combination Windows + I to access the Settings charm. Touch users can swipe in from the right side and tap Settings.
2. Click Change PC settings.

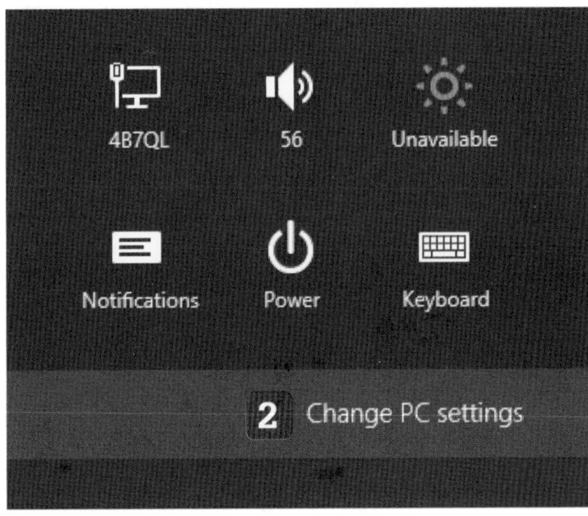

? DID YOU KNOW?

If you sign up for a data plan that offers a very limited amount of usage, say 300 MB of data per month, you won't be able to do much. If you want to watch a one-hour TV episode on Netflix, for instance, you'll use approximately 110 MB of data, almost a third of your allocation. That's where Wi-Fi comes in. What you do when connected to a free Wi-Fi network doesn't count against your paid data amount.

3 Click the Wireless tab and verify Airplane mode is turned off and that Wi-Fi is turned on.

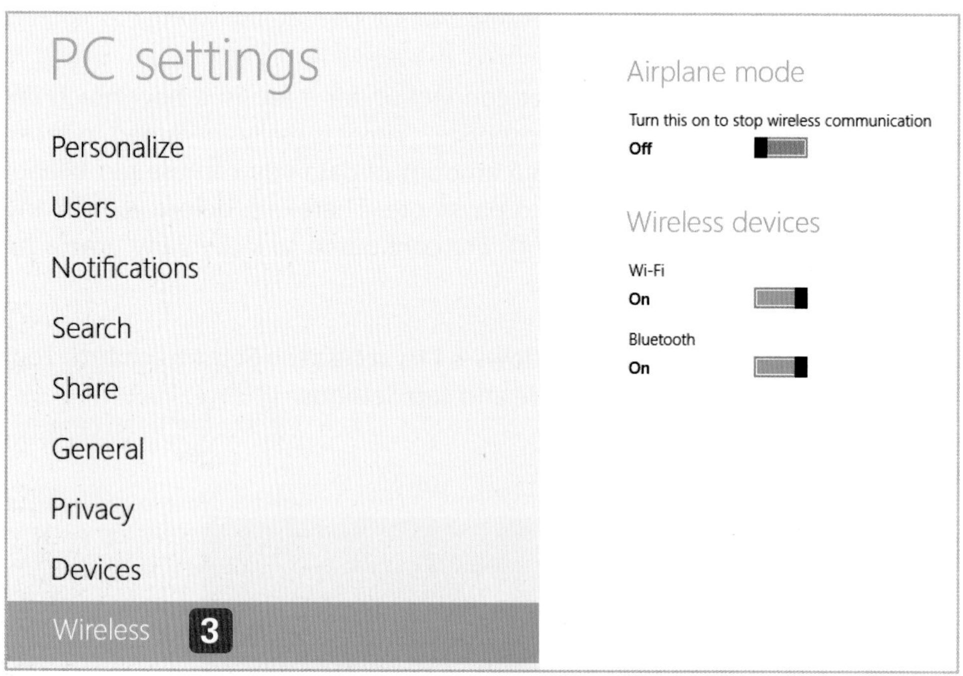

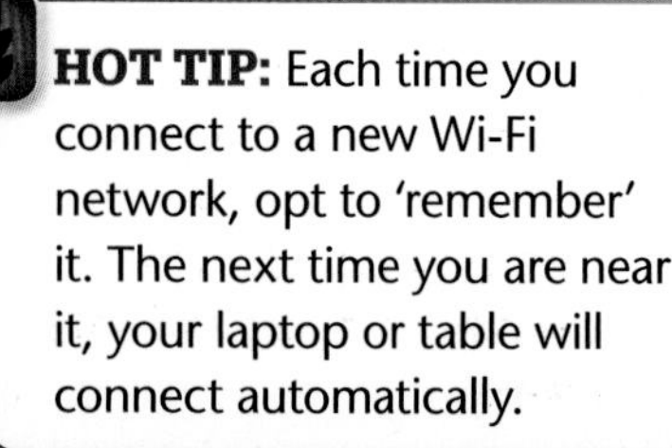

HOT TIP: Each time you connect to a new Wi-Fi network, opt to 'remember' it. The next time you are near it, your laptop or table will connect automatically.

Understand your needs

Before you start shopping for an always-available Internet connection, you should figure out exactly what you want and need, and what your options are. You may have to refer to your laptop or tablet's User's Guide or return to the store where you purchased it to find the answers to some of the questions here.

- If you have a mobile phone, can you turn that phone into a wireless hotspot that you can connect your laptop or tablet to?
- If you purchased your laptop or tablet from a mobile phone store, can you connect through a mobile network they provide?
- If you already subscribe to the Internet through an ISP at home, can you add your laptop to your current plan? If so, what kind of hardware is required?
- Does your laptop or tablet have a USB port you can connect a Wi-Fi device to? If so, you can probably connect using one of many mobile phone providers.
- If you live in the country and far away from any city, what types of services do you have in your area? (A mobile connection may be spotty, for instance, and your only option may be a satellite connection).

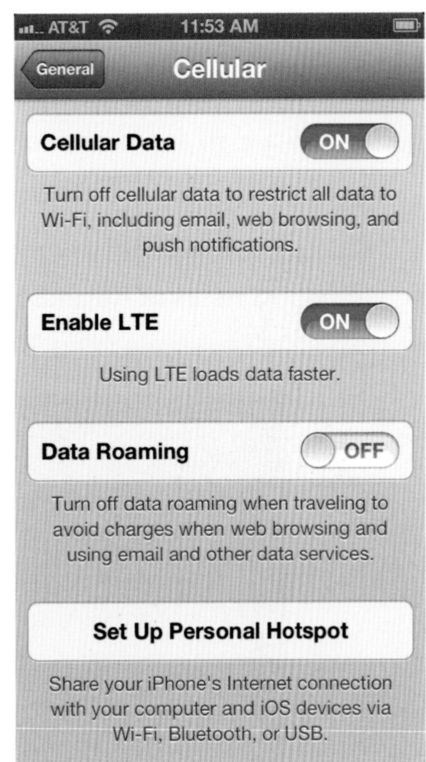

ALERT: If you set up a personal hotspot using your mobile phone, data you use from your laptop or tablet is added to your phone's data plan usage.

HOT TIP: Once you understand your options for connecting, you can then begin the process of comparing prices and data plans.

Know what to ask before committing to a plan

Once you've narrowed down your options for an always-available Internet connection, you need to estimate how much data you're going to need per billing cycle. You may need unlimited access, which is expensive (if you can find this deal at all), but you'll more likely have to decide how much data you want to purchase per billing cycle. Some companies offer data plans that start at 300 MB (megabytes) and go up to 12 or more GB (gigabytes). (1,000 MB equals approximately 1 GB.) These facts will help you decide and are an approximation:

- Sending 1,000 emails per month = 1 GB of data usage.
- Visiting 3,000 websites per month = 3 GB of data usage.
- Viewing 15 hours of streaming video per month = 4 GB of data usage.
- Uploading or downloading 300 pictures per month = 1.5 GB of data usage.

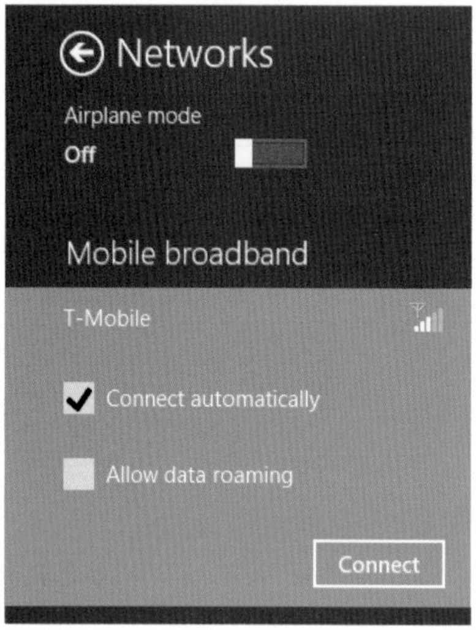

HOT TIP: If given an option, don't enable data roaming.

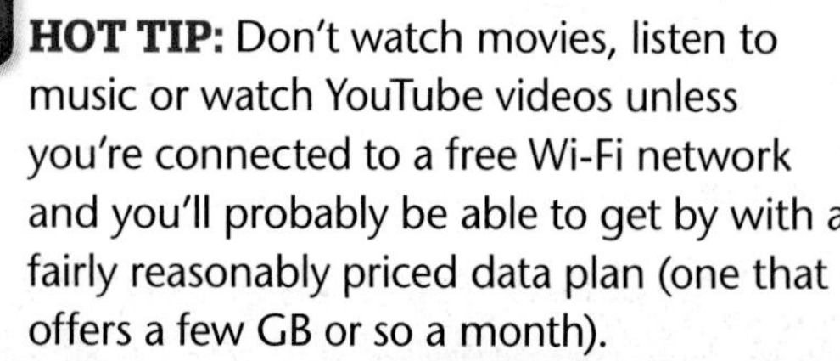

HOT TIP: Don't watch movies, listen to music or watch YouTube videos unless you're connected to a free Wi-Fi network and you'll probably be able to get by with a fairly reasonably priced data plan (one that offers a few GB or so a month).

DID YOU KNOW?

Online gaming doesn't use much data. You can play most online games for 120 hours a month and use only about 0.5 GB of data.

Consider a mobile provider

If you decide to go with a mobile provider, make sure you ask some important questions. You can use the answers to compare the various mobile plans you are considering.

- Do I have to sign a contract for a year or two years or do you have a pay-as-you-go plan?
- Is there a limit on how much data I can use each month? Is there a limit on how many hours I can be online? How much does it cost if I go over that limit?
- How much is the service per month? How much will taxes and fees add to that?
- Are there any set-up costs or activation fees?
- Am I required to purchase additional hardware? If so, is it a universally recognised unit like the one shown here, perhaps one that connects via USB?

- Is there a 30-day return policy or grace period, in case the connection is not as good or as strong as I had hoped?

ALERT: Try to stay away from one- and two-year contracts; you may decide later you don't really need the service, the service is poor, or you might find something cheaper.

ALERT: Whichever service you choose, make sure you know you'll be informed via email when you are nearing your data limit.

Consider an ISP

If you already subscribe to the Internet at home through an ISP, that ISP may offer an option for connecting your device. Here are a few things to ask when you contact your current provider:

- Can I add my laptop or tablet to my current plan and receive a bundled rate?
- Do you have a pay-as-you-go plan?
- What kind of hardware do I need to purchase or rent to make the connection from my laptop or tablet?
- Is there a limit to how much data I can use or how many hours I can be online?
- How large is your coverage area?

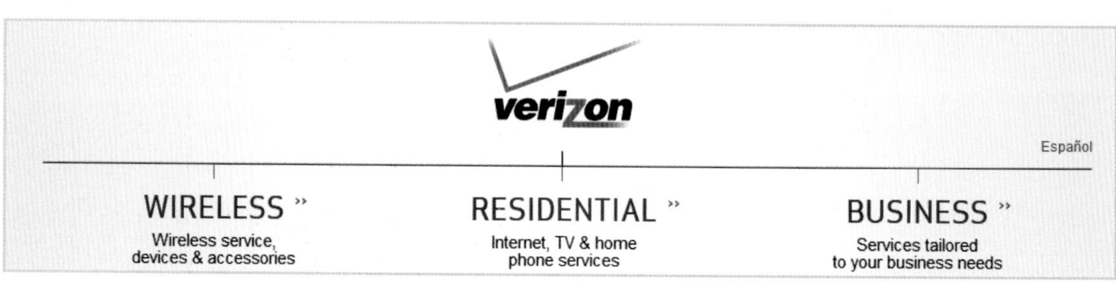

? DID YOU KNOW?
Many ISPs do more than provide cable TV and Internet. Many also provide a mobile service. This means that although you may opt to obtain service using what you believe to be a broadband ISP, it may really provide a mobile connection.

HOT TIP: Make sure your ISP provider will tell you when you are nearing your data limit for the billing cycle.

Consider a satellite provider

If you live way out in the country or between two large mountains, you may not be able to get a strong enough mobile signal to connect to the Internet reliably. If you travel with your laptop to remote areas, you may not be within range of a mobile tower when you arrive there. In these cases (and others) you should consider a satellite provider. Perform an Internet search for satellite providers in the UK for more information.

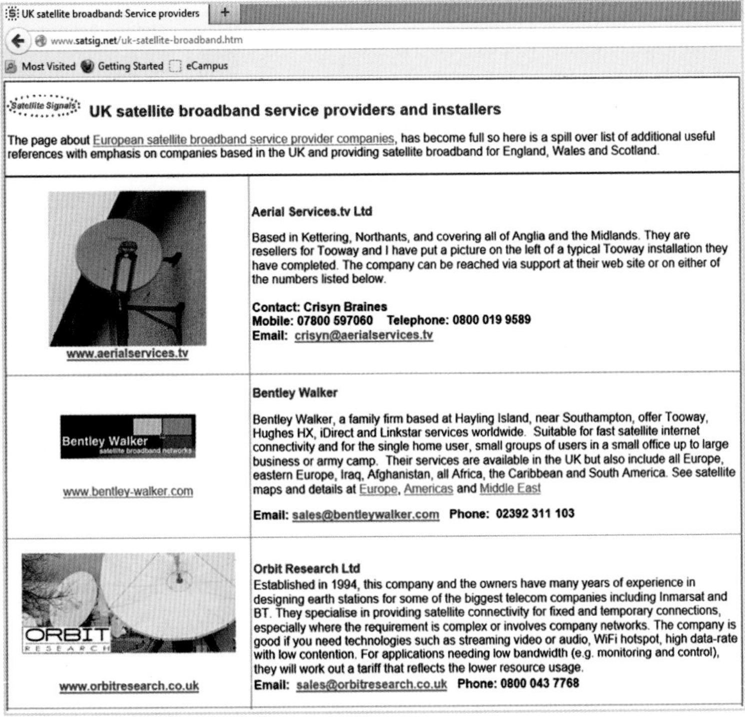

UK satellite broadband: Service providers

www.satsig.net/uk-satellite-broadband.htm

Most Visited Getting Started eCampus

Satellite Signals UK satellite broadband service providers and installers

The page about European satellite broadband service provider companies, has become full so here is a spill over list of additional useful references with emphasis on companies based in the UK and providing satellite broadband for England, Wales and Scotland.

www.aerialservices.tv

Aerial Services.tv Ltd

Based in Kettering, Northants, and covering all of Anglia and the Midlands. They are resellers for Tooway and I have put a picture on the left of a typical Tooway installation they have completed. The company can be reached via support at their web site or on either of the numbers listed below.

Contact: Crisyn Braines
Mobile: 07800 597060 Telephone: 0800 019 9589
Email: crisyn@aerialservices.tv

Bentley Walker satellite broadband networks

www.bentley-walker.com

Bentley Walker

Bentley Walker, a family firm based at Hayling Island, near Southampton, offer Tooway, Hughes HX, iDirect and Linkstar services worldwide. Suitable for fast satellite internet connectivity and for the single home user, small groups of users in a small office up to large business or army camp. Their services are available in the UK but also include all Europe, eastern Europe, Iraq, Afghanistan, all Africa, the Caribbean and South America. See satellite maps and details at Europe, Americas and Middle East

Email: sales@bentleywalker.com **Phone: 02392 311 103**

ORBIT RESEARCH

www.orbitresearch.co.uk

Orbit Research Ltd

Established in 1994, this company and the owners have many years of experience in designing earth stations for some of the biggest telecom companies including Inmarsat and BT. They specialise in providing satellite connectivity for fixed and temporary connections, especially where the requirement is complex or involves company networks. The company is good if you need technologies such as streaming video or audio, WiFi hotspot, high data-rate with low contention. For applications needing low bandwidth (e.g. monitoring and control), they will work out a tariff that reflects the lower resource usage.

Email: sales@orbitresearch.co.uk **Phone: 0800 043 7768**

Satellite providers generally offer the following:

- Options for Internet speeds. Faster speeds cost more; slower speeds cost less.
- Hardware that is compatible with your device.
- A connection to the Internet in places where cable and DSL won't reach.

? DID YOU KNOW?
You need a clear view of the sky for best satellite access and performance.

! ALERT: Satellite Internet is generally more expensive than other options, so use it as a last resort.

Obtain the proper settings

Once you've decided on a provider, you'll need to call them to set up the subscription, follow the directions offered on the device or with it, or follow the instructions offered online. There are some important things to know, and you must write these things down and keep them in a safe place. Keep in mind that not all of these are required in all instances.

- Phone number – mobile devices are associated with a phone number, even if you can't use them to make a phone call.
- Passcode/passphrase – mobile devices include a passcode or passphrase for connection.
- SSID – mobile devices that can be configured as hotspots that others can connect to are configured with an SSID. This is the name of the network.
- Device ID – devices come with an ID, sometimes called an ESN, IMEI or MEID.
- User name – might be required to log on to the Internet.
- Account name (this may be the same as user name) – the name used to log on to the Internet.
- Password – a group of numbers, letters and symbols often used to secure your Internet connection.

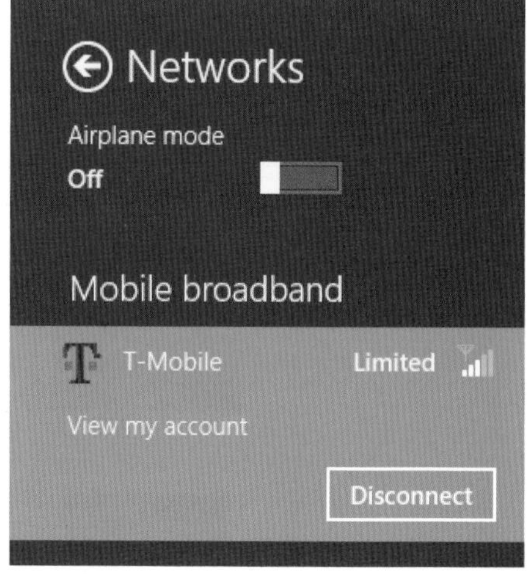

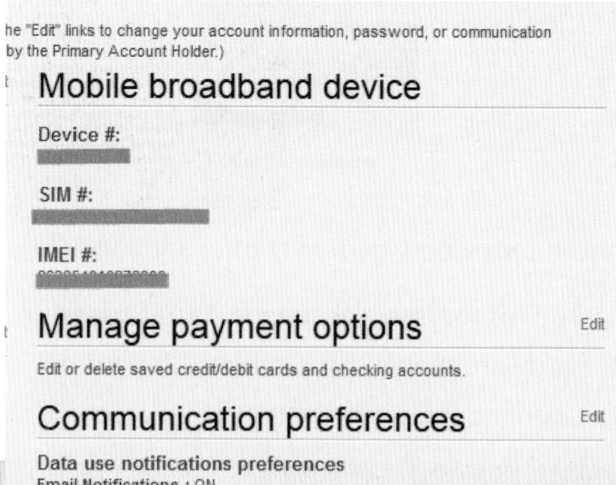

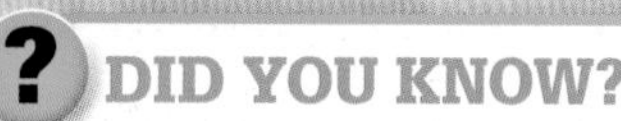

DID YOU KNOW?

Sometimes you can obtain the information you need by logging on to the provider's website by clicking View my account or something similar.

HOT TIP: Once your subscription and hardware are set up, you won't be required to input this information again.

Make the connection

Before you can connect to the Internet, you need to install any hardware you've received. This may mean inserting a USB adapter or installing a program from a CD or DVD. Generally, the first time the USB stick or CD/DVD is inserted, the installation program runs automatically.

1. Insert the USB Wi-Fi adapter and work through the installation process, if applicable.
2. If no installation is required, follow the instructions provided by your ISP, satellite or mobile provider.
3. The first time you connect to any network you'll be prompted to choose how to share. Choose No, don't turn on sharing or connect to devices.

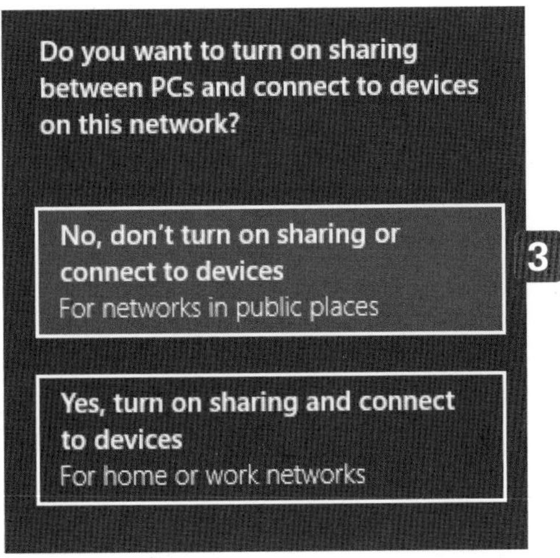

? DID YOU KNOW?

Once you've set up your device or connection, use the Settings charm and the Network icon there to connect.

6 Perform computer basics on the Desktop

Introduction

Now that you know a little about the Start screen, apps, charms, and other Windows 8 features, it's time to learn a few Desktop techniques. You may already be familiar with the Desktop, and some of this may be old hat to you. For instance, you may already know how to access programs, files, folders and the like from the taskbar. You may also know how to open a file or folder, and what options are available for organizing your data. However, there are other things to learn, including how to back up your data and work at the desktop while still maintaining access to other areas of the computer.

Explore the Desktop

No matter what kind of device you have, if it has Windows 8 installed on it, you have access to the Desktop. This is the familiar, traditional computing environment you're used to (if you've used a computer before, that is).

1 Use any method to access the Start screen. (You can tap the Windows key on the keyboard.)

2 From the Start screen, click or tap Desktop.

3 Note the Desktop features:

a. The Recycle Bin.
b. The taskbar.
c. The Internet Explorer icon. IE is open here.
d. The File Explorer icon (we've opened File Explorer here).
e. The Notification area.
f. Personal items.
g. Open programs.
h. Programs pinned to the taskbar.

ALERT: The Start button was not available on the taskbar when this book was written. If you'd like to access something like it, press the Windows + X key combination.

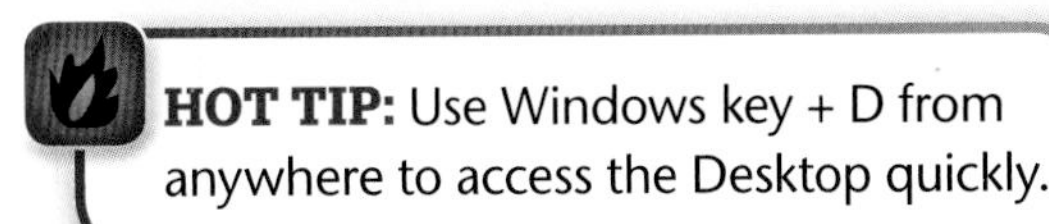

HOT TIP: Use Windows key + D from anywhere to access the Desktop quickly.

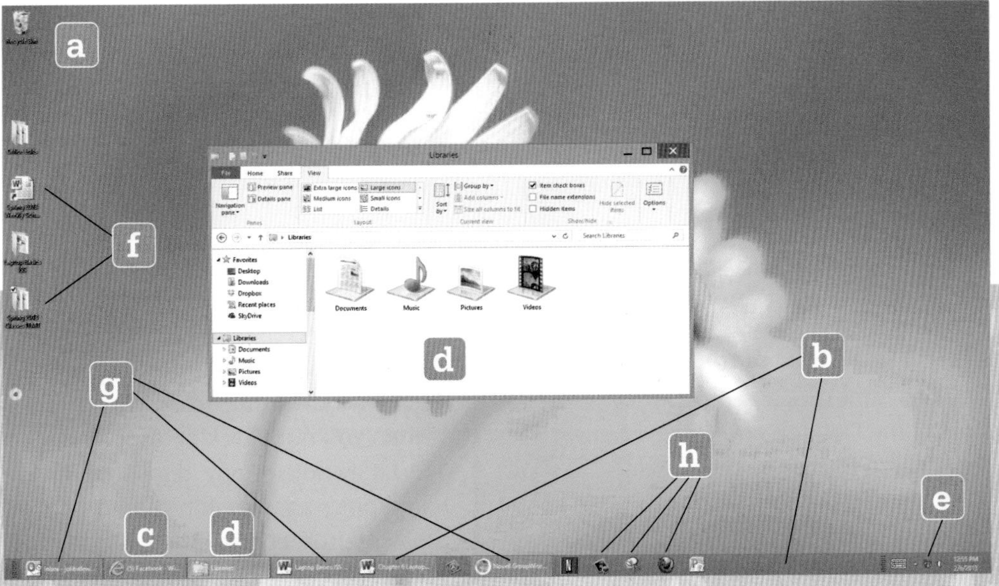

Learn Desktop techniques

While at the Desktop you can apply a few techniques to perform tasks, such as using a right-click to access a contextual menu and dragging and dropping to move icons.

1. If you aren't on the Desktop, use Windows + D to get there.
2. Right-click (or tap and hold on a touch screen) to access various Desktop options.

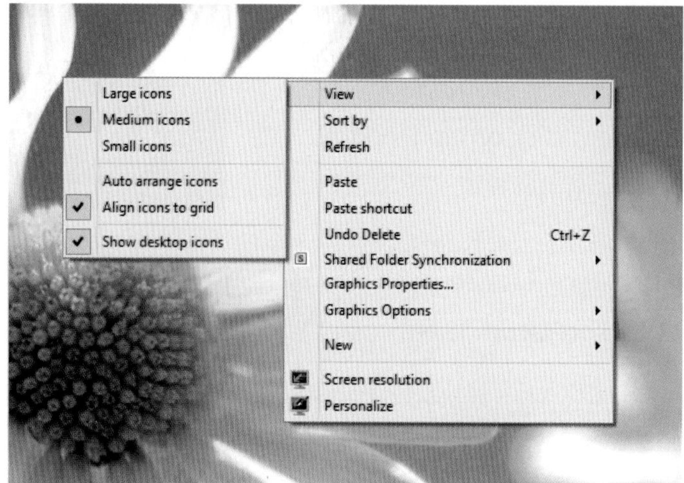

3. Click outside of these options to hide the contextual menu.
4. Left-click and drag the Recycle Bin to another area of the screen.
5. Drop it there.

DID YOU KNOW?
You can right-click an empty area of the Desktop and click Personalize to change the Desktop background, among other things.

ALERT: Some computer manufacturers add their own touches to what's available when you right-click on the Desktop. You may not see any items that involve a graphics adapter, for instance, but you may see something else that isn't.

Explore the taskbar

The taskbar runs across the bottom of the Desktop and holds icons for File Explorer and Internet Explorer, among others. You can click or tap the icon to open the item it represents. Additionally, you can personalise the taskbar by adding your own icons for programs, folders and so on that you use often. You'll learn how to do this in Chapter 7. The taskbar also holds the Notification area.

1. Locate the taskbar.
2. Locate the Notification area.
3. Locate the Internet Explorer icon.
4. Locate the File Explorer icon.
5. Right-click an empty area of the taskbar to access personalisation options.

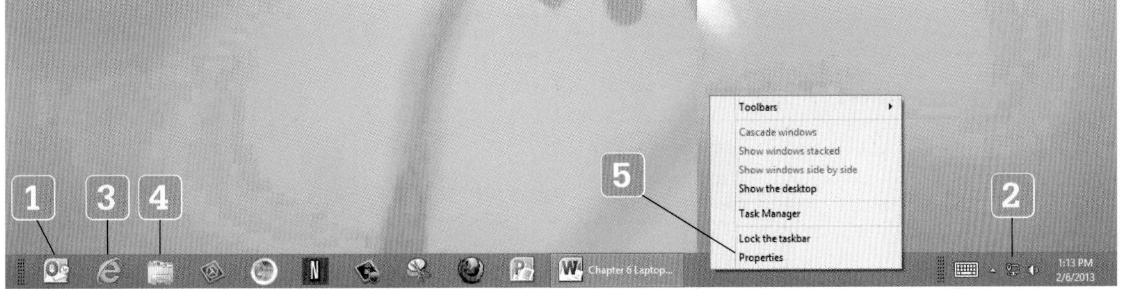

? DID YOU KNOW?
You can drag the taskbar to another side of the screen – left, right or top – provided it is not locked (right-click the taskbar to find out).

HOT TIP: Right-click an empty area of the taskbar and choose Properties, then opt to hide the taskbar when you aren't using it. Position the cursor where the taskbar should be to show it once hidden.

Understand libraries in File Explorer

Libraries offer a place to access related data. The Documents library lets you access documents stored in the My Documents folder, the Public Documents folder, and any subfolders you've created in those folders. Likewise, the Pictures library offers access to the My Pictures and Public Pictures folders, and any subfolders you've created there.

1. Click the folder icon on the taskbar.
2. Click Libraries in the left pane.
3. Click any library icon in the resulting right pane to view its contents. Here, we've selected Pictures. Pictures becomes the selected item in the left pane.

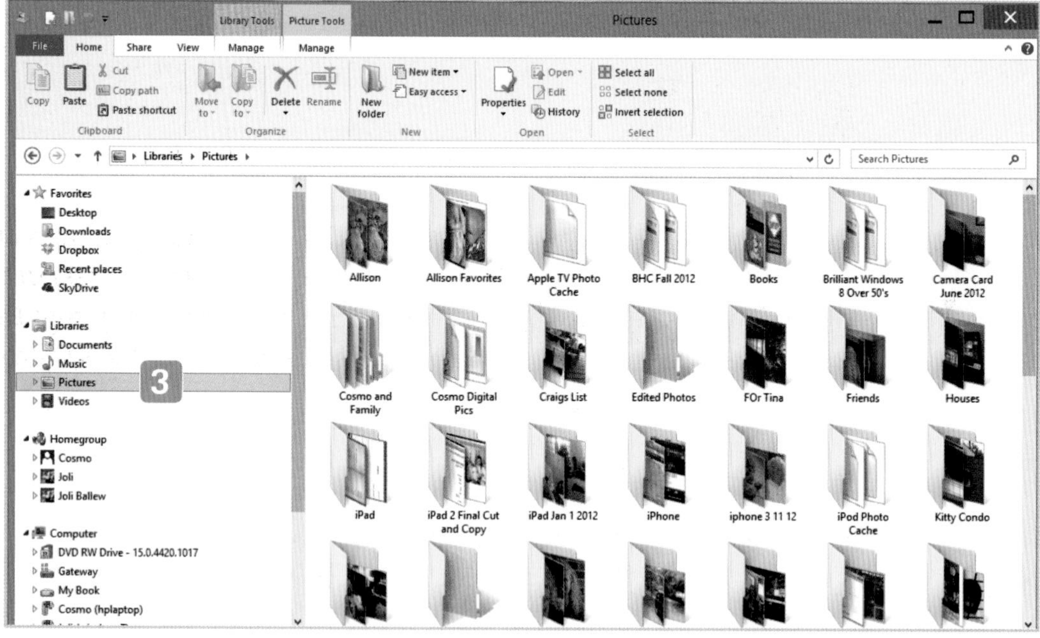

HOT TIP: You can create your own libraries or add folders to any library to personalise them.

? DID YOU KNOW?

To include a folder in a library's results, right-click the library name under Libraries and choose Properties. From there you can click Include a folder to get started.

Open, close, resize the File Explorer window

A window can be minimised (on the taskbar), maximised (filling the entire Desktop) or in restore mode (not maximised or minimised but showing on the Desktop). When in restore mode, you can drag from any corner or edge to resize it. (You can't do that when it is maximised because every corner is a hot corner!)

- A maximised window is as large as it can be and takes up the entire screen. You can maximise a window that is on the Desktop by clicking the square in the top right corner. If the icon shows two squares, it's already maximised. (You can drag down from the middle of the title bar to change its size.)

DID YOU KNOW?
Every corner of the Windows 8 screen is a hot corner. This means you can move your mouse there and something will become available, like charms or the last app used, or quick access to the Start screen.

- When a window is in restore mode, you can resize the window by dragging from any corner or edge. An icon is in restore mode if there is a single square in the top right corner. You can access this mode from the maximised position by dragging from the title bar downwards. Here you can see the Desktop background behind the window.

- When a window is minimised, it does not appear on the screen and instead is relegated to the taskbar. You cannot resize the window while on the taskbar.

DID YOU KNOW?
Holding down the Alt key and pressing the Tab key repeatedly allows you to move through open windows on the Desktop. When you stop, the selected window will become the active window.

HOT TIP: To bring any window to the front of the others, click its title bar. This makes it the active window.

Change the view in a window

When you open most File Explorer windows, you will see additional folders inside them. You'll use these subfolders to organise the data you create and save, such as documents, pictures and songs. You can change the appearance of these folders so that you can more easily view them on your laptop or tablet.

1. Open File Explorer.
2. In the Navigation pane, click Pictures.
3. From the View tab, select a new layout. For Pictures, try Extra large icons.

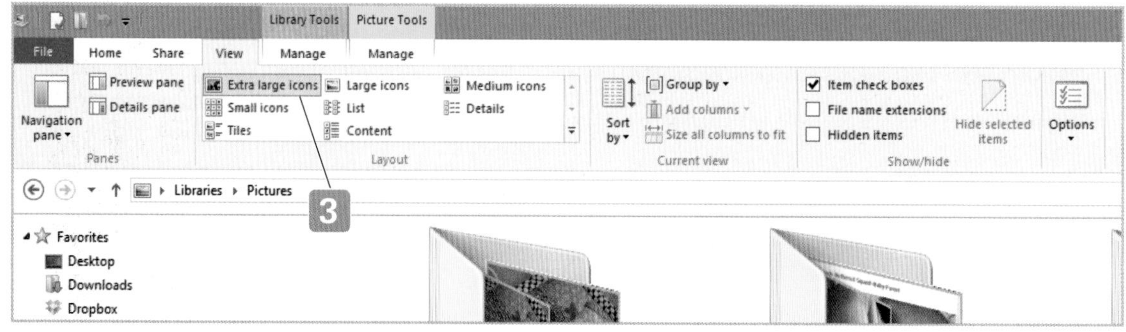

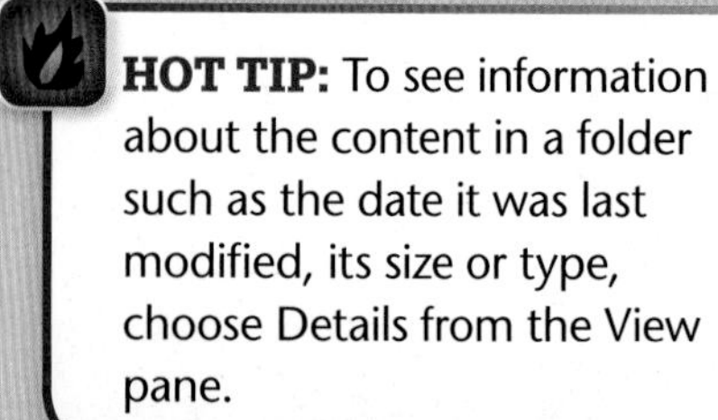

HOT TIP: To see information about the content in a folder such as the date it was last modified, its size or type, choose Details from the View pane.

DID YOU KNOW?
You can opt to show the Preview pane or Details pane in any File Explorer window. These options are also on the View tab.

Snap a window to the side of the Desktop

When working on the Desktop with multiple open windows, sometimes minimising, maximising and restoring or resizing isn't exactly what you want to do. Perhaps you want to make two windows share the screen equally, see what is behind the open windows, or minimise all the open windows except one quickly. You can do this with Snap, Peek and Shake.

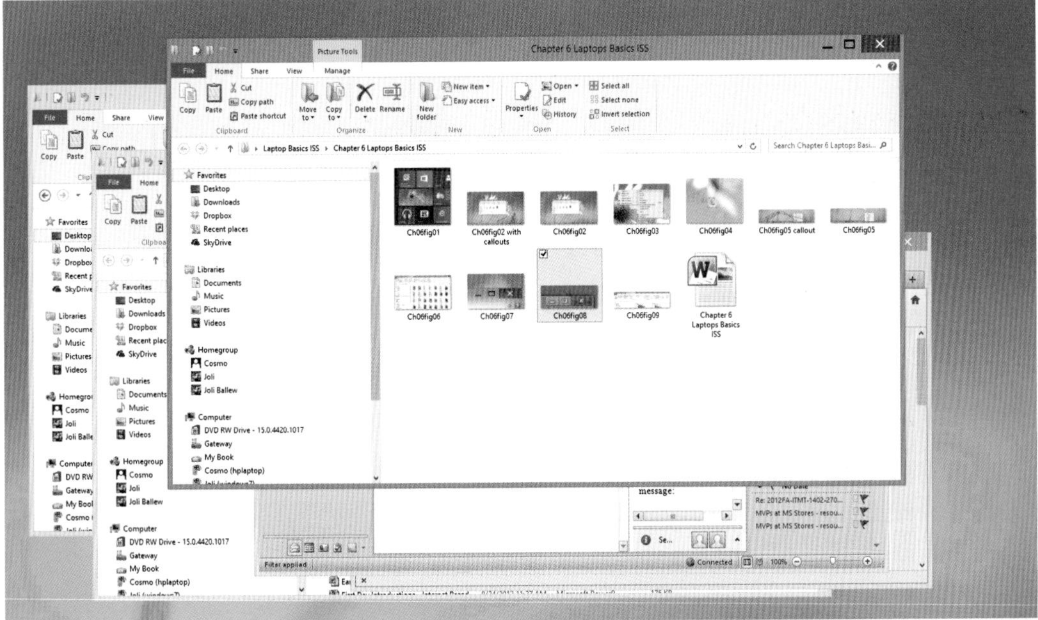

- Snap – to position two open windows so that each takes up half of the screen, using their title bars, drag one quickly to the left and the other quickly to the right. Each will 'snap' into place.
- Peek – to view what's on the Desktop, position your mouse in the bottom right corner of the Desktop. The windows will become transparent and you can see behind them.

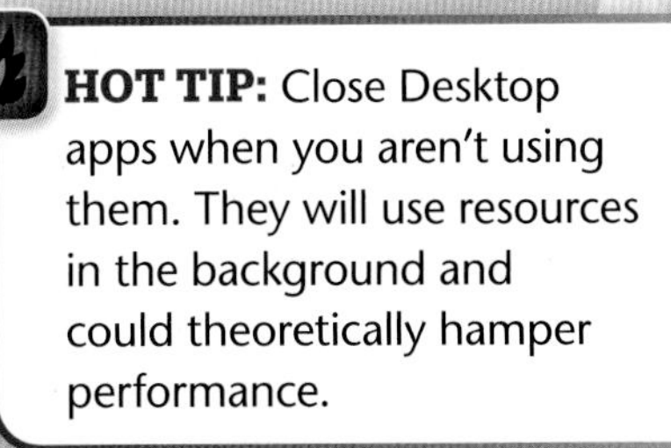

HOT TIP: Close Desktop apps when you aren't using them. They will use resources in the background and could theoretically hamper performance.

- Shake – to minimise all but one window, click, hold and quickly move your mouse left and right on the window to keep. This 'shaking' motion will make the others fall to the taskbar.
- If you have an app open, you can position the app to take up a third of the screen by dragging it in from the left side. Position your mouse in the top left corner, drag downwards to find the app to position, and drag inwards. It will snap into place.

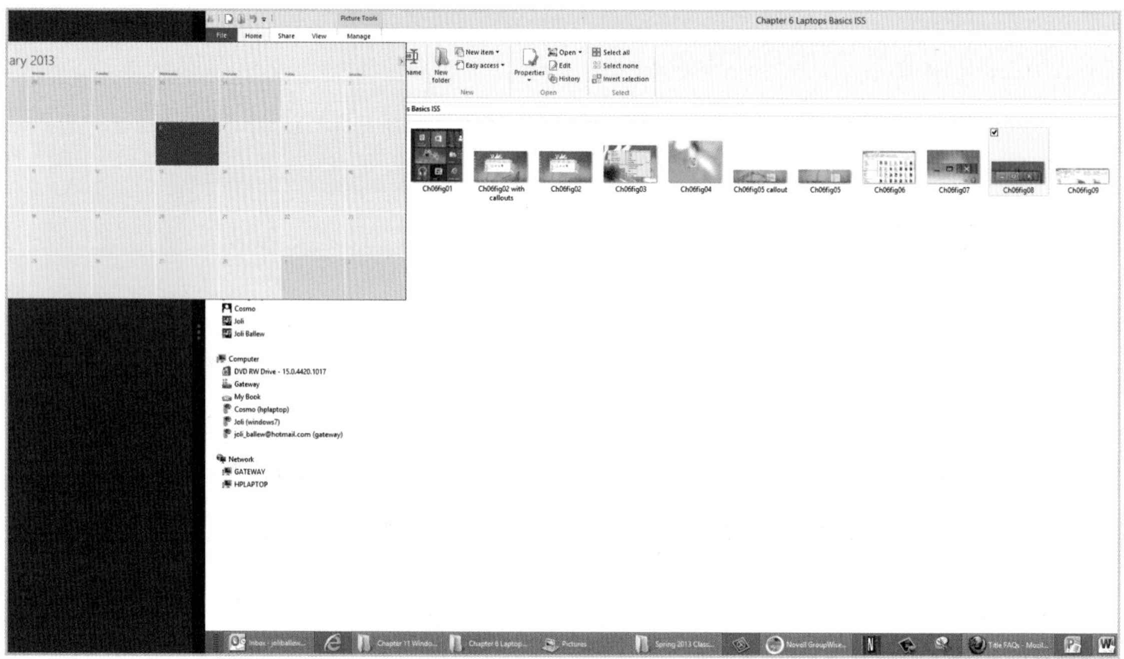

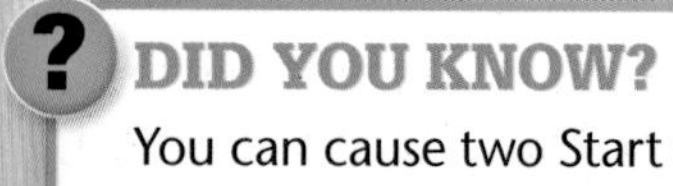

DID YOU KNOW?

You can cause two Start screen apps to share a single screen by dragging one inwards from the left side of the screen. Touch users, use your finger.

Create a folder or subfolder

The default folders and subfolders will suit your needs for a while, but soon you'll want to create your own subfolders to manage your data and keep it organised. You could create subfolders inside My Pictures named Children, Pets, Holidays and Friends, and then move related photos into them, for example. Likewise, you could create subfolders inside My Documents named Taxes, Health, CVs and Letters.

1. On the Desktop, from the taskbar, open File Explorer.
2. In the Navigation pane, select the folder to hold the new folder you'll create. (We've chosen My Videos.)
3. From the Home tab, click New folder.

? DID YOU KNOW?
You can right-click the Desktop or inside any folder, point to New and then click Folder to create a subfolder.

! ALERT: If you can't type a name for the folder or if you'd like to rename it, click the folder and from the Home tab, click Rename. (You can also right-click the folder to rename it.)

4 Name the folder and press Enter on the keyboard.

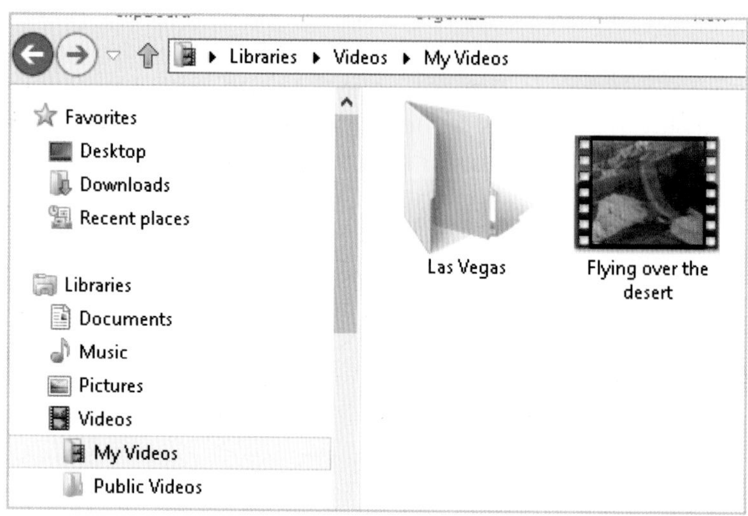

DID YOU KNOW?

You can drag the folder to another area of the Desktop or even to another area of the hard drive to move it there. (To make sure you're moving and not copying though, right-click while you do it.)

HOT TIP: Create a folder to hold data related to a hobby, tax information, work or family.

Move a folder or file

Folders contain files. Files can be documents, pictures, music, videos and more. Sometimes you'll need to copy a file to another location. Perhaps you want to copy files to an external drive, memory card or USB thumb or flash drive for the purpose of backing them up. In most other instances though, moving is a better option, such as when you create a subfolder to organise data in a parent folder and want to propagate the folder with data.

1. In File Explorer, locate a file to copy or move. Click it once to select it.
2. If the subfolder is available in the open folder, right-click the file and drag it there. Let go. You can then choose whether to move or copy the file.

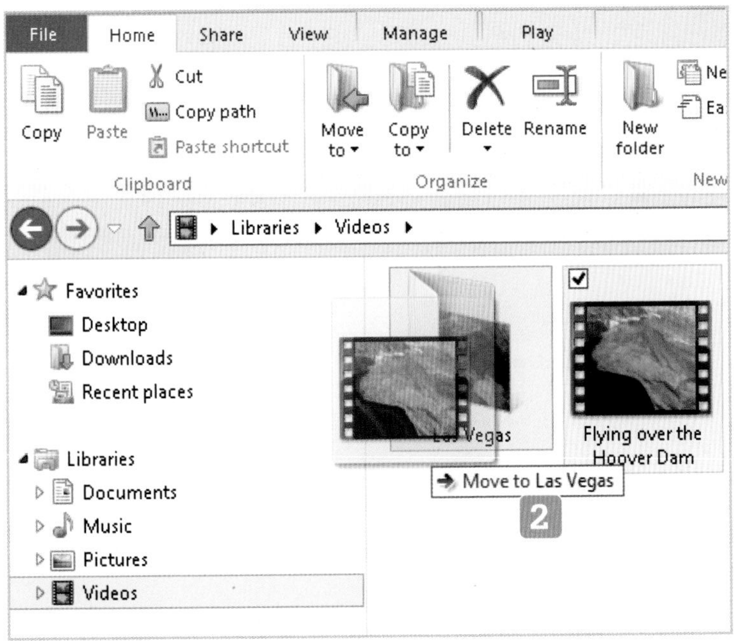

DID YOU KNOW?

When you copy something, an exact duplicate is made. The original copy of the data remains where it is and a copy of it is placed somewhere else. For the most part, this is not what you want to do when organising data because you generally want to move the data.

3 If the subfolder is not readily available:

a. Click the file once to select it.
b. From the Home tab, click either Move to or Copy to.
c. Choose the desired location from the list. If you don't see it, click Choose location.

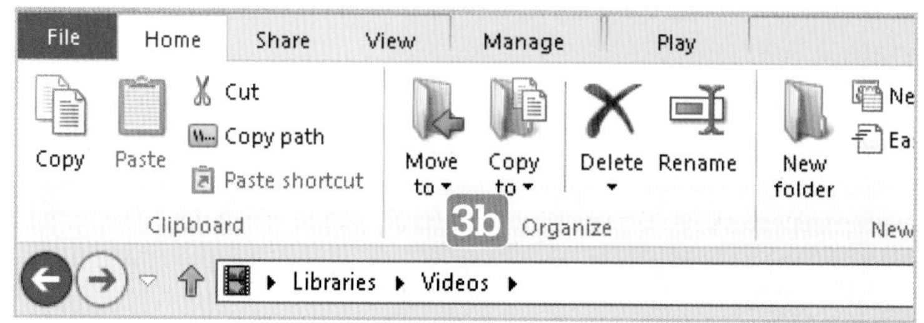

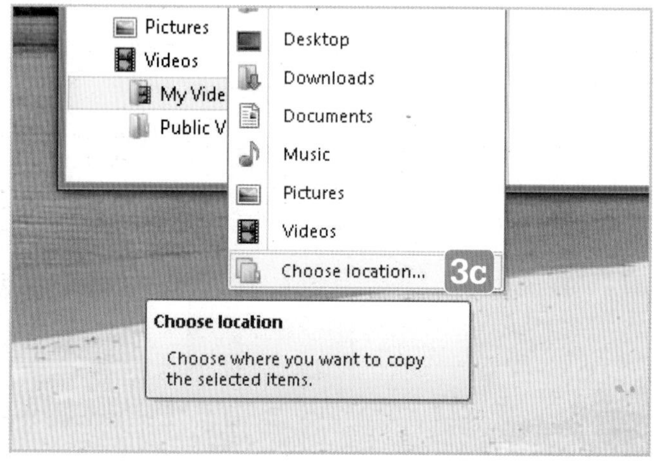

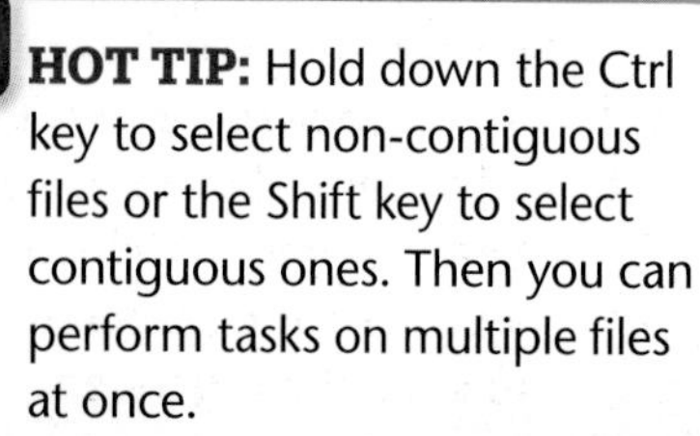
HOT TIP: Hold down the Ctrl key to select non-contiguous files or the Shift key to select contiguous ones. Then you can perform tasks on multiple files at once.

Search for a file or other item

After you create data, such as a Notepad document, you save it to your hard drive. When you're ready to use the file again, you have to locate it and open it. There are several ways to locate a saved file. If you know the document is in the My Documents folder, you can open File Explorer and click Documents. Then you can double-click the file to open it. However, if you aren't sure where the file is, you can search for it from the Start screen. Here, we'll search for a video.

1. Click the Windows key on the keyboard to return to the Start screen.
2. Start typing the name of the file or a unique word in the file.
3. Click Files in the Search pane.
4. Click the desired result.

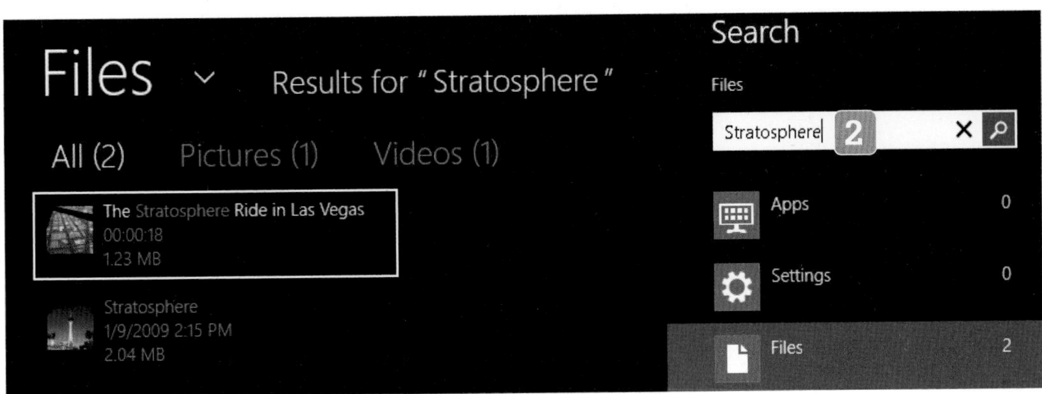

DID YOU KNOW?

You can search for a word *in a file*, such as a word in a document or presentation slide. You don't have to search using a word in the file name. The word will need to be unique though, so that the results don't offer too many files to browse through.

HOT TIP: If you have to search for files often, it may be because your file system isn't organised very well. Consider spending some time creating subfolders and moving data into them to be better organised.

Back up a folder to an external drive

One way to back up your data is to copy it to an external drive. You can copy data to a DVD drive, a USB drive, a network drive or a larger external backup drive (among others). You copy the folder to the external drive the same way you'd copy a folder to another area of your hard drive – you use the Copy command from the Home tab of any File Explorer window.

1. Using File Explorer, select the data to copy.
2. From the Home tab, click Copy to.
3. Click Choose location. (Steps 2 and 3 are not shown here.)
4. Click Copy.

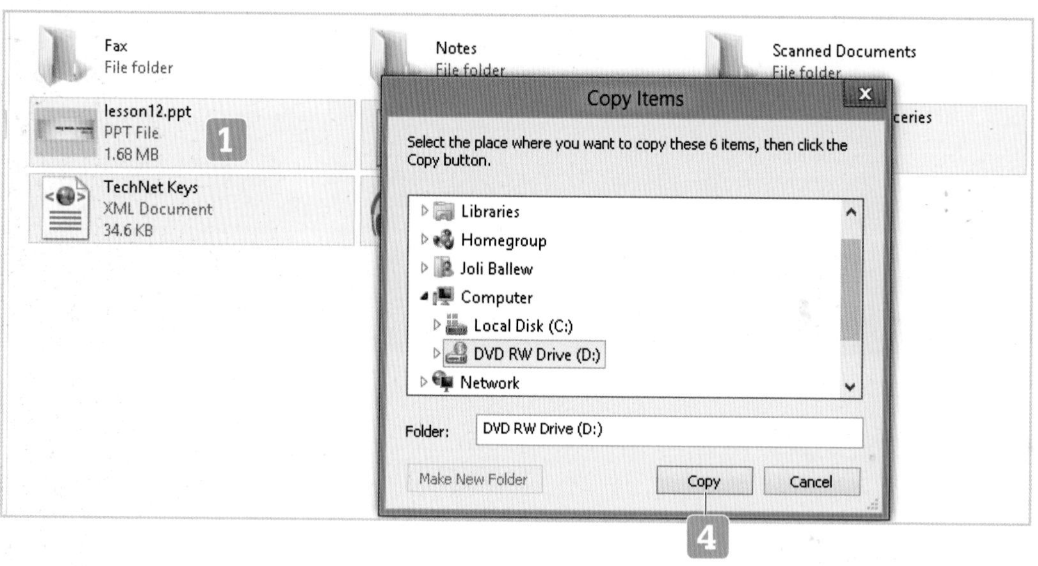

ALERT: Before you begin, plug in and/or attach the external drive if applicable.

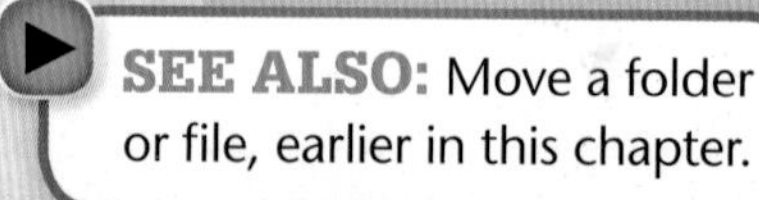

SEE ALSO: Move a folder or file, earlier in this chapter.

7 Explore Desktop apps

Introduction

Desktop applications open on the Desktop, the traditional computing environment (as opposed to the newer Start screen apps that offer charms and do not require the Desktop to function). These applications can be programs you install, such as Adobe Photoshop Elements or Mozilla Firefox, or less complex applications that come with printers, cameras or scanners. They can be Windows accessories too, like the Calculator, WordPad, the Snipping Tool and Sound Recorder. There are lots of programs that need access to the Desktop to run.

In this chapter you'll learn how to locate the Desktop apps from the Start screen and how to use a few of them. After that, whenever an application opens on the Desktop, you'll understand how to use it and why it's a Desktop app.

Search for an application from the Start screen

The Start screen offers access to the applications, programs, accessories and features available on your laptop or tablet, including the Desktop applications (Desktop apps). If they aren't available on the Start screen, you can find them in the All apps screen instead.

1. Access the Start screen. You can press the Windows key to get there.
2. Scroll through what's shown. For the most part, what you see as squares with a blue background are Desktop apps (or features, folders or something similar).
3. Right-click and click All apps.
4. Scroll right and look for additional Desktop apps. A few are shown here.

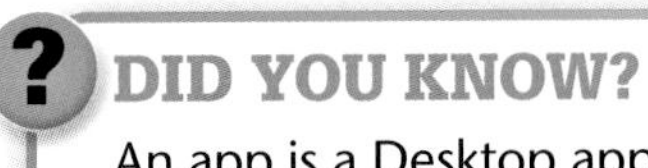

DID YOU KNOW?

An app is a Desktop app if it opens on the Desktop.

WHAT DOES THIS MEAN?

Desktop: the traditional computing environment and offers the taskbar, the Recycle Bin, the Notification area and so on.

Write a letter with WordPad

If you need to create and print a simple document such as a grocery or to-do list, or need to put together a weekly newsletter that you send via email, there's no reason to purchase a large office suite like Microsoft Office (and learn how to use it) when WordPad will do just fine.

1. At the Start screen, type WordPad, then click WordPad.

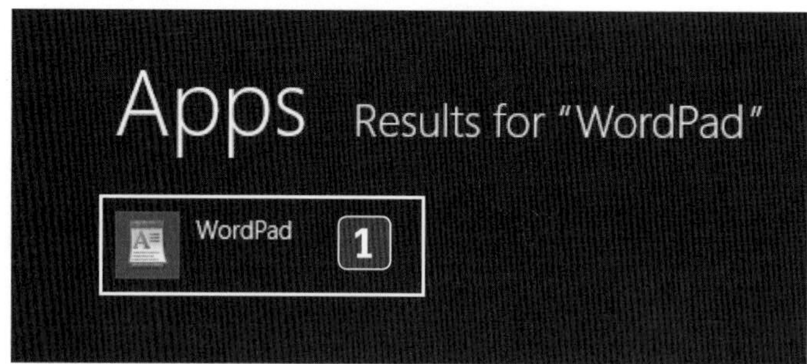

2. Click once inside WordPad and start typing.

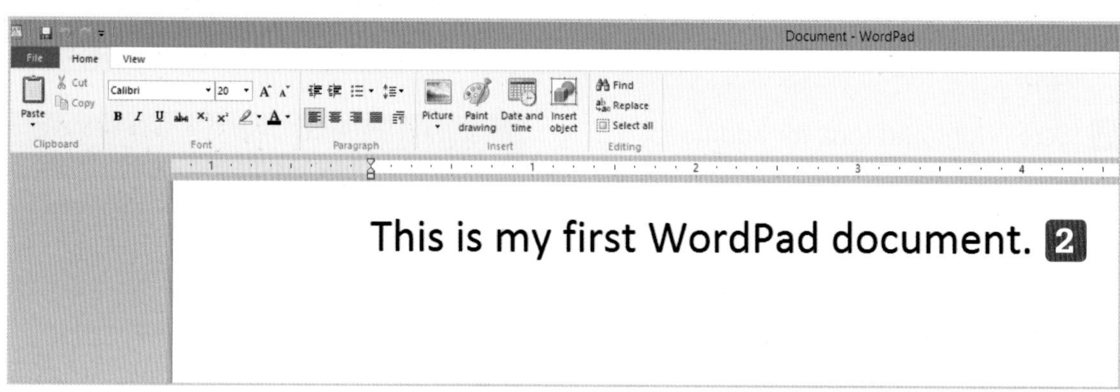

ALERT: If you close WordPad before saving the file, your work will be lost!

ALERT: WordPad has two tabs: Home and View. Each tab group holds related tools. You'll see similar tabs and tab groups in other programs. If time allows, explore these tabs to see what is available there.

DID YOU KNOW?
WordPad's Home tab offers options for setting the font, font style, font size and more.

Save a letter with WordPad

If you want to save a letter, document or similar item you've written in WordPad so you can work with it later, you click the File tab and then click Save as. This will allow you to choose a file type, name the file and save it to your hard drive. The next time you want to view the file, in WordPad, click File and then click Open. You can browse for the file in the resulting dialogue box. The file may also appear in the Recent Documents area of WordPad (under the File tab). Or you can always search for the file from the Start screen by typing the file name and clicking File.

1 With WordPad open and a few words typed, click File.

2 Point to Save as and click Rich Text document.

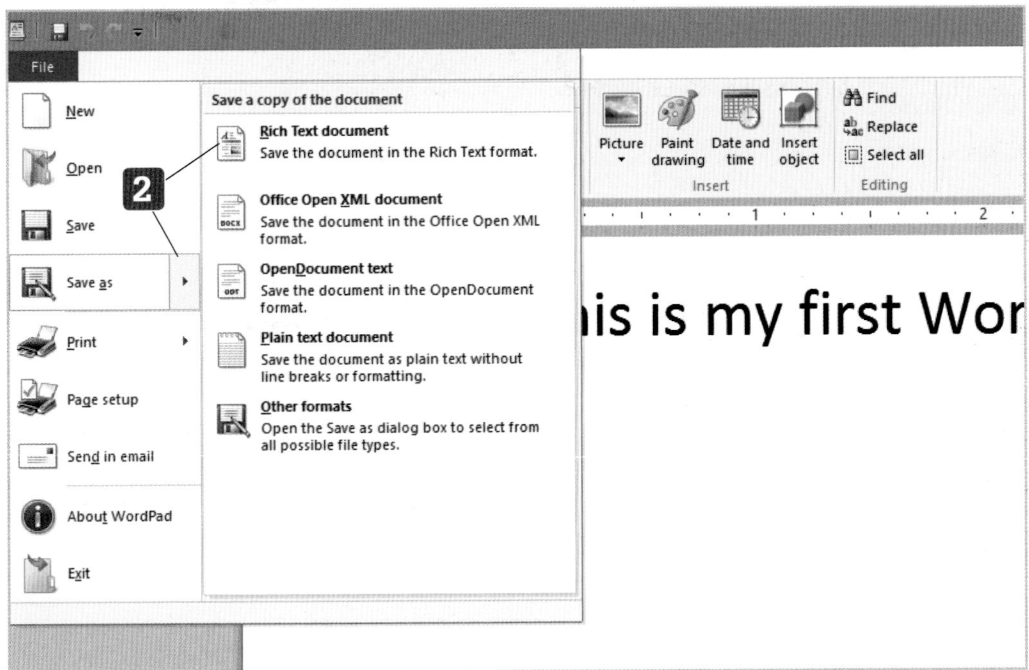

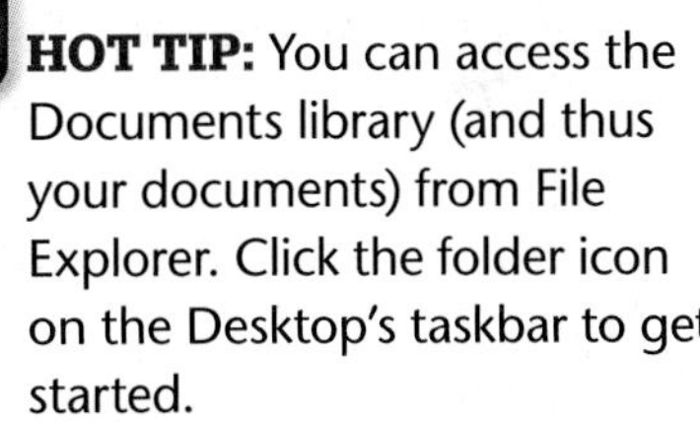

HOT TIP: You can access the Documents library (and thus your documents) from File Explorer. Click the folder icon on the Desktop's taskbar to get started.

DID YOU KNOW?

You can open a saved file and make changes to it and then resave it. Your changes will be saved automatically.

3 Type a unique name for the file. Notice that the default folder for saving a document is the Documents library.

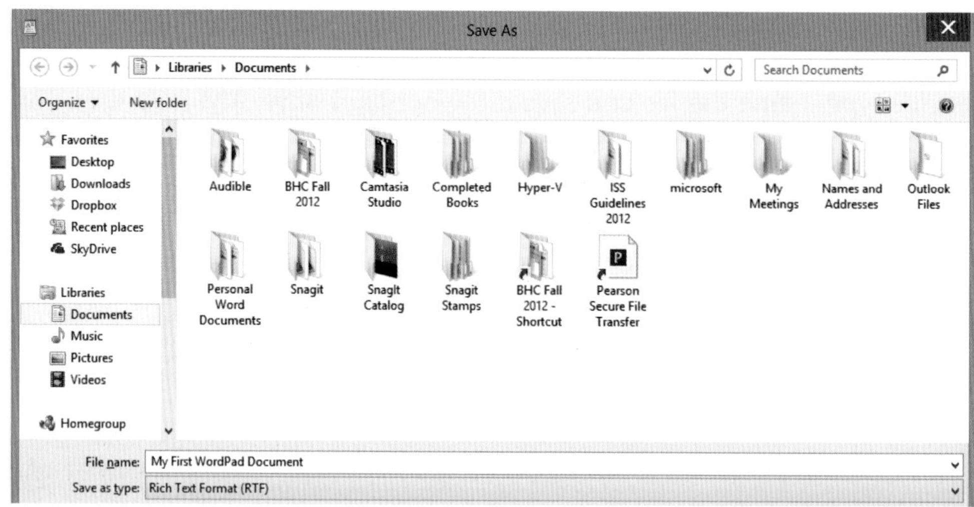

4 Click Save.

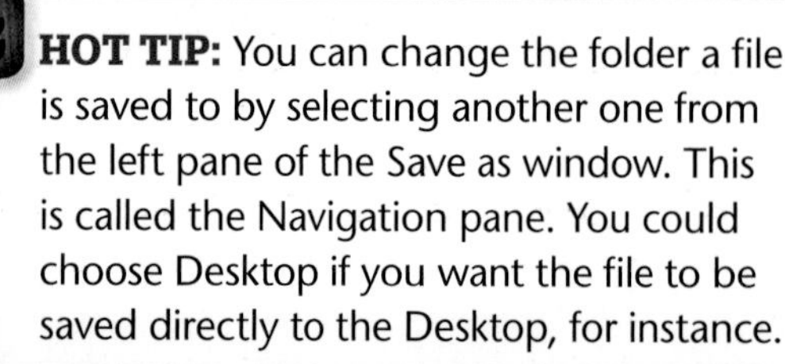

HOT TIP: You can change the folder a file is saved to by selecting another one from the left pane of the Save as window. This is called the Navigation pane. You could choose Desktop if you want the file to be saved directly to the Desktop, for instance.

Print a letter with WordPad

Sometimes you'll need to print a letter so you can post it, print a grocery list to take on a shopping trip, or print a list of steps to follow in order to complete a task. You can access the Print command from WordPad's File menu. If WordPad isn't open, from the Windows 8 Start screen, type the name of the file, and from the Search pane click Files. Then, click the file in the resulting list.

1. With the document open in WordPad, click File.
2. Click Print in the left pane. Note the additional options in the right pane.
3. Select a printer (if more than one exists).
4. Increase the number of copies if you wish. Click Print.

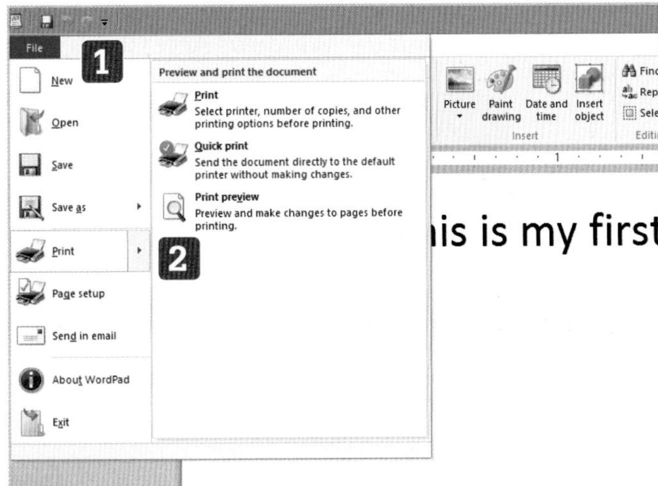

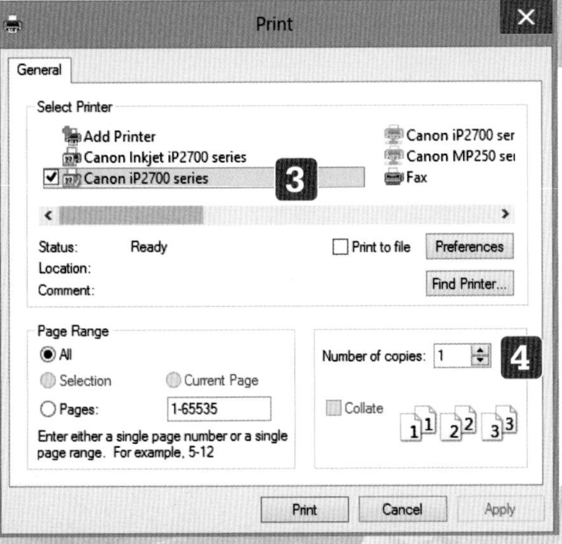

HOT TIP: You must have a printer installed, plugged in and turned on to print. Additionally, the Print dialogue box must show that the printer is 'Ready' before you can print to it.

WHAT DOES THIS MEAN?

Printer Preferences: lets you select the page orientation, print order and type of paper you'll be printing on, among other features.

Page range: lets you select which pages to print.

Use the calculator

You've probably used a calculator before, and using the Windows 8 calculator is not much different from a hand-held one, except that you input numbers with a mouse click, a keyboard, a number pad or your finger. There are four calculators available, and Standard is the default. Calculator is available from the All apps screen.

1. From the Start screen, right-click and then click All apps.
2. Scroll right and under Windows Accessories, click Calculator.

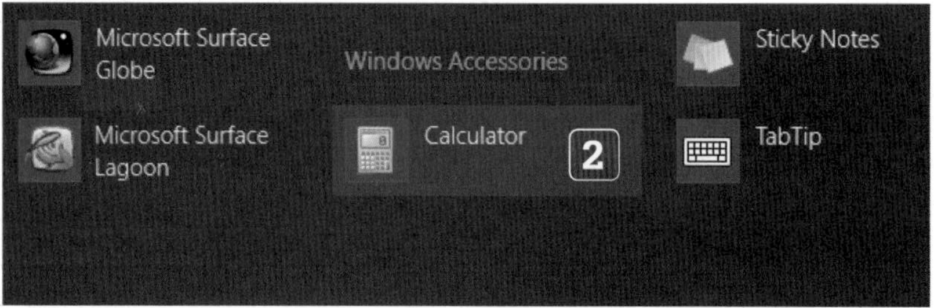

3. Input numbers and operations using any applicable method.
4. Click the View menu to see other calculator options. This is the Scientific calculator. Note the other options.
5. Close Calculator by clicking the X in its top right corner.

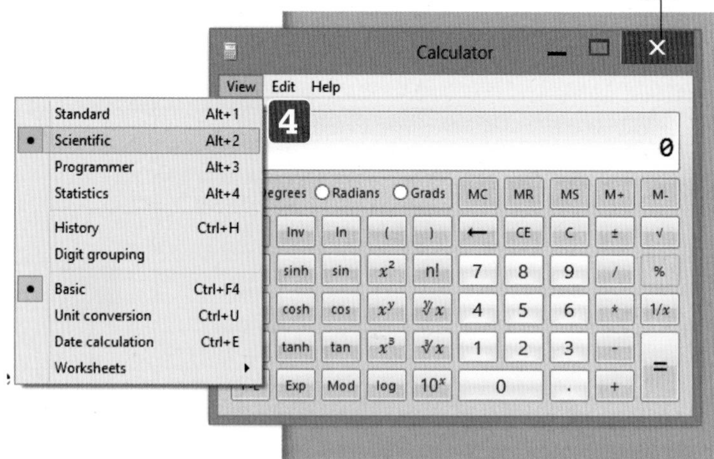

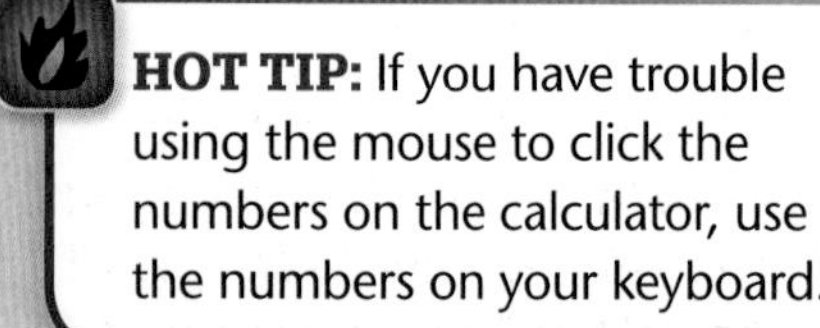
HOT TIP: If you have trouble using the mouse to click the numbers on the calculator, use the numbers on your keyboard.

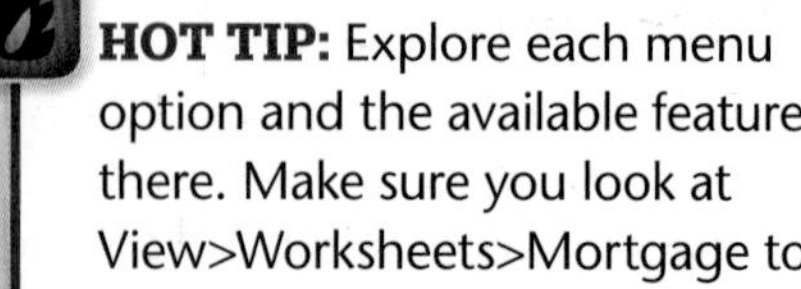
HOT TIP: Explore each menu option and the available features there. Make sure you look at View>Worksheets>Mortgage to see how worksheets function.

Use the Snipping Tool

Sometimes you'll see something on your screen you want to capture to keep or share. It may be the newest, hottest, laptop computer, an article about a place you'd like to visit, or a photo from a webpage that you'd like to share with others. It doesn't matter what it is – you can capture anything that appears on your laptop's screen with the Snipping Tool. Once captured, you can save it, edit it and/or send it to an email recipient.

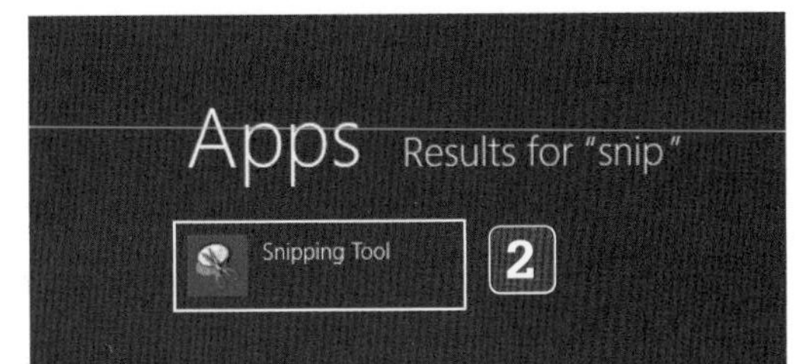

1. From the Start screen, type Snip.
2. In the results, click Snipping Tool.
3. Click New.
4. Drag your mouse across any part of the screen. When you let go of the mouse, the snip will appear in the Snipping Tool window. Here, I've captured the page I'm currently writing.
5. Explore each menu – File, Edit, Tools and Help – and the options on the toolbar. Refer to the next task for more information.

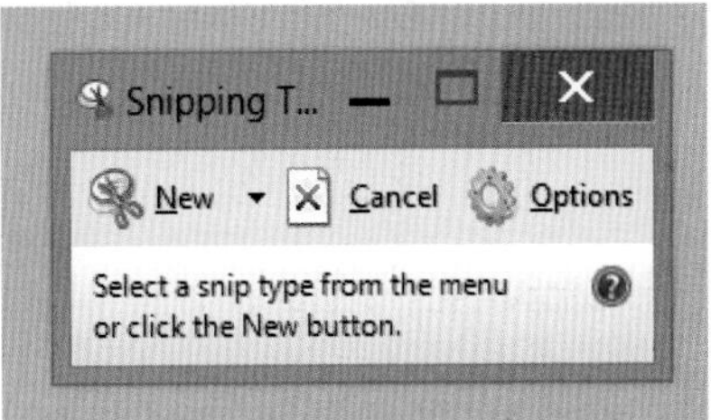

HOT TIP: Editing tools become available after creating a snip. You can write on a clip with a red, blue, black or customised pen or a highlighter, and if you mess up, you can use the eraser.

DID YOU KNOW?
You can open the Snipping Tool from the Start screen's All apps page. If you think you'll use it often, pin it to the taskbar. This is explained at the end of the chapter.

Email a snip

You can use the Snipping Tool to take a picture of your screen as detailed in the previous section. You can even write on it with a 'pen'. You can also email that snip if you'd like to share it with someone.

1. Take a shot of your screen with the Snipping Tool.
2. If you wish, use the pen, highlighter and other tools to write on the image.
3. Click File and click Send To.
4. Click Email Recipient.

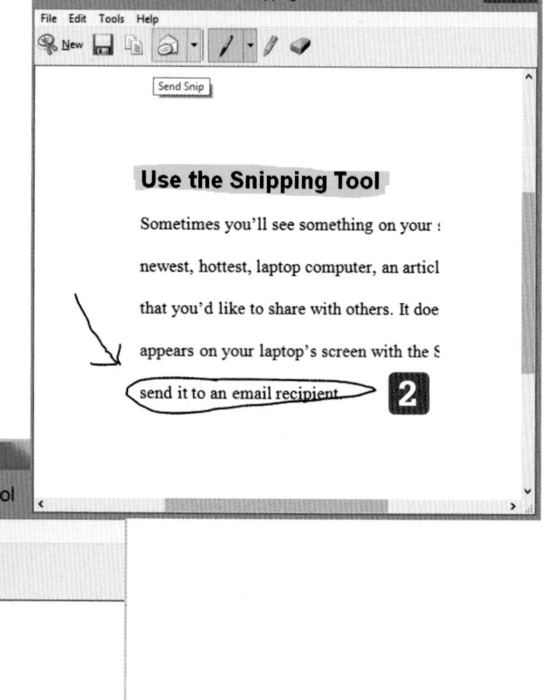

5. Insert the recipients' names, change the subject if you wish, type a message and click Send.

SEE ALSO: For more information on sending an email, refer to Chapter 9.

ALERT: If you select Email Recipient, this will insert the snip inside an email. Note that you can also send the snip as an attachment.

DID YOU KNOW?

If you need more editing tools than the Snipping Tool provides, press Print Screen on your keyboard, open Paint (a Desktop application) and click Paste. The capture will appear there and you can use Paint to finalise the screenshot.

Record a sound clip

Sometimes the spoken word is best. With the Sound Recorder, you can record a quick note to yourself or others instead of writing a letter or sending an email. Sound Recorder is a simple tool with only three options: Start Recording, Stop Recording and Resume Recording. To record, click Start Recording; to stop, click Stop Recording; to continue, click Resume Recording. You save your recording as a Windows Media audio file, which will play by default in Windows Media Player.

1. From the Start screen, type Sound Recorder.
2. Select Sound Recorder in the results.
3. Click Start Recording, then Stop Recording. If prompted to save the file, click Cancel.
4. Click Resume Recording.

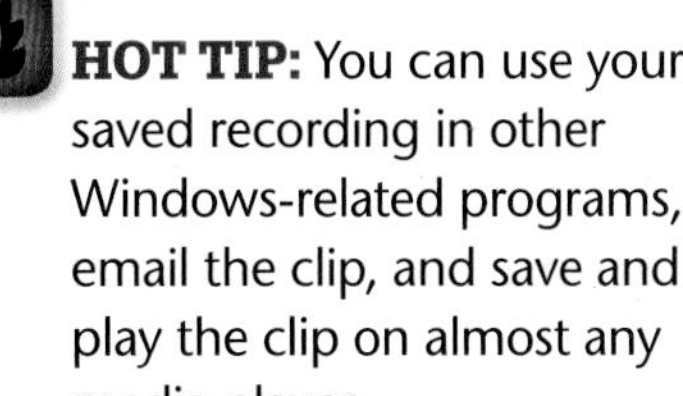

HOT TIP: You can use your saved recording in other Windows-related programs, email the clip, and save and play the clip on almost any media player.

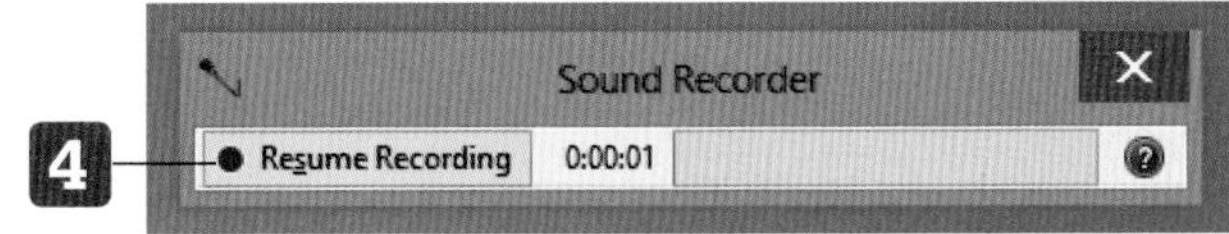

5. Click Stop Recording to complete the recording.
6. In the Save As dialogue box, type a name for your recording and click Save.
7. Click the X in the Sound Recorder to close it.

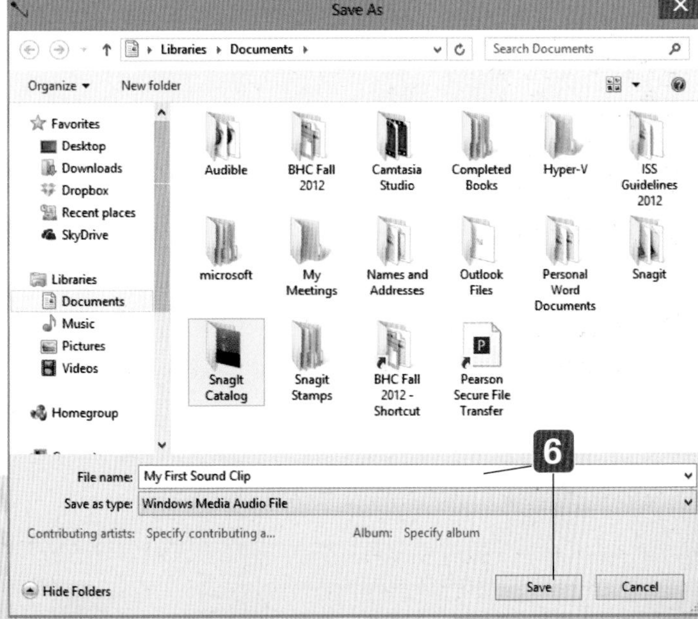

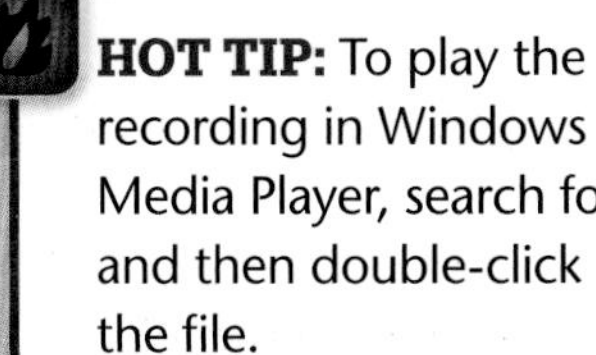

HOT TIP: To play the recording in Windows Media Player, search for and then double-click the file.

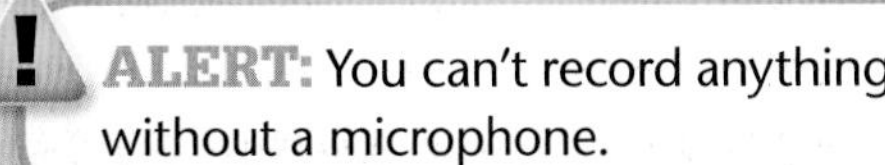

ALERT: You can't record anything without a microphone.

Explore other Desktop apps

There are many more Desktop apps available than those introduced here. All are available from the All apps screen, or you can simply start typing at the Start screen to locate them. Here are a few to try before moving on:

- Math Input Panel – write an equation with your finger, stylus or pen and this application will type it for you. You can then copy and paste the equation anywhere that accepts text.
- Paint – create flyers, signs, flowcharts and other artwork.
- Sticky Notes – create your own digital sticky notes.

- Control Panel– use this to personalise all aspects of your laptop or tablet.

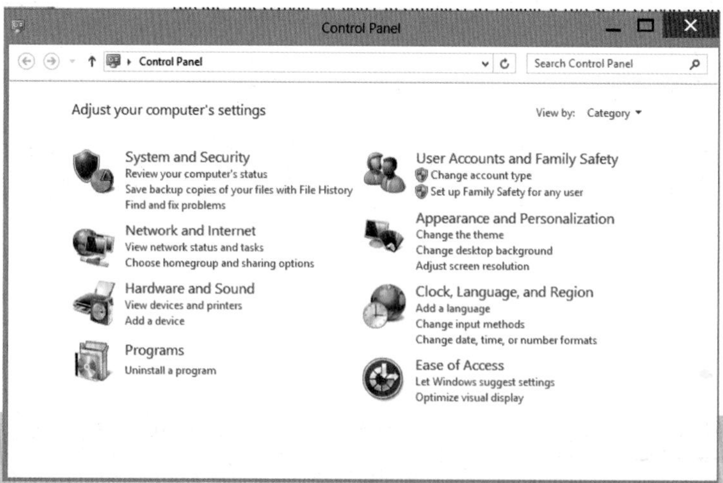

HOT TIP: If you need help at any time, search for and open Help and Support. It's a Desktop app and is easy to use.

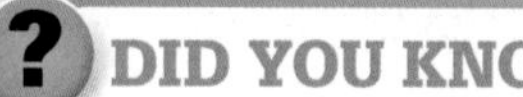

DID YOU KNOW?

You may have installed a few Desktop apps yourself – iTunes and Photoshop are both Desktop applications.

Pin your favourite Desktop apps to the taskbar

If there is a Desktop app you use often and you don't want to have to access the Start screen to find it each time you need it, you can pin a shortcut to the taskbar for easy access.

1. Locate the app's tile on the Start screen or the All apps screen.
2. Right-click the tile.
3. Click Pin to taskbar.

DID YOU KNOW?

You can also pin any Desktop app's tile to the Start screen if it isn't already there.

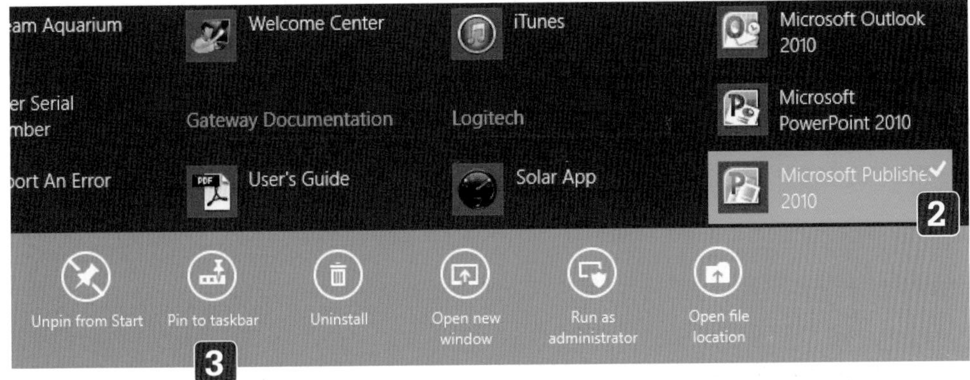

4. Return to the Desktop to see the item on the taskbar.

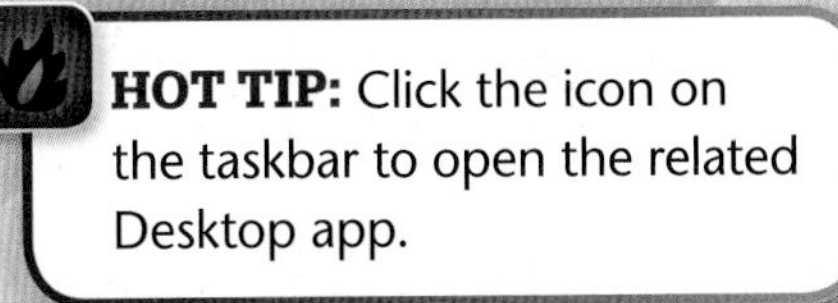

HOT TIP: Click the icon on the taskbar to open the related Desktop app.

DID YOU KNOW?

If you use touch only, tap, hold and drag downwards a little to select the tile and thus access the options to pin an item.

8 Use the Internet Explorer Desktop app

Introduction

You use Internet Explorer to access the Internet and browse websites. Windows 8 comes with two versions of this application. You learned about the Internet Explorer Start screen app in Chapter 4; in this chapter, you'll learn about the Internet Explorer Desktop app.

If you recall, the IE Start screen app (the IE app) provides limited functionality, but is streamlined to offer a clean and efficient web browsing experience. You should use this version when you want to visit your favourite websites and do some basic web surfing, especially if you have a small screen, such as you find on tablet computers and smaller laptops. The IE Desktop app is the fully functional version of IE that you may already be familiar with. It offers what the IE Start screen app offers and much, much more, including the ability to save a list of Favorites, use the familiar tabbed browsing features, and enable the Favorites bar, among other things. You may prefer this version on larger laptops, so at the end of this chapter we'll show you how to make it the default web browser, should you prefer.

Explore the Internet Explorer Desktop app

If you've used a Windows-based computer before, you've probably used the traditional version of Internet Explorer. You open this from the Desktop, specifically by clicking the big blue E on the taskbar. Microsoft has made a few changes from previous versions though: the Menu bar is hidden, the 'Do not track' feature is enabled, and performance is improved, among other things.

1 If you are on the Start screen, click or tap the Desktop tile or use the Windows + D keyboard shortcut to get to the Desktop.

2 Tap the Internet Explorer icon on the taskbar.

3 To go to a website you want to visit, type the name of the website in the window at the top of the page. This is called the Address bar. Press Enter on the keyboard.

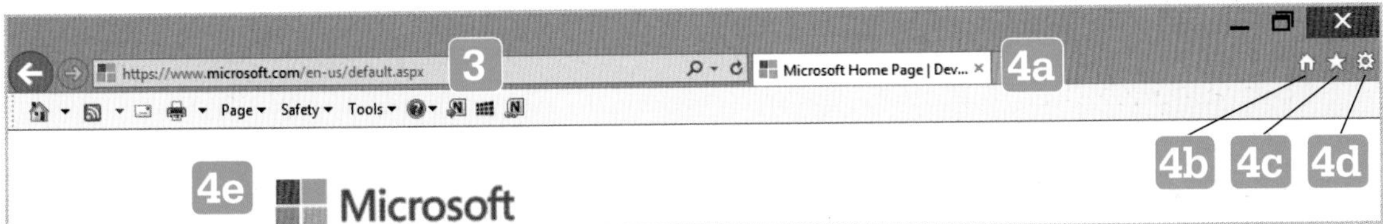

4 Explore these features:

a. Tabs – click any tab to access the related webpage.
b. Home – click to access your configured home page(s).
c. Add to Favorites – click to view favourites or to add a webpage as a favourite.
d. Tools – click to access all available settings.
e. Web content – click to read the information offered on the webpage.

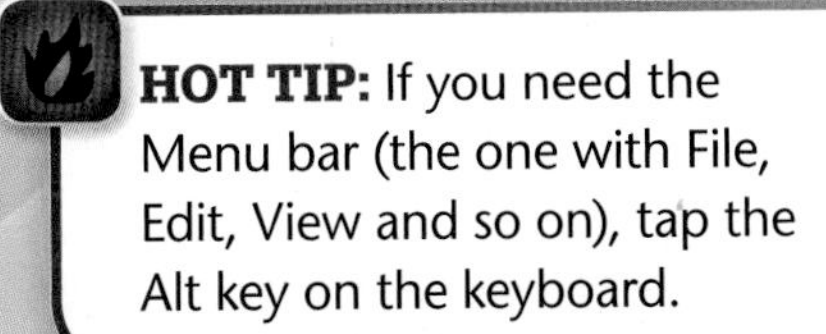

HOT TIP: If you need the Menu bar (the one with File, Edit, View and so on), tap the Alt key on the keyboard.

HOT TIP: Right-click just above the area where you type the website name to enable hidden toolbars.

Use tabs

You can open more than one website at a time in the Internet Explorer Desktop app. To do this, click the tab that appears to the right of the open webpage. Then type the name of the website you'd like to visit.

1. Open Internet Explorer.
2. Click an empty tab.
3. Type the name of the website you'd like to visit in the Address bar.
4. Press Enter on the keyboard.

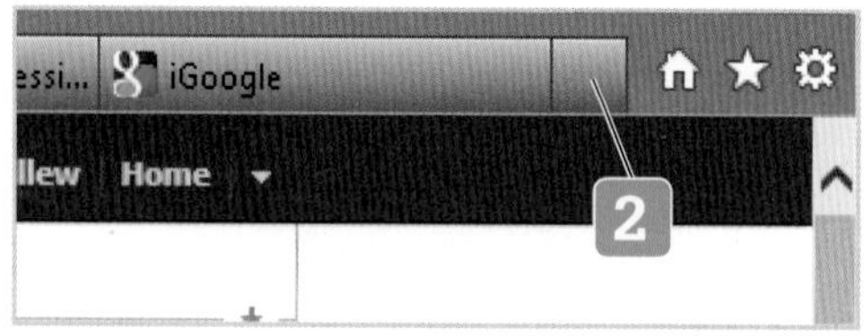

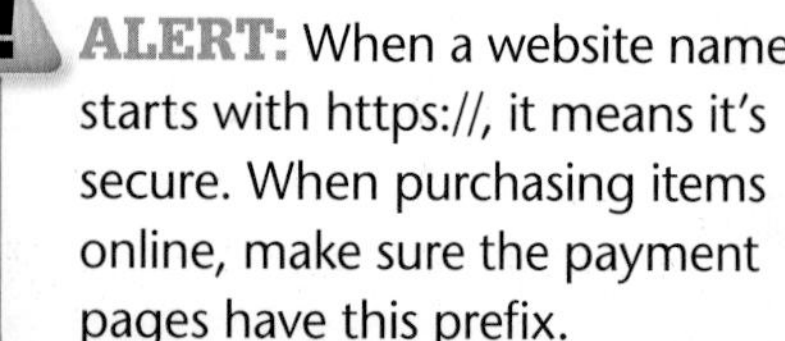

ALERT: When a website name starts with https://, it means it's secure. When purchasing items online, make sure the payment pages have this prefix.

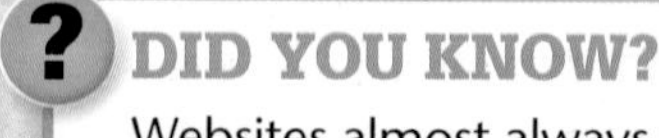

DID YOU KNOW?
Websites almost always start with http://www.

Set a home page

You can select a single webpage or multiple webpages to be displayed each time you open the Internet Explorer Desktop app. In fact, there are three options for configuring home pages:

- Use this webpage as your only home page – select this option if you only want a single web page, the one you have open and selected, to serve as your home page.
- Add this webpage to your home page tabs – select this option if you want the page you have open and selected to be added to the other home pages you've already configured.
- Use the current tab set as your home page – select this option if you've opened multiple tabs and you want all of them to be home pages.

1. Use the Address bar to locate a webpage (and use the empty tab button to repeat to open additional webpages).
2. Right-click the Home icon and click Add or change home page. (Note you have additional choices, including showing various toolbars.)
3. Make a selection using the information provided regarding each option.
4. Click Yes.

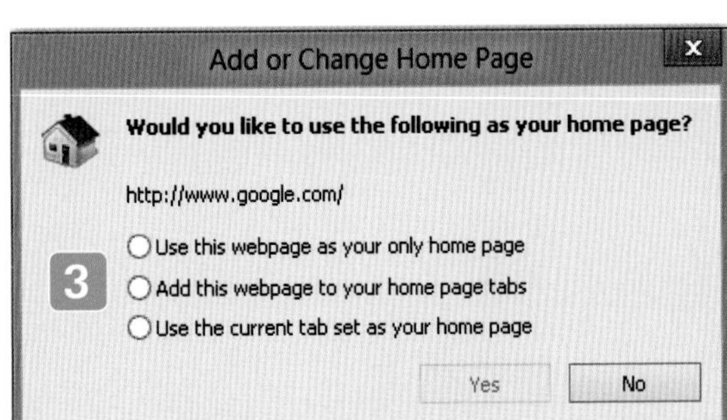

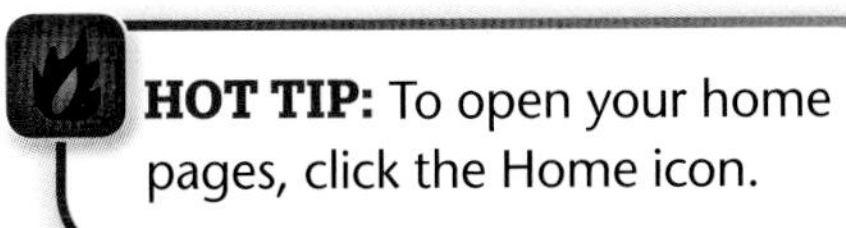

HOT TIP: To open your home pages, click the Home icon.

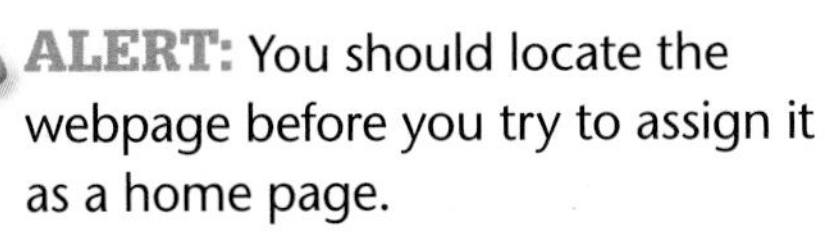

ALERT: You should locate the webpage before you try to assign it as a home page.

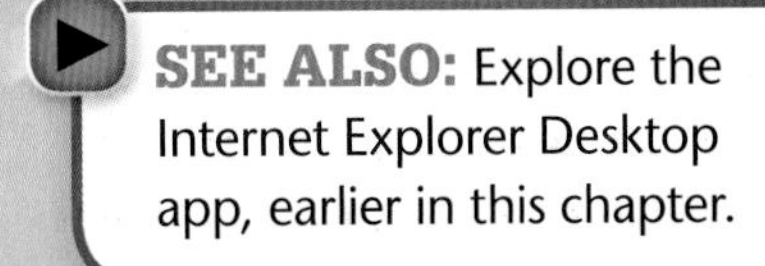

SEE ALSO: Explore the Internet Explorer Desktop app, earlier in this chapter.

Mark a favourite

Favourites are websites you save links to for accessing more easily at a later time. They differ from home pages because by default they do not open when you start the Internet Explorer Desktop app. The favourites you save appear in the Favorites Center. You can also save favourites to the Favorites bar, an optional toolbar you can enable in IE.

1 Go to the webpage you want to configure as a favourite.

2 Click the Add to favorites icon (it's the star).

3 Click Add to favorites. (To add the website to the Favorites bar, click the arrow beside the Add to favorites option.)

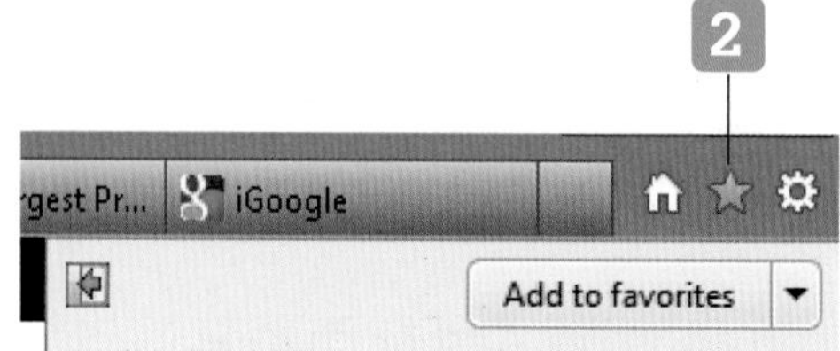

HOT TIP: To show the Favorites bar, right-click just above the tabs or the Address bar and click Favorites bar.

HOT TIP: You can organise your favourites in your personal Favorites folder. To get started, click the arrow next to Add to favorites in the Favorites Center.

Zoom in or out

If you have trouble reading what's on a webpage because the text is too small, use the Page Zoom feature. Page Zoom preserves the fundamental design of the webpage you're viewing. This means that Page Zoom intelligently zooms in on the entire page, which maintains the page's integrity, layout and look.

1. Open the Internet Explorer Desktop app and browse to a webpage.
2. If you have a physical keyboard, use the Ctrl + = and the Ctrl + – combinations to zoom in and out.
3. If you have a touch screen, pinch in and out with two or more fingers to zoom in and out.
4. If you prefer to use a mouse or track pad, right-click the area above the tabs and Address bar and place a tick by Status bar, then click the arrow on the right end of the Status bar to zoom to a specific amount.

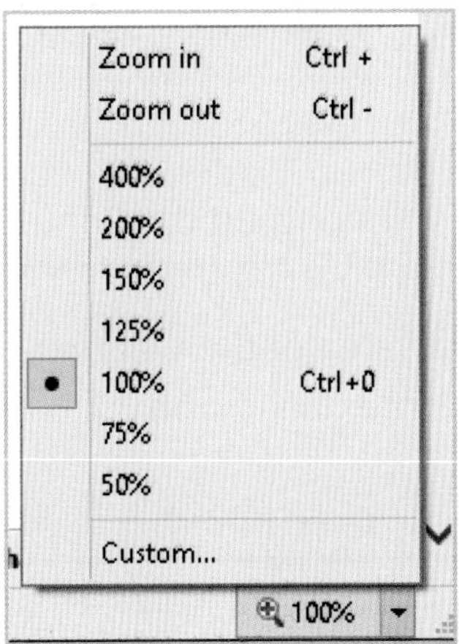

DID YOU KNOW?

The term browse is used to describe both locating a file on your hard drive and locating something on the Internet.

DID YOU KNOW?

On a laptop it's easiest to zoom with Ctrl + = and Ctrl + –.

Print a webpage

You can print a webpage in several ways. When you do though, remember that the pictures and ads will be printed too, so you may want to copy the text and paste it in a word document first.

- The Print icon is available from the Command bar. To show the Command bar, right-click just above the tabs and Address bar and place a tick by it. The Command bar and the Print option are shown here.

DID YOU KNOW?

A long tap on a touch screen is often equivalent to a right-click on a mouse or track pad.

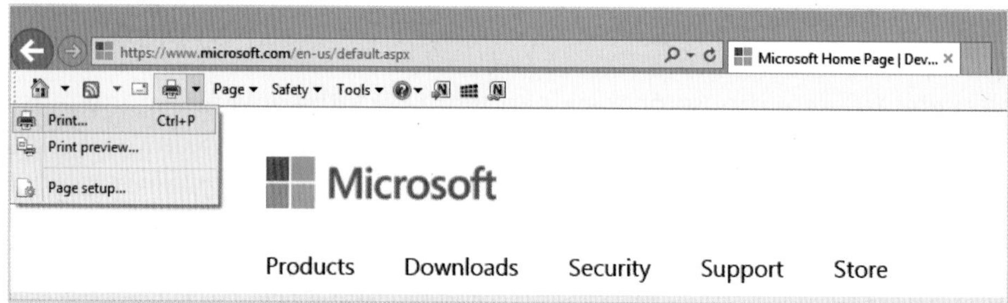

- The key combination Ctrl + P will bring up the Print dialogue box.
- You can right-click on an empty area of the webpage and click Print from the resulting contextual menu.

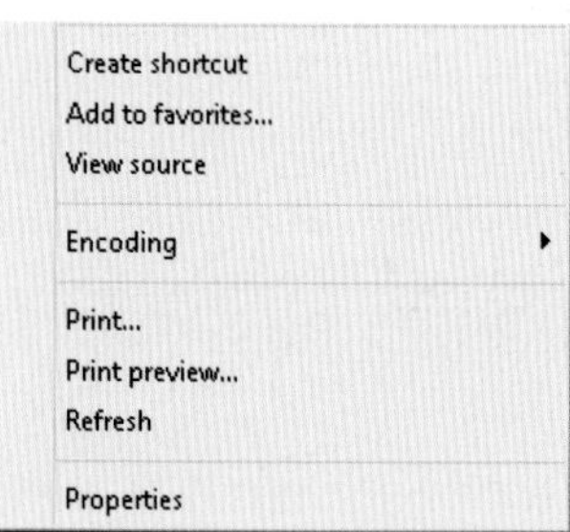

WHAT DOES THIS MEAN?

There are three menu options under the Print icon:

Print: opens the Print dialogue box where you can configure the page range, select a printer, change page orientation, change print order and choose a paper type. Additional options include print quality, output bins and more. Of course, the choices depend on what your printer offers. If your printer can print only at 300 × 300 dots per inch, you can't configure it to print at a higher quality.

Print Preview: opens a window where you can see before you print what the printout will actually look like. You can switch between portrait and landscape views, access the Page Setup dialogue box and more.

Page Setup: opens the Page Setup dialogue box. Here you can select a paper size, source and create headers and footers. You can also change orientation and margins, all of which is dependent on the features your printer supports.

Clear history

If you don't want people (who have access to your computer) to be able to snoop around on your laptop and find out which websites you've been visiting, you'll need to delete your 'browsing history'. Deleting your browsing history lets you remove the information stored on your computer related to your Internet activities.

1. Open the Internet Explorer Desktop app.
2. Click the Alt key on the keyboard if you do not see the menu shown here.
3. Click Tools.
4. Click Delete browsing history.

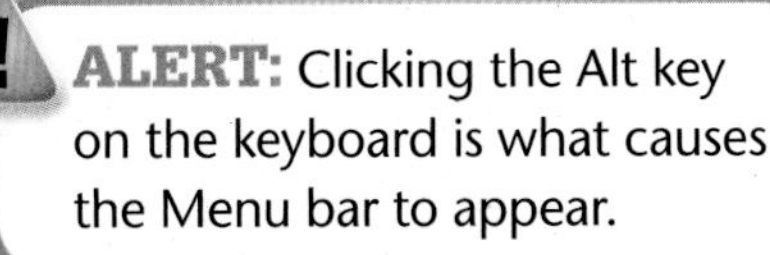

ALERT: Clicking the Alt key on the keyboard is what causes the Menu bar to appear.

DID YOU KNOW?

You can also click the Tools icon, Internet Options, and from the General tab, opt to delete your browsing history.

5 Select what to remove and click Delete. (You may want to keep Preserve Favorites website data selected.)

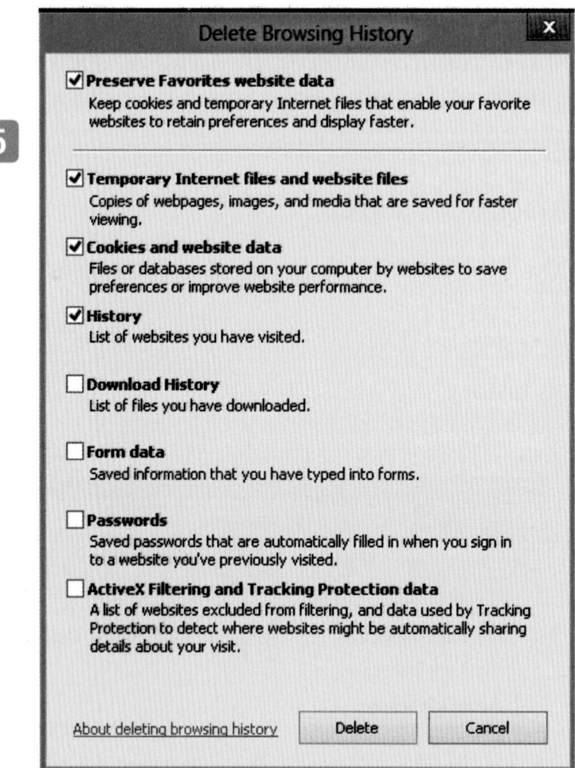

WHAT DOES THIS MEAN?

Temporary Internet Files: files that have been downloaded and saved in your Temporary Internet Files folder. A snooper could go through these files to see what you've been doing online.

Cookies: small text files that include data that identifies your preferences when you visit particular websites. Cookies are what allow you to visit, say, www.amazon.com and be greeted with 'Hello <your name>, We have recommendations for you!' Cookies help a site offer you a personalised web experience.

History: the list of websites you've visited and any web addresses you've typed. Anyone with access to your laptop can look at your history list to see where you've been.

Form data: information that's been saved using Internet Explorer's autocomplete form data functionality. If you don't want forms to be filled out automatically by you or someone else who has access to your computer and user account, delete this.

Passwords: passwords that were saved using Internet Explorer autocomplete password prompts.

InPrivate Blocking data: data that was saved by InPrivate Blocking to detect where websites may be automatically sharing details about your visit.

Stay safe on the Internet

Although you can rely somewhat on anti-virus software, pop-up blockers, secure websites and such to keep you safe while surfing the Internet, most tasks that have to do with staying secure online have more to do with common sense. When you're online, make sure you follow the guidelines listed below.

- If you are connecting to a public network, make sure you select Public when prompted by Windows 8.
- Always keep your computers updated with Windows Updates.
- Limit the amount of confidential information you store on the Internet.
- When making credit card purchases or travel reservations, or when logging on to a service such as Twitter, always make sure the website address starts with https:// and use a secure site.

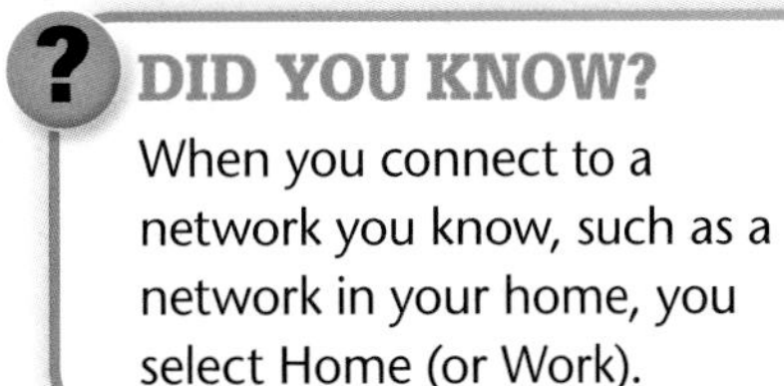

DID YOU KNOW? When you connect to a network you know, such as a network in your home, you select Home (or Work).

- Always sign out of any secure website you enter.

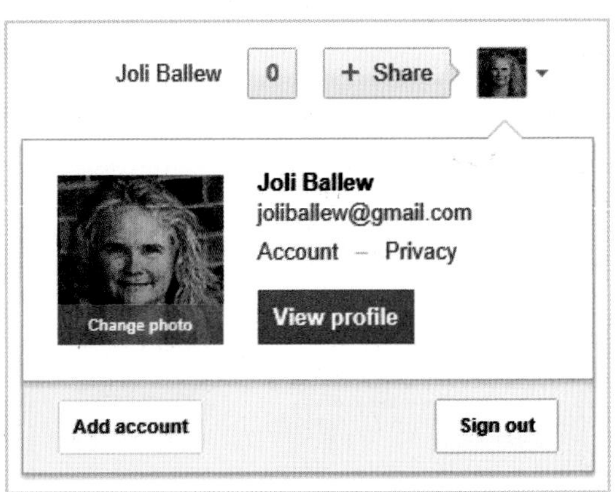

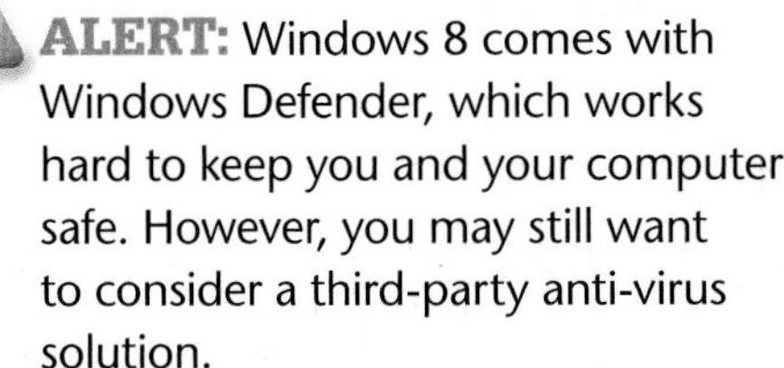

ALERT: Windows 8 comes with Windows Defender, which works hard to keep you and your computer safe. However, you may still want to consider a third-party anti-virus solution.

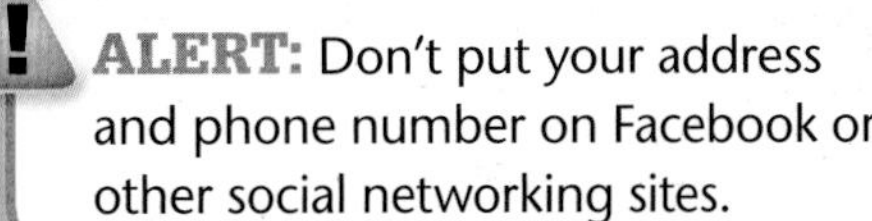

ALERT: Don't put your address and phone number on Facebook or other social networking sites.

Configure the IE Desktop app as the default

If you'd prefer the Internet Explorer Desktop app to open when you click a link in an email, message, document and so on, instead of the simpler IE app, you can configure it in Internet Explorer's settings. Doing so will make the Desktop app the default.

1. Open Internet Explorer on the Desktop.
2. Click the Tools icon, then Internet Options.
3. Click the Programs tab.
4. Click the arrow beside Let Internet Explorer decide.
5. Click Always in Internet Explorer on the desktop.
6. Click OK.

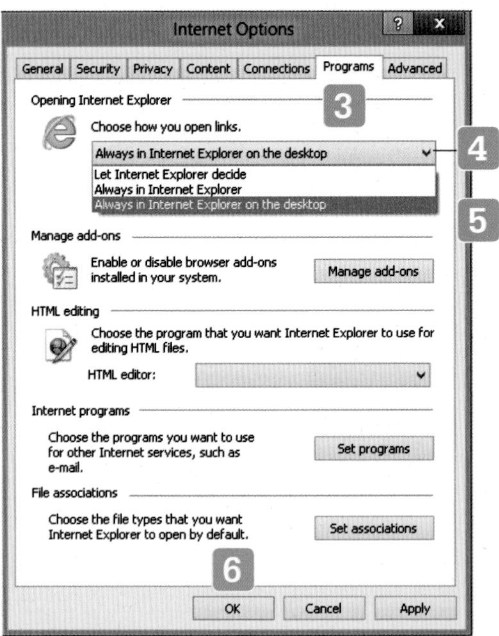

HOT TIP: While you have the Internet Options dialogue box open, explore the other options available. From the General tab, for instance, you can configure IE to start each time with tabs from the last session (instead of your configured home page(s).)

DID YOU KNOW?
If you configure the IE Desktop app as the default, when you click the IE app tile on the Start screen, the IE Desktop app will open.

9 Configure and use Mail

Introduction

Mail is an app available from the Start screen that enables you to view, send and receive email, and manage sent, saved and incoming mail using various techniques. It's an app, so it offers minimal features compared with more complex applications such as Windows Live Mail, Microsoft Office Outlook and Mozilla Thunderbird. It is meant to be that way though, and because of its minimalistic approach it may be just what you're looking for.

If you have signed in to your Windows 8 laptop or tablet with a compatible Microsoft account like one from Hotmail.com or Live.com, Mail is already set up and ready to use. If you have a third-party email account, you'll have to add that manually. Once your email accounts are ready, accessing new mail and composing your own is a simple process.

Access email

If you haven't used Mail yet but you know you logged in to your Windows 8 laptop or tablet with a Microsoft account, open Mail and see whether the account is configured. You may be in for a surprise!

1. Locate the Mail icon on the Start screen and click it.

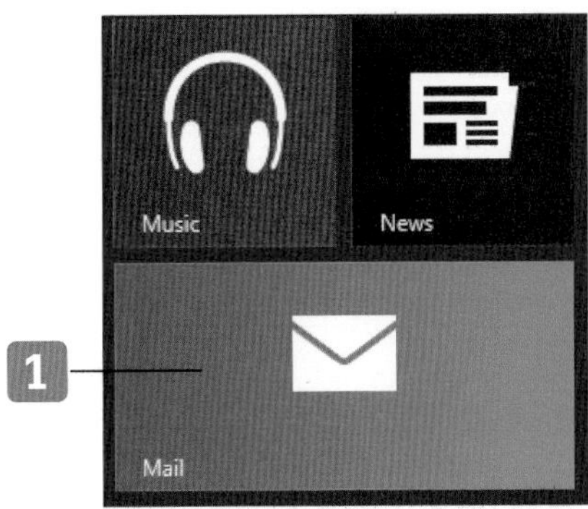

2. If an email account is already configured, you'll see the related inbox and folders. You may even have email.

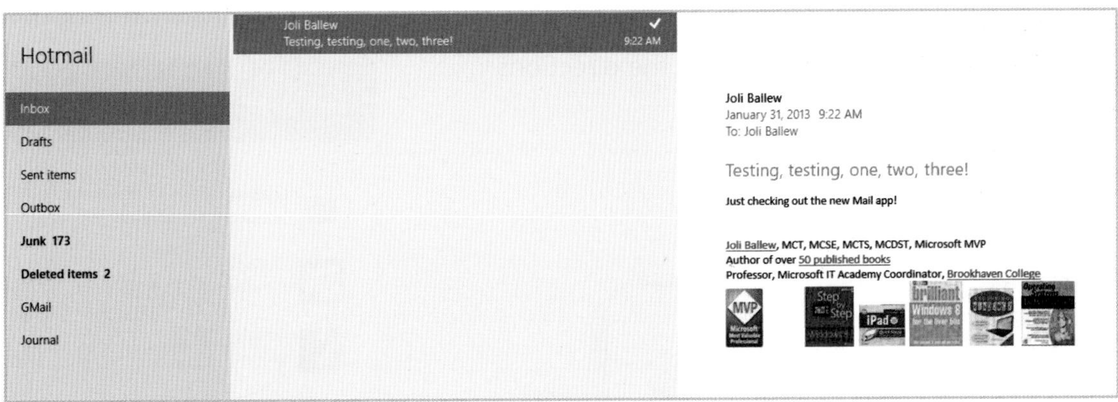

3. If you see mail there, click once to read it.

DID YOU KNOW?
If you have been using a web-based email account from Hotmail or Live.com and you've created folders to store your mail, you'll see them in Mail when you open it.

HOT TIP: If you need an email account, get one from Microsoft at https://signup.live.com.

Set up a third-party email account

If you use an email account you obtained from an entity other than Microsoft (such as Gmail), you'll have to set up the account manually. You access the option to add an account from the Settings charm while inside the Mail app.

1. Open Mail and then access the charms. You can use the Windows key + C or flick inwards from the right side of a touch screen. Click Settings.
2. From the Settings options, click Accounts.
3. Click Add an account (not shown).
4. Choose the type of account to add.
5. Fill out the information when prompted, including your email account and password.
6. Click Connect.
7. If you receive an email that requires you to finish setting up your account, follow the directions provided to do so.

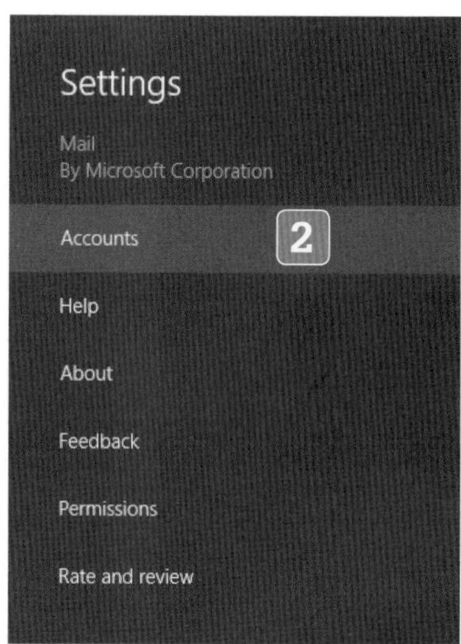

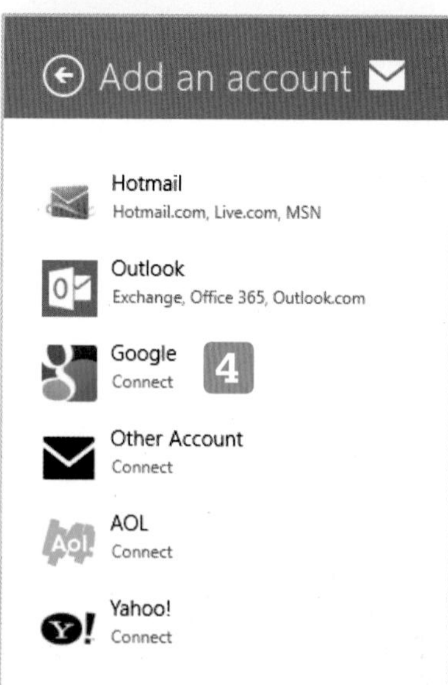

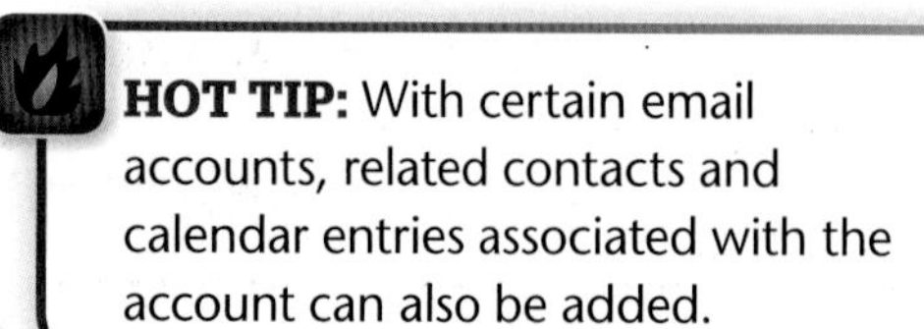

HOT TIP: With certain email accounts, related contacts and calendar entries associated with the account can also be added.

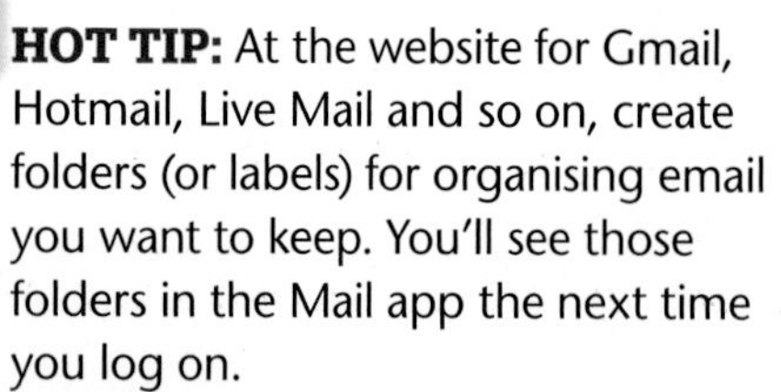

HOT TIP: At the website for Gmail, Hotmail, Live Mail and so on, create folders (or labels) for organising email you want to keep. You'll see those folders in the Mail app the next time you log on.

DID YOU KNOW?

Mail supports Exchange email accounts. These are corporate email accounts.

Open and read email

Mail gets email almost immediately after it's been sent. If you want to check for email manually though, you can click the Sync charm any time you want.

1 If you have more than one email account configured, select the account to use.

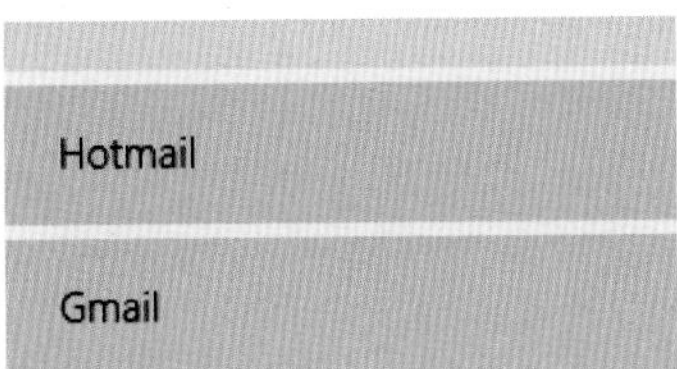

2 Right-click the screen or flick upwards to view the charms. Click Sync.

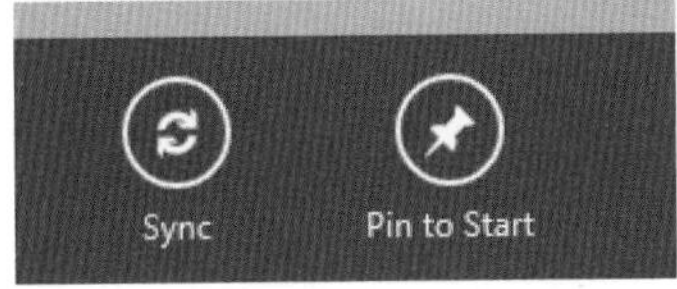

3 Click the email to read.

ALERT: Each email account you configure has its own inbox. Click the inbox to switch between multiple accounts.

HOT TIP: Always delete email immediately after you read it if you don't need to keep it for future reference. This will help keep your inboxes clean and tidy.

WHAT DOES THIS MEAN?

Inbox: holds mail you've received.

Outbox: holds mail you've written but have not yet sent (or has not been sent).

Sent Items: stores copies of messages you've sent.

Deleted Items: holds mail you've deleted.

Drafts: holds messages you've started and saved but not completed. Click the X in a new message and click Save draft to put an email in progress here.

Junk: holds email that is probably spam. You should check this folder occasionally since Mail may put email in there you want to read.

Compose and send a new email

You compose an email message by clicking the + sign in the upper right corner of the Mail interface. You input who the email should be sent to and the subject, then you type the message. If you like, you can click the + sign that is located just to the right of the To line and choose your recipient(s) from the People app.

1. Click the + sign.

2. Type the recipient's email address in the To line. You can type multiple addresses.

3. Type a subject in the Add a subject field.
4. Type the message in the body pane under the subject field.
5. Click the Send icon.

DID YOU KNOW?
If you want to send the email to someone and you don't need them to respond, you can put them in the CC line. This is a carbon copy. If you want to send the email to someone and you don't want other recipients to know you have included them in the email, click Show more. Then add the address in the resulting Bcc line. This is a blind carbon copy.

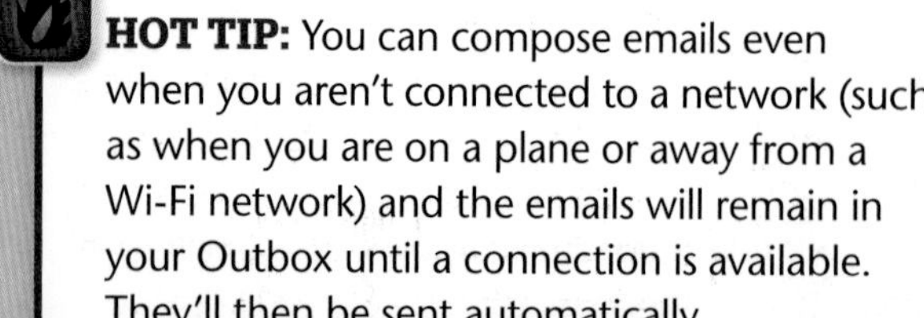

HOT TIP: You can compose emails even when you aren't connected to a network (such as when you are on a plane or away from a Wi-Fi network) and the emails will remain in your Outbox until a connection is available. They'll then be sent automatically.

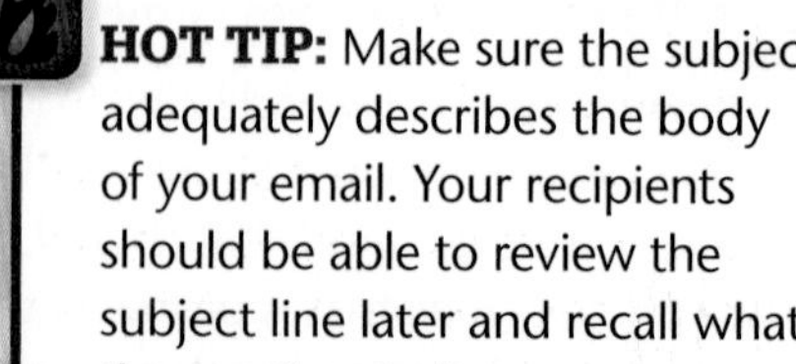

HOT TIP: Make sure the subject adequately describes the body of your email. Your recipients should be able to review the subject line later and recall what the email was about.

Format email text

Formatting options are hidden away in the Mail toolbar. You access those options with a right-click of a mouse or track pad, or a flick upwards with your finger on a touch screen. Once the options are available, you apply them as you would any formatting tools in any word-processing program. You can only format text in the body of the email though; you can't format text in the subject line.

1. Compose a new email and then click in the body pane.
2. Right-click to see the formatting options. (Note that you can click More to see additional options.)

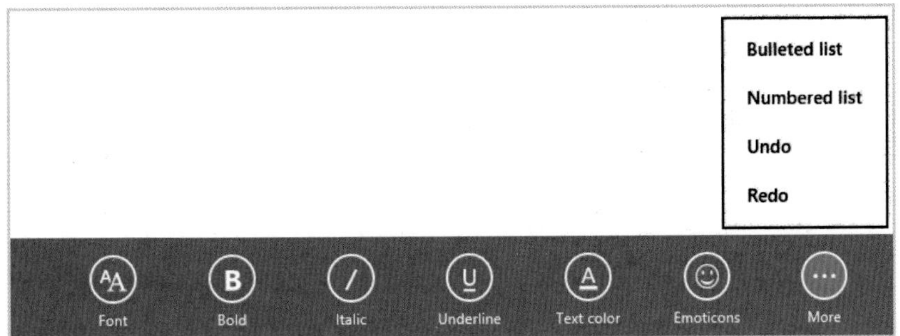

3. Click any formatting option (perhaps Bold) and then click another (perhaps Italic).
4. Click Font and choose a new font and font size.
5. Type a few words in the body of the email.

? DID YOU KNOW?
If you apply formatting options without any text selected, those options will be applied to all future text until you change it. If you select text and then apply formatting, the formatting is applied to the selected text only.

! ALERT: If the new font choices aren't applied when you type, try clicking in a new line, pressing Enter to go to a new line, or click under the signature. Sometimes this type of application of the formatting tools is a little tricky.

Reply to or forward an email

When someone sends you an email, you may need to send a reply to them. You do that by selecting the email and then clicking the appropriate 'respond' button. You can forward the email to others using the same technique.

1. Select the email you want to reply to or forward.
2. Click the respond button, then click the appropriate option.

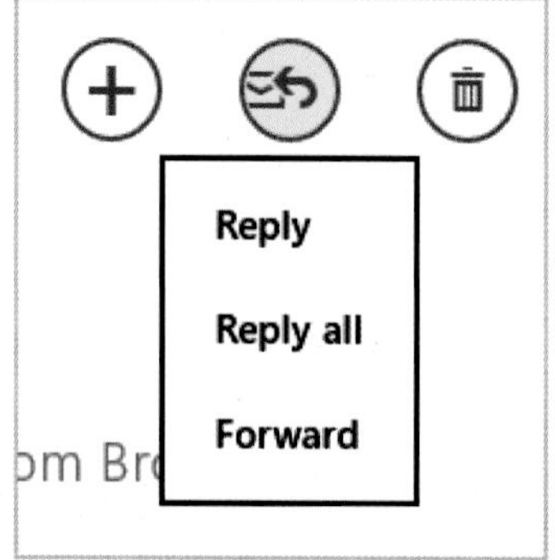

3. If you wish, change the subject, then type the message in the body pane.
4. Click Send.

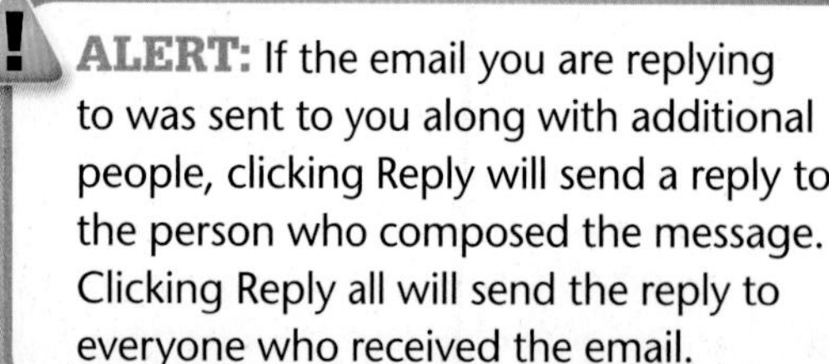

ALERT: If the email you are replying to was sent to you along with additional people, clicking Reply will send a reply to the person who composed the message. Clicking Reply all will send the reply to everyone who received the email.

HOT TIP: Mail offers formatting tools that you can use to change the font, font colour, font size and more. Right-click or flick upwards to access these options.

Print an email

Sometimes you'll need to print an email or its attachment. You access your printer from the Devices charm. Since it's likely that you do not have a printer attached to your laptop or tablet, you'll have to look for a shared printer.

1. Select the email to print.
2. Bring up the default charms (Windows + C will show these) and click Devices.
3. Select the printer to use (not shown). We'll choose a printer that is shared from a Windows 7 desktop computer.
4. Configure the print options and click Print.

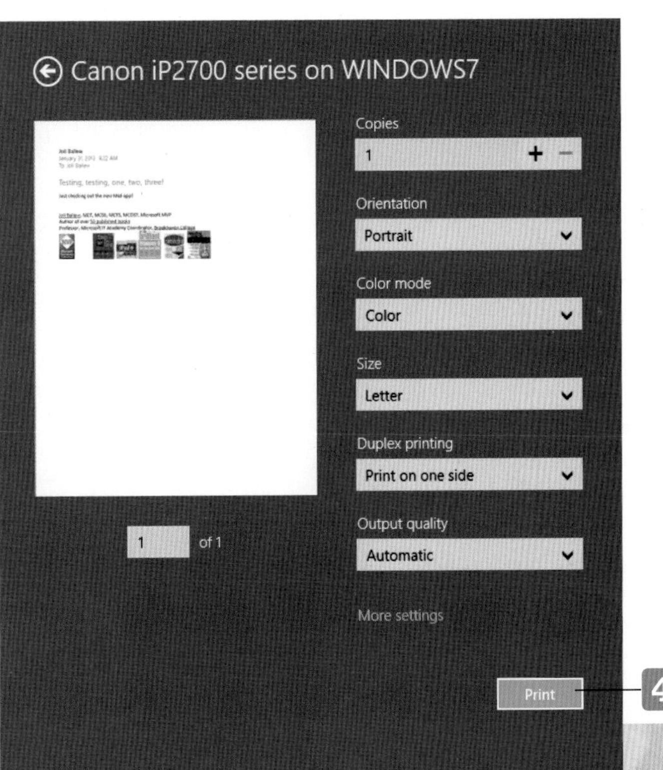

? DID YOU KNOW?

If you use a keyboard, the shortcut Ctrl + P will open the Print window. From there, select the printer and configure printer options, then print.

Attach something to an email

Although email that contains only a message serves its purpose quite a bit of the time, often you'll want to send a photograph, a short video, a sound recording, a document or other data. When you want to add something other than text to your message, it's called adding an attachment.

1. Click the + sign to create a new mail message. Select the recipients, type a subject and compose the email.
2. Right-click the screen and click Attachments.

3. Locate the file to attach and click it. You can select multiple files.
4. Click Attach (not shown).

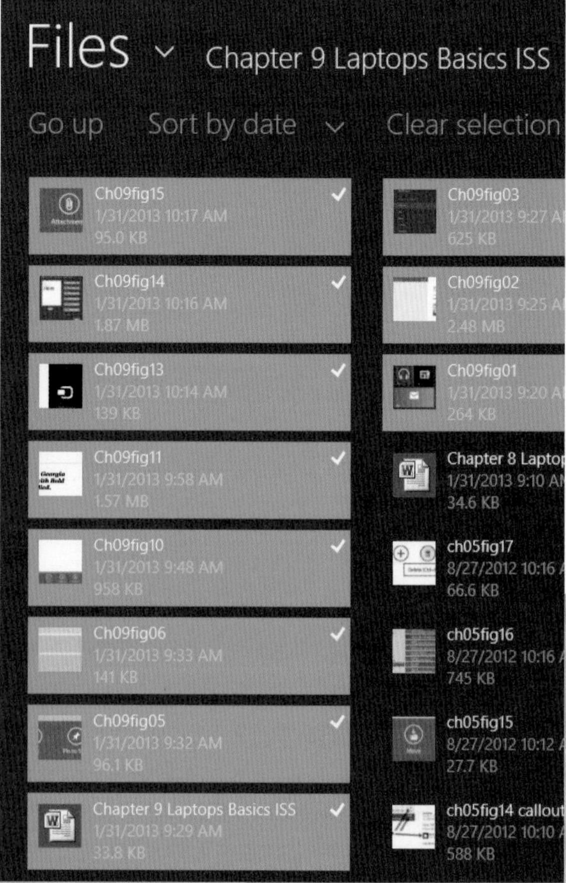

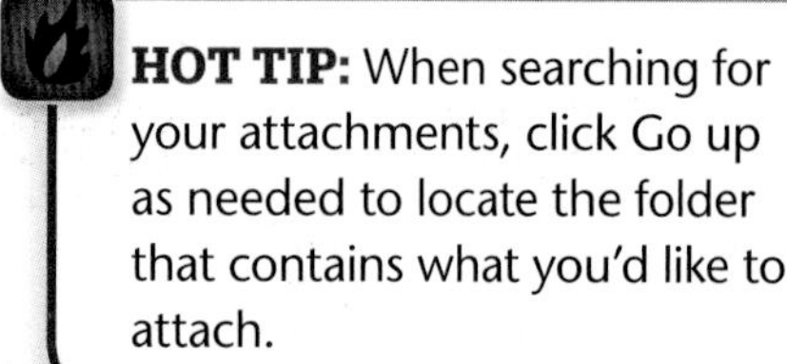

HOT TIP: When searching for your attachments, click Go up as needed to locate the folder that contains what you'd like to attach.

ALERT: Anything you attach won't be removed from your computer; instead, a copy will be created for the attachment.

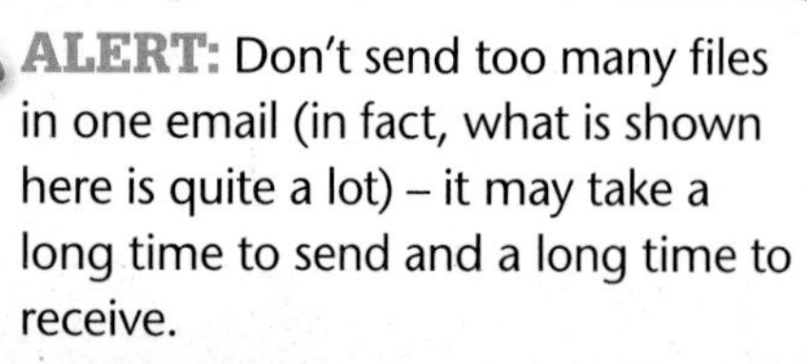

ALERT: Don't send too many files in one email (in fact, what is shown here is quite a lot) – it may take a long time to send and a long time to receive.

View an attachment in an email

If an email you receive from someone else contains an attachment, you'll see a paperclip. To open the attachment, first select the email and then click the attachment to open. If you are prompted to download the rest of the message, do that too.

1 Click the email that contains the attachment.

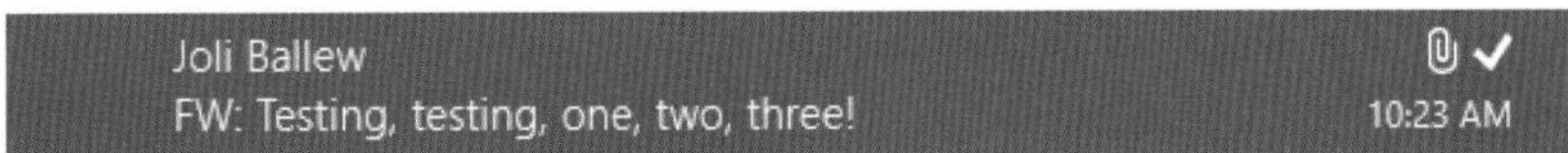

2 If applicable, click Download to download the attachment(s) to your laptop.

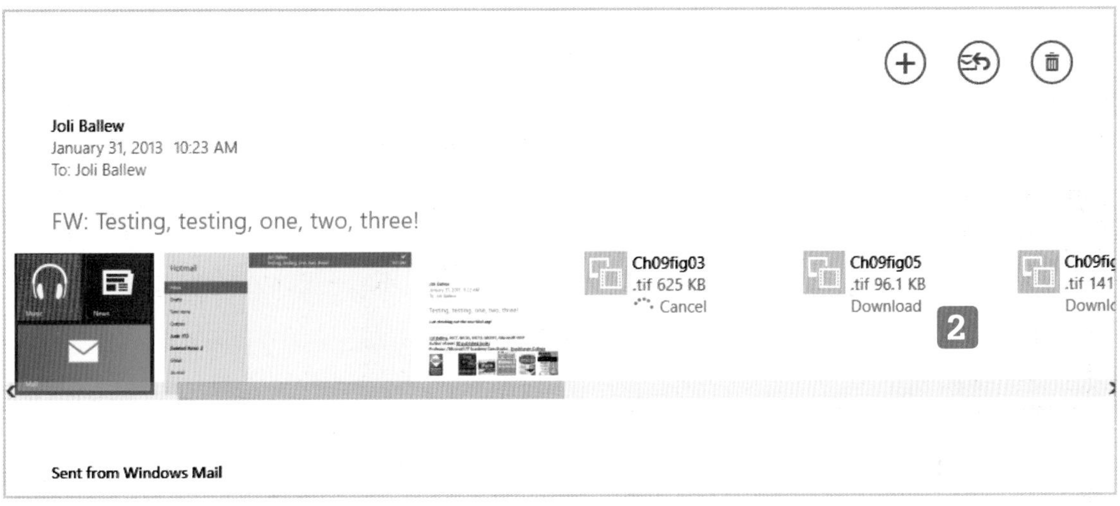

3 Once the download has completed, click the attachment name and choose to open the item.

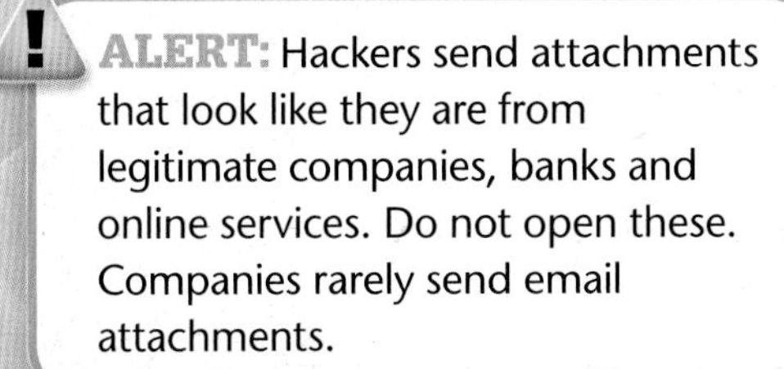

ALERT: Hackers send attachments that look like they are from legitimate companies, banks and online services. Do not open these. Companies rarely send email attachments.

ALERT: Attachments can contain viruses. Never open an attachment from someone you don't know.

View junk email

All email accounts have some version of a *Junk* folder. If an email is suspected to be spam, it gets sent there. (Spam is another word for junk email.) Unfortunately, sometimes email that is actually legitimate gets sent to the Junk folder. Therefore, once a week or so you should look in this folder to see whether any email you want to read is in there.

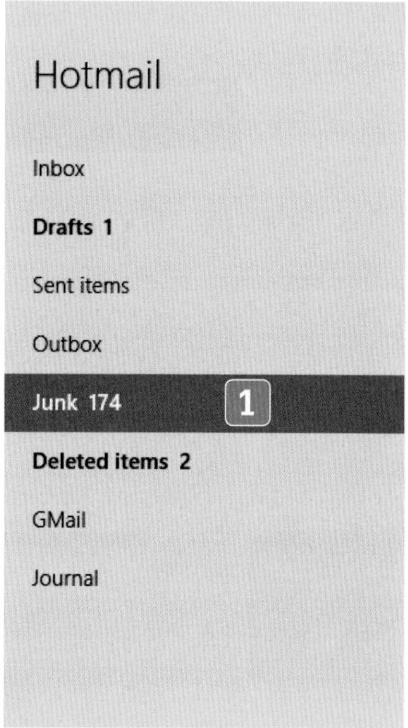

1. Click the Junk folder once. (Depending on the email account you use, it may say Junk Email, Junk, or something else.)
2. Use the scroll bars if necessary to browse through the email in the folder.
3. If you see an email that is legitimate, click it once.
4. Right-click to access the charms and click Move.

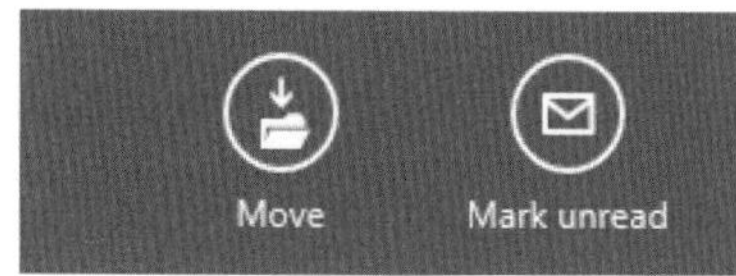

5. Click Inbox.

? DID YOU KNOW?
The Mail app doesn't have all the features that fully fledged programs (such as Microsoft Office Outlook) do, so it's not possible to, say, add contacts from an email (easily), create subfolders and so on.

! ALERT: Mail requires routine maintenance which generally involves deleting email from various folders. You'll learn how to delete items in a folder next.

Delete email in a folder

It's easy to delete a single email: click the email once and then click the Trash icon. It's a little more difficult to delete more than one email at a time.

1. Click any folder that contains email you'd like to delete. You may want to choose Sent items, Inbox or even Junk.
2. Click the first entry in the list to delete, hold down the Shift key and then click the last entry. This will select these two emails and all those in between.

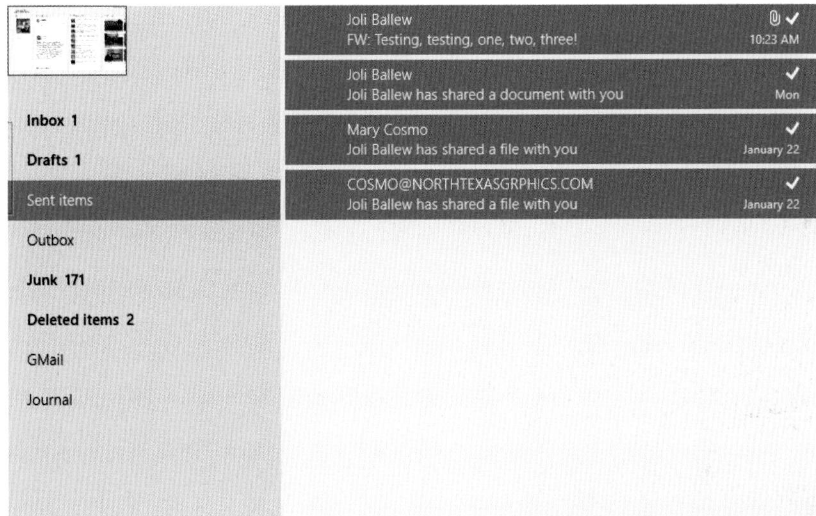

3. Click the Trash icon.
4. Repeat Step 2. This time, hold down the Ctrl key while selecting non-contiguous email.
5. Click the Trash icon.

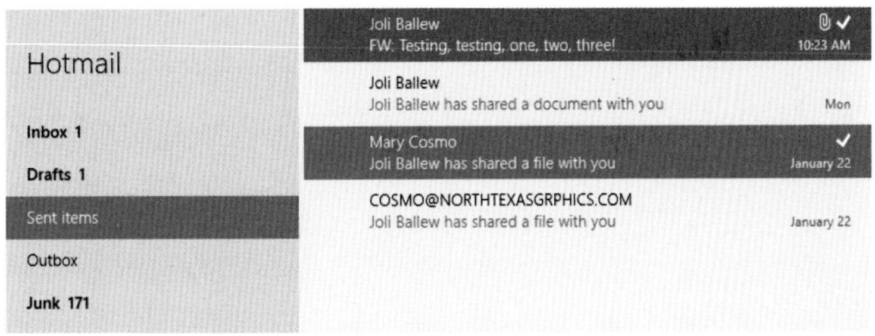

HOT TIP: If you use an email provider that lets you create folders on its website, do so. Those folders will appear in Mail. You can then move email you want to keep to those folders and you won't have to delete them.

DID YOU KNOW?
Even if you delete an important email and decide you want it back, you can get it in the Deleted items folder (at least until you empty that folder).

10 Personalise Windows 8

Introduction

You should take some time now to personalise your Windows 8 laptop to make it easier to use and uniquely yours. You may want to create a PIN for logging on quickly, choose a new picture for the Lock screen or change the items which show there, create shortcuts on the Desktop for items you access often, and personalise which tiles appear on the Start screen (and which don't). You may also want to learn how to access data that has been shared by others or share your own across a network.

You'll learn how to do all of this and more in this chapter, with the focus of the tasks applying specifically to laptop and tablet users. As an example of the latter, as a tablet or laptop owner you probably won't want to create a homegroup, but you'll probably want to join one. You won't share your own printer but you may want to print to one that is shared on the network. Likewise, it's probably more important to you (as a mobile user) to be able to get important information about new email and messages from the Lock screen than it is to a Desktop PC user.

Switch from a local account to a Microsoft account

When you first set up your laptop or tablet, you were prompted to create an account. In fact, you were strongly encouraged to create and use a Microsoft account. If you opted not to do that, then you created a local user account instead. At some point you'll probably want to change from the local account to a Microsoft account. Here's how.

1. Access the Windows 8 charms. You can flick in from the right on a touch screen or use the Windows key + C key combination with a keyboard.
2. Settings.
3. Click Change PC settings.
4. Tap or click Users.
5. Tap or click Switch to a Microsoft account. (If you see Switch to a Local account instead, you're already using a Microsoft account.)

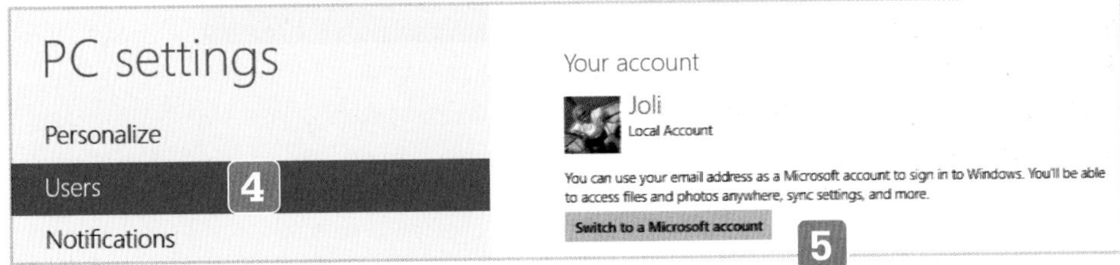

6. Enter your existing Microsoft account, one you recently obtained, or your favourite email address. You can also get a new email address from this screen.
7. Complete the process as instructed.

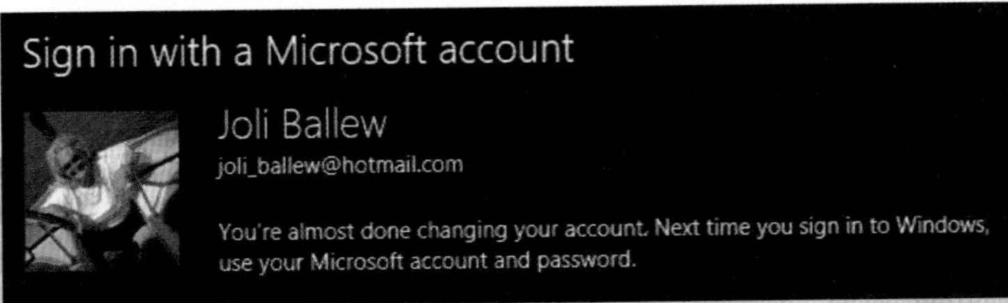

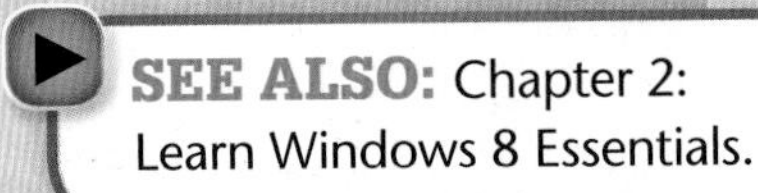

SEE ALSO: Chapter 2: Learn Windows 8 Essentials.

ALERT: You won't be able to use SkyDrive, Calendar, Store and lots of other apps unless you are signed on with a Microsoft account.

Log on faster: create a PIN

When you log on to your Windows 8 device, you have to type a password. This can become tiring after a while, especially if you don't have a physical keyboard. Even if you do have a keyboard, typing a complex password still takes time. You can change your login requirements so that you need only enter a numeric personal identification number (PIN) instead.

1. At the Start screen, type PIN. (If you don't have access to a physical keyboard, from the Settings charm, tap Keyboard and tap Touch keyboard and handwriting panel.)
2. On the right side of the screen, click Settings.
3. Click Create or change PIN.

4. Click Create a PIN.

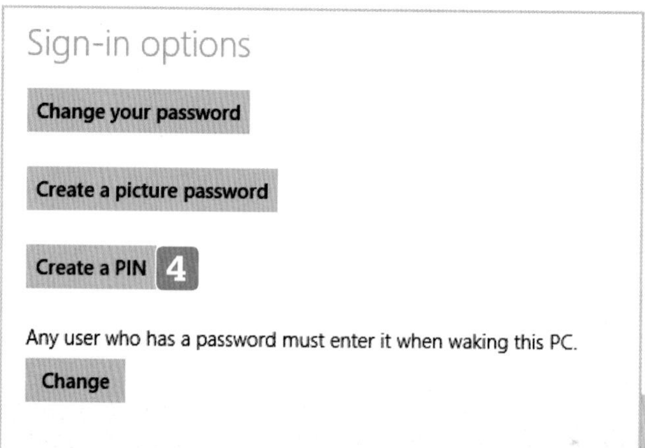

ALERT: When creating a PIN, try to avoid things like 12345 or 9876. Avoid using your birthday, too. (Make it at least a little difficult to guess!)

5 Type your current password, click OK, then enter the desired PIN twice.

6 Click Finish.

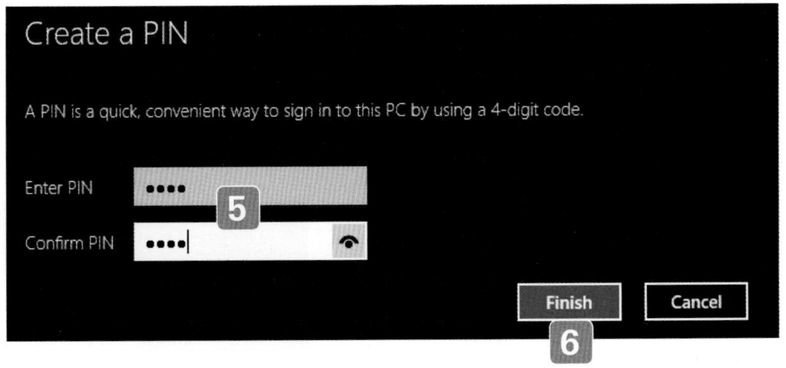

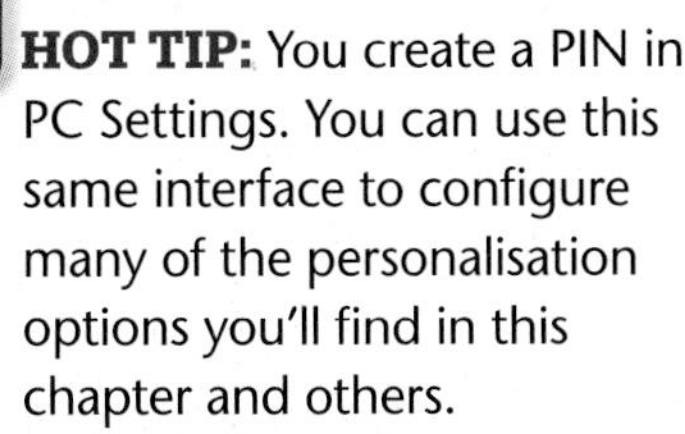

HOT TIP: You create a PIN in PC Settings. You can use this same interface to configure many of the personalisation options you'll find in this chapter and others.

Change the picture on the Lock screen

You can change the picture that appears on the Lock screen from the same PC Settings interface you used when you created a PIN. As you'll learn here, there is more than one way to open the PC Settings window.

1. At the Start screen, click your user name in the top right corner.
2. Click Change account picture. (This is simply another way to open the PC Settings interface.)
3. In the left pane, click Personalize.
4. In the right pane, click Lock screen.
5. Click one of the images provided or click Browse to locate a picture you'd like to use.

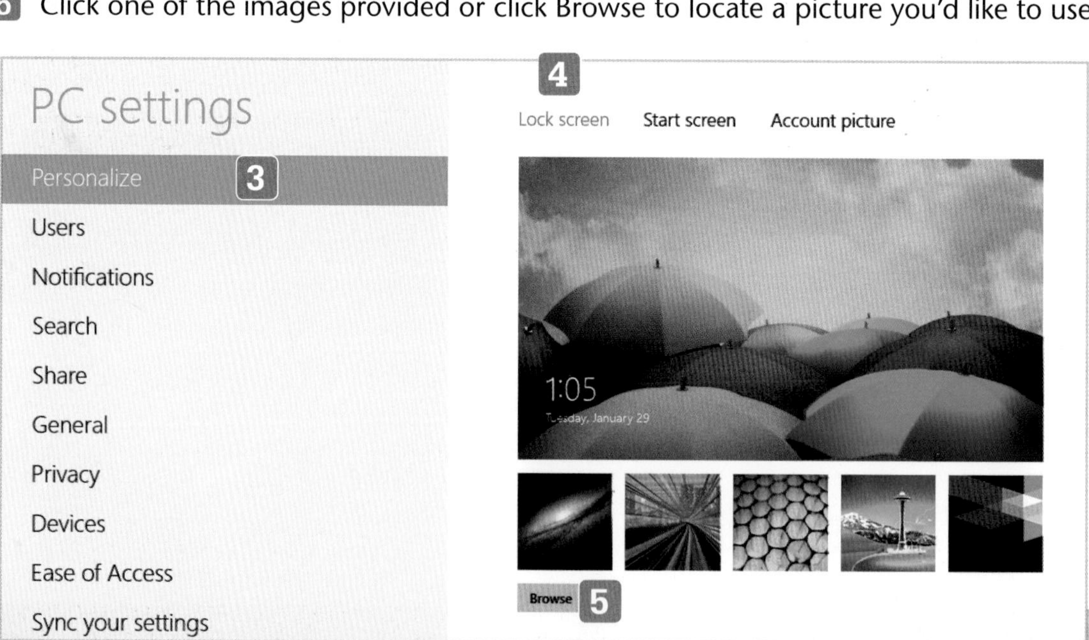

DID YOU KNOW?

PC Settings isn't technically an app, and it's not a window either. Most people refer to the group of PC Settings commands as an 'interface' or a 'hub'.

DID YOU KNOW?

You can type just about anything at the Start screen and find what you're looking for under one of the categories shown in the Search window.

Choose Lock screen apps

You may have noticed after using your Windows 8 computer for a while that a few app icons appear on the Lock screen (and they sometimes have numbers with them). By default these include Messages, Mail and Calendar. Numbers appear when new information is available, such as a new email or a new message. You can add more icons if you wish and remove the ones you don't want.

1. From the PC Settings interface, click Personalize. (Click the Settings charm to access PC Settings.)
2. In the right pane, click Lock screen.
3. Scroll down to the Lock screen apps section and click a + sign.
4. Choose an app to add.
5. To remove an app icon from the Lock screen, click the icon and then click Don't show quick status here.

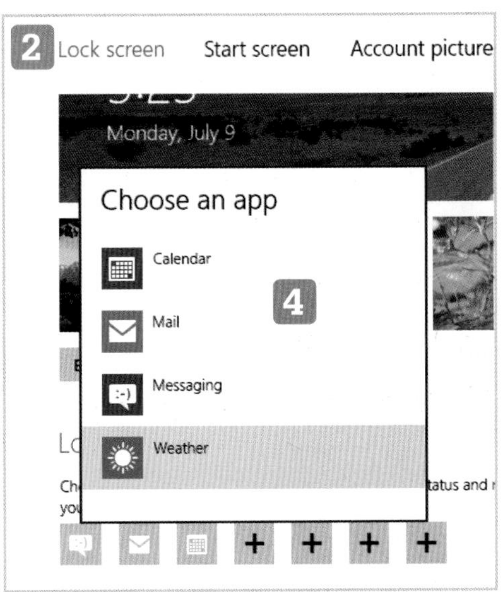

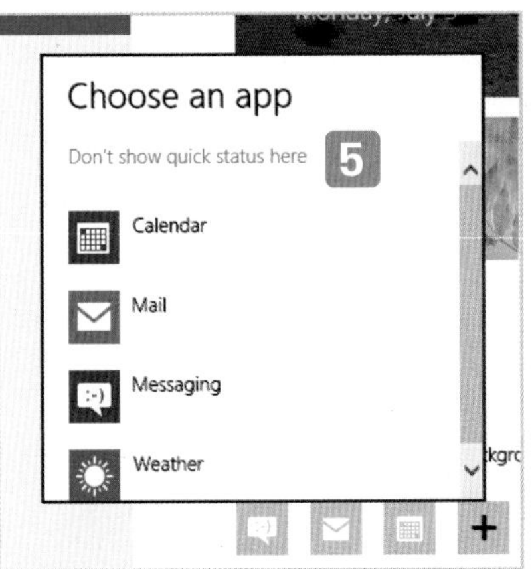

HOT TIP: Lock screen app icons can be particularly helpful to laptop and tablet users whose Lock screen is easily available. (Often you only need to press the Sleep/Wake/On/Off button to show this screen.)

HOT TIP: So far you've explored the Personalize and Users categories in the left pane of the PC Settings interface. Note how many other categories are available (including Notifications, General, Devices and so on).

Personalise the Start screen background

When you set up your Windows 8 computer, you chose the colour of the Start screen's background. You can change it again from the PC Settings interface.

1. Bring up the charms and click Settings. (You can use the keyboard shortcut Windows + C, flick in from the right side of the screen using your thumb, or position the cursor in the bottom right or top right corner of the screen.)
2. Click Change PC Settings.
3. In the left pane click Personalize; in the right pane click Start screen.
4. Move the slider to the desired colour and click the design you like.

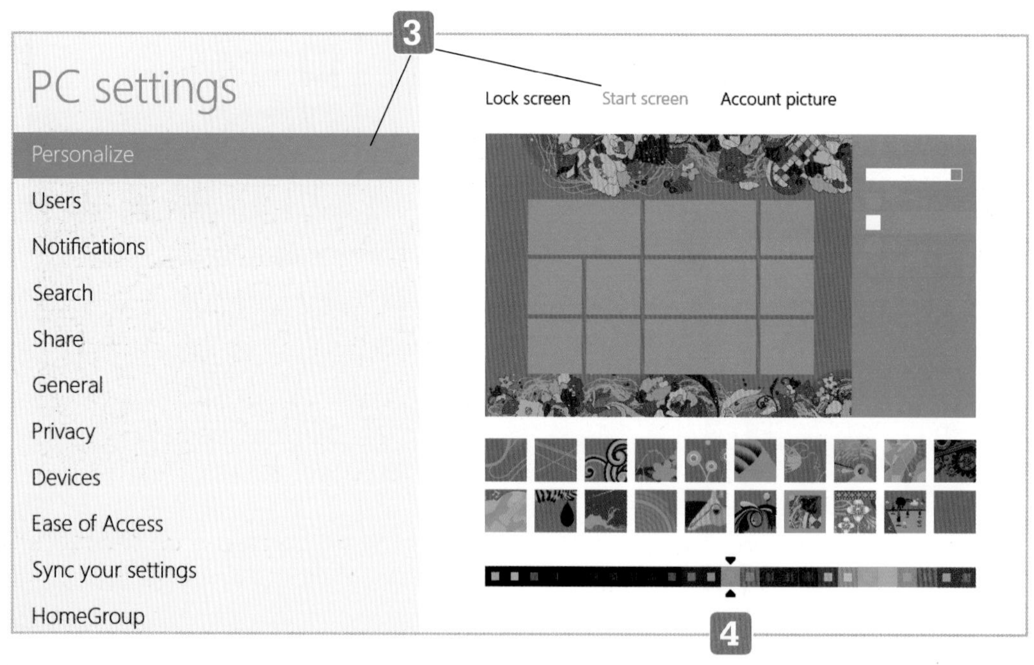

DID YOU KNOW?
If you use a Microsoft account to log in to your Windows 8 computer, and if you make changes to how your computer looks as outlined in this chapter, then when you log on to any other Windows 8 computer or tablet with that same Microsoft account, those changes will be applied there, too.

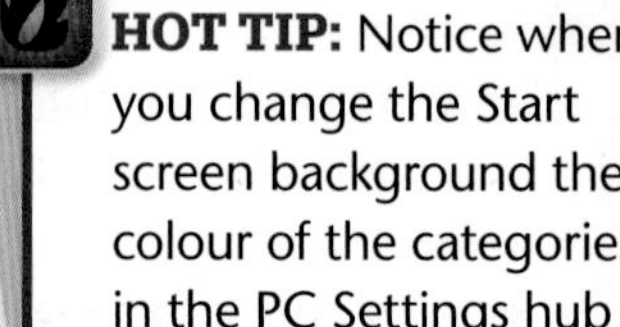

HOT TIP: Notice when you change the Start screen background the colour of the categories in the PC Settings hub changes, too.

Add a tile to the Start screen

There are more windows, apps, programs and applications available than those that appear on the Start screen by default. There's the Calculator, for instance, and Windows Media Player, Control Panel, Windows Explorer and WordPad, to name a few. You can add any item to the Start screen to have easier access to it.

1 Right-click an empty area of the Start screen. On a touch screen, flick upwards from the bottom of the screen.

2 Click All apps.

3 Right-click (or tap, hold and drag downwards) an item you'd like to add.

4 From the bar that appears at the bottom of the page, click Pin to Start.

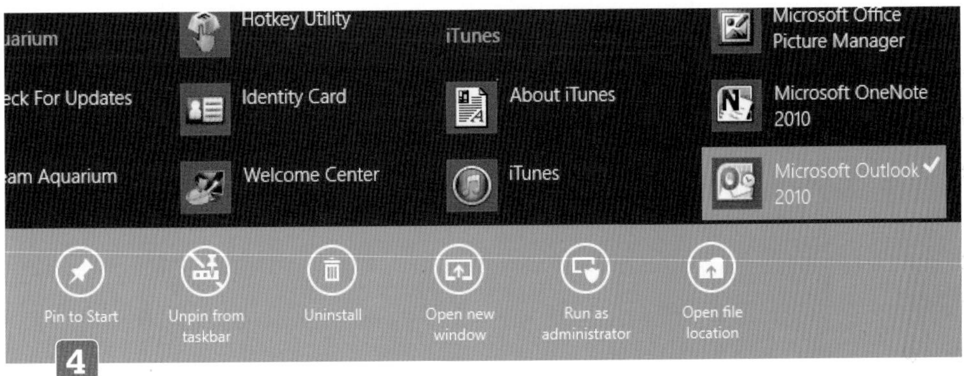

5 Return to the Start screen and locate the new tile. It will be placed on the far right. You may want to drag it left to reposition it.

DID YOU KNOW?
You can open an app from the All apps screen by clicking it once.

HOT TIP: Add tiles for apps, applications, system tools, windows and other items that you know you'll use often. You may want to add Control Panel if you're familiar with that feature, for instance.

Remove a tile from the Start screen

You remove an unwanted tile from the Start screen by selecting it and then choosing Unpin from Start. If you like, you can select multiple tiles to remove at one time.

1. Right-click or tap, hold and drag downwards on any tile you'd like to remove.
2. Repeat as often as you like to select additional tiles.
3. Click or tap Unpin from Start.

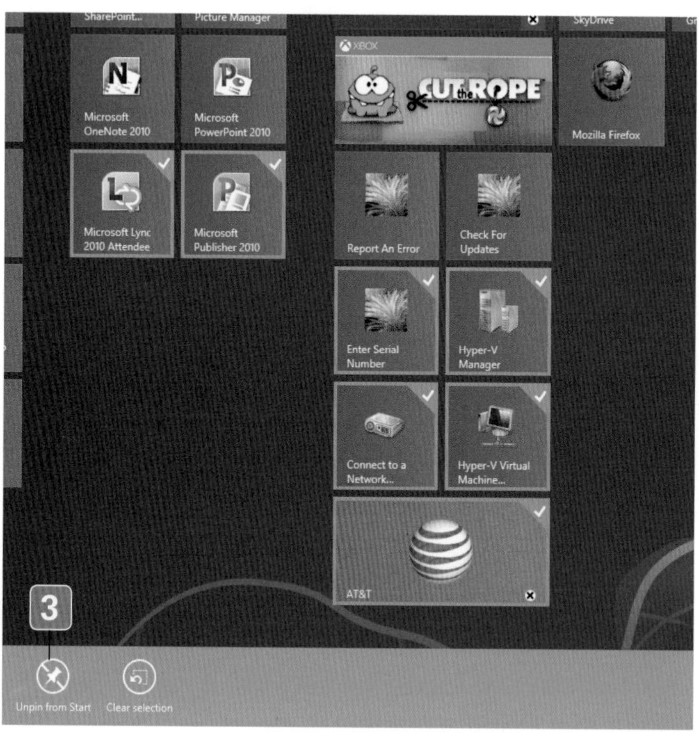

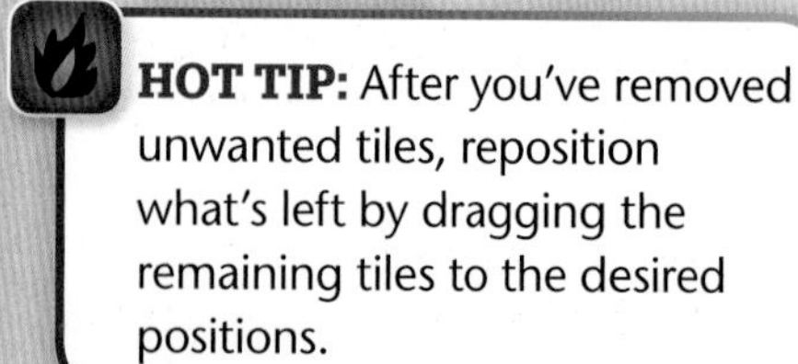

HOT TIP: After you've removed unwanted tiles, reposition what's left by dragging the remaining tiles to the desired positions.

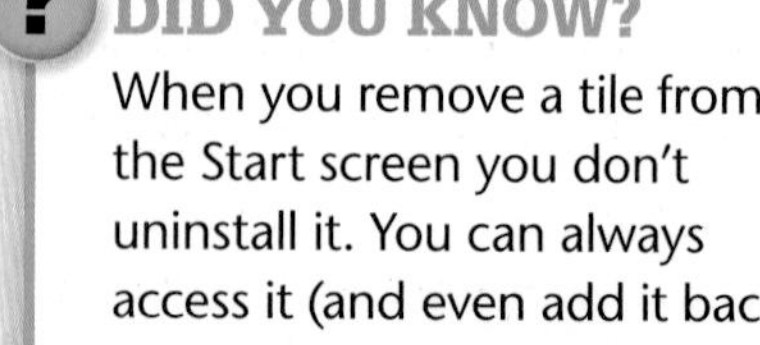

DID YOU KNOW?
When you remove a tile from the Start screen you don't uninstall it. You can always access it (and even add it back) from the All apps screen.

Create a shortcut for a folder or library on the Desktop

If you work at the Desktop regularly you can create shortcuts there for folders and libraries you use often. This makes it easier to open those items when you need them. You can locate the items in File Explorer.

1. From the Start screen, click Desktop.
2. On the Desktop, from the taskbar, click the folder icon. This opens File Explorer and gives access to your Libraries.

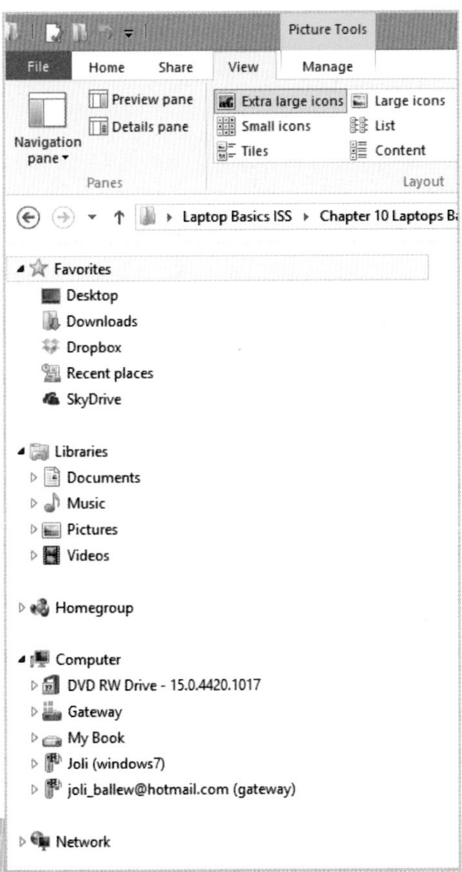

WHAT DOES THIS MEAN?

Library: a container that offers access to two or more folders. The Pictures library offers access to both your personal Pictures folder and the Public Pictures folder, for instance. You can create new and manage existing libraries.

3 To create a shortcut to any library or folder:

a. Right-click the item. (On a touch screen, use a long tap.)

b. Click Send to.

c. Click Desktop (create shortcut).

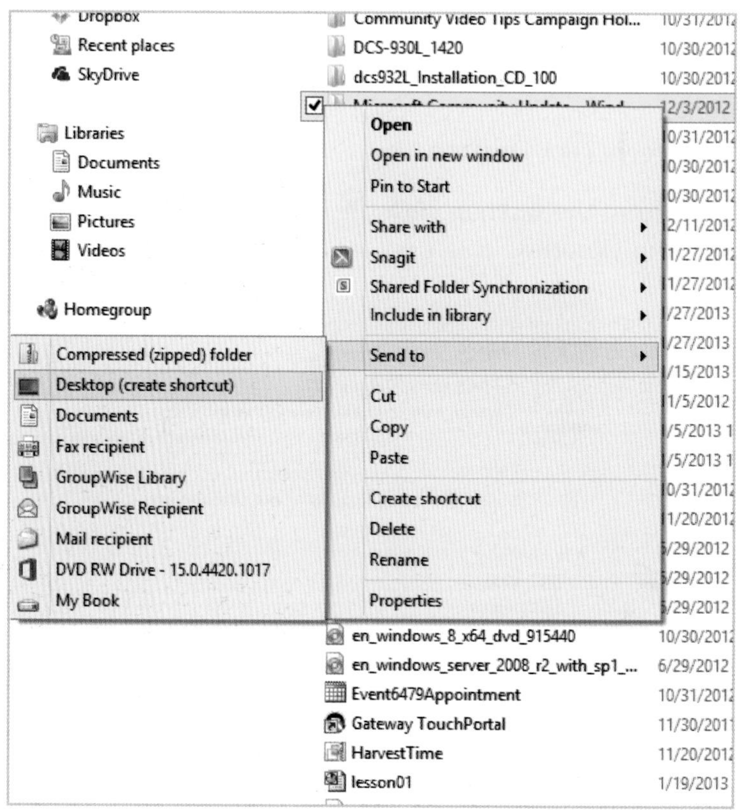

4 Repeat as desired.

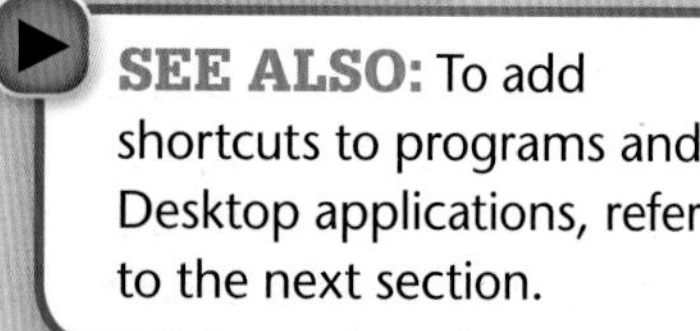

SEE ALSO: To add shortcuts to programs and Desktop applications, refer to the next section.

Create a shortcut for a program, accessory, system tool and more

You have to locate the item you want to add to the Desktop before you can right-click it (or long tap it) to access the Send to command. The easiest way to do this is to use the Start screen.

1. Right-click an empty area of the Start screen and click All apps. (Flick upwards on a touch screen.)
2. Use the scroll bar to move to the right of the screen and right-click the application, tool, accessory or program to add.
3. Click Open file location. (If you don't see this, you can't create a shortcut for it.)
4. Right-click (long tap) the item and click Send to.

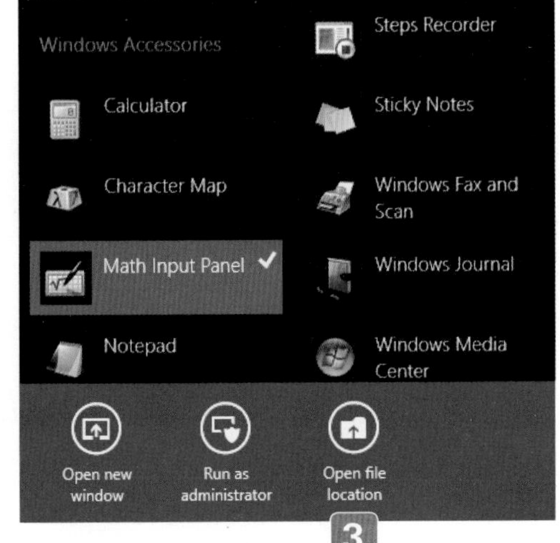

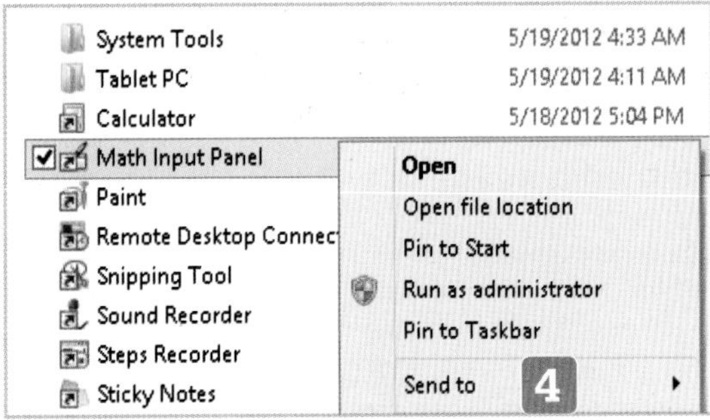

5. Click Desktop (create shortcut).

DID YOU KNOW?

You can't add shortcuts for any of the Start screen apps to the Desktop. You can only add shortcuts for Desktop apps, Windows Accessories, Windows System tools and similar items.

HOT TIP: You don't always have to add a shortcut on the Desktop. You can pin the item to the Desktop's taskbar instead. You may see this option along with the Send to command in a contextual menu, or you may not. It depends on what you're trying to add.

Add an item to the taskbar

If you'd rather not clutter up your Desktop with shortcuts, you can opt to add icons for items to the taskbar. This is called 'pinning' an item. You already know you can choose Pin to Start to add tiles to the Start screen. Another option is Pin to taskbar.

1. From the Start screen (or the All apps screen), right-click an item you'd like to add to the taskbar.
2. Click Pin to taskbar. If you don't see this option, it can't be pinned.

3. Repeat as desired and then note the new items that are pinned.

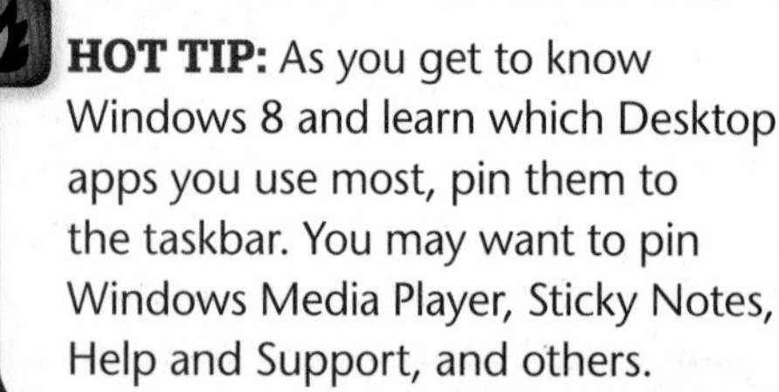

HOT TIP: As you get to know Windows 8 and learn which Desktop apps you use most, pin them to the taskbar. You may want to pin Windows Media Player, Sticky Notes, Help and Support, and others.

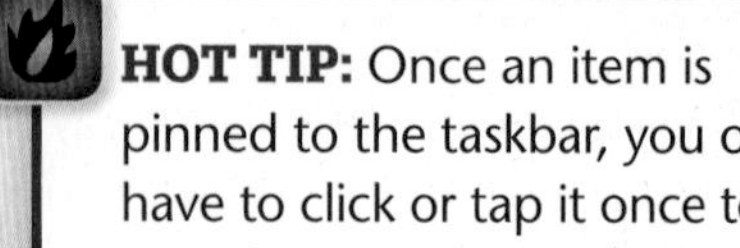

HOT TIP: Once an item is pinned to the taskbar, you only have to click or tap it once to open it.

Choose which Desktop icons appear

By default, the Recycle Bin is the only icon on the Desktop. You can add icons for commonly used items from the Personalization options in Control Panel.

1. Right-click an empty area of the Desktop and click Personalize.
2. Click Change desktop icons.

3. Place a tick by the items you'd like to add to the Desktop and click OK.

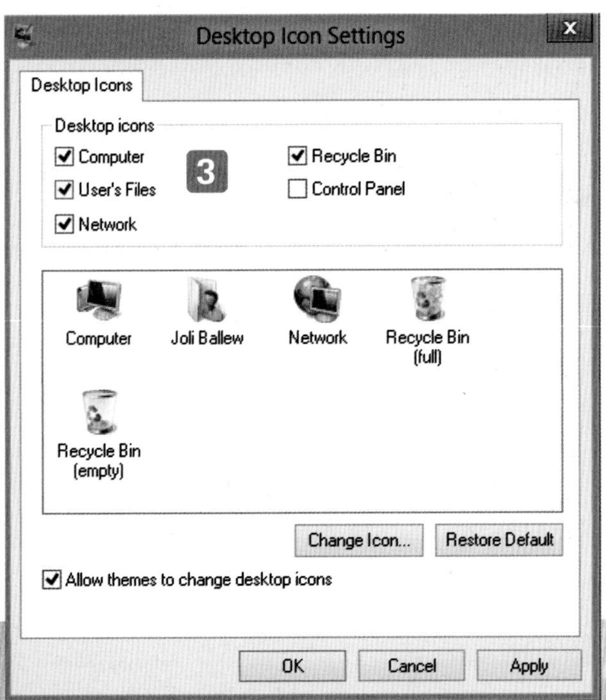

HOT TIP: Remember, in many instances, a long tap is equivalent to a right-click of a mouse.

HOT TIP: Continue to explore the various personalisation options as time allows.

Join a homegroup

You can share data, printers, media and so on in many ways using various techniques; likewise, there are lots of options for accessing the items and data shared by others. Using a homegroup facilitates sharing the most easily. If you know that a homegroup is available, you will probably want to join it.

1 At the Desktop, right-click the Network icon on the taskbar.

2 Click Open Network and Sharing Center.

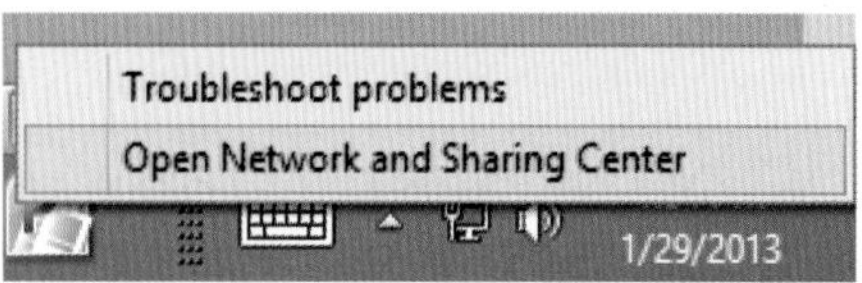

3 If a homegroup exists on the network already, you'll see Available to join. Click this.

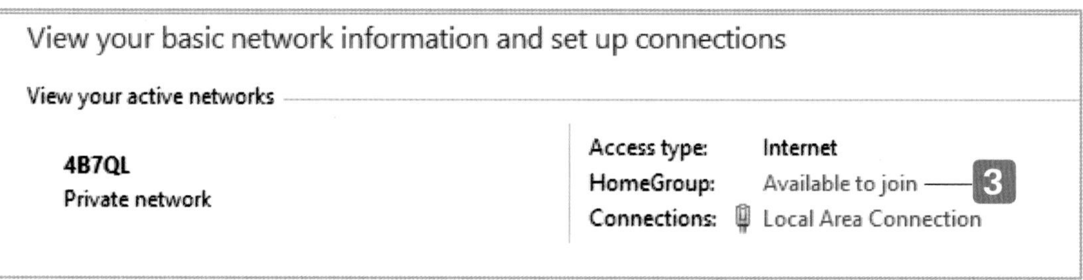

4 Click Join now.

HOT TIP: Homegroups are for sharing data with others you trust. It's okay to share your data in this manner.

5 Proceed through the wizard by clicking Next and choosing what to share.

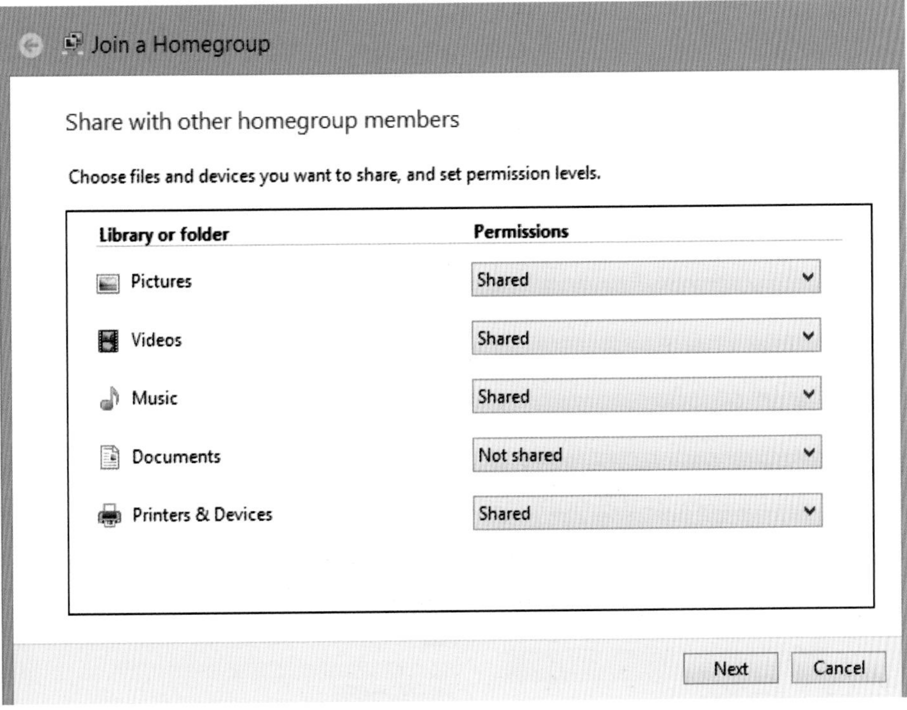

6 Type the existing homegroup password. You can find the password on another network computer.

Create a new user

You created your user account when you first turned on your new Windows 8 laptop or tablet. Your user account is what defines your personal folders as well as your settings for Desktop background, screen saver and other items. If you share the computer with someone else, they should have their own user account, too. If every person who accesses your computer has their own standard user account and password, and if every person logs on using that account and then logs off each time they've finished using it, you'll never have to worry about anyone accessing anyone else's personal data.

1. Click the Settings charm.
2. Click Change PC settings.
3. If applicable, click Users in the left pane. Then select Add a user in the right pane.

ALERT: You must be logged on with an administrator account to create a new user.

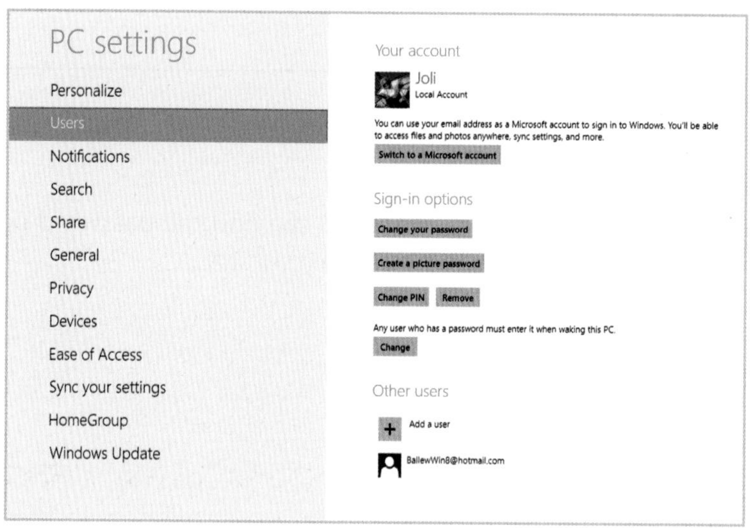

4. Work through the process to add a new user. It's the same process you worked through when you set up Windows 8.

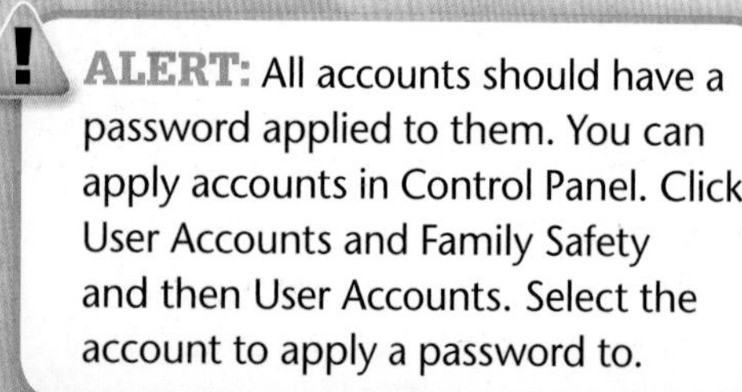

ALERT: All accounts should have a password applied to them. You can apply accounts in Control Panel. Click User Accounts and Family Safety and then User Accounts. Select the account to apply a password to.

DID YOU KNOW?

The first account you created, probably your own, is an administrator account. Administrators have full access to the computer. Subsequent accounts you create are standard accounts. Standard users have limited access, permissions and rights on the computer for security reasons. You can change the account type in Control Panel if you wish.

Share with the Public folder

Windows 8 comes with Public folders you can use to share data easily with others on your network or others who share your computer. The Public folders are located on your local disk, generally C:, under Users.

1. From the Desktop, open File Explorer.
2. Click Computer in the left pane, double-click the disk that contains your data and double-click Users.
3. Double-click the Public folder.

HOT TIP: Create a shortcut for the Public folder on the Desktop so that it's easy to access.

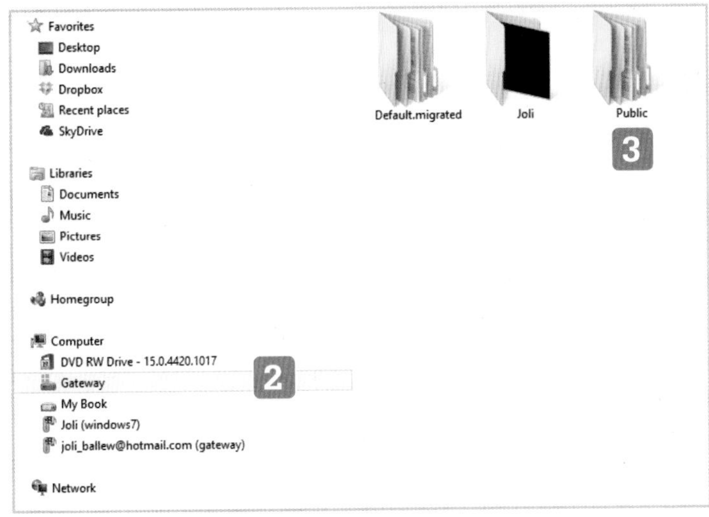

4. Now save, move or copy data to these folders as desired.

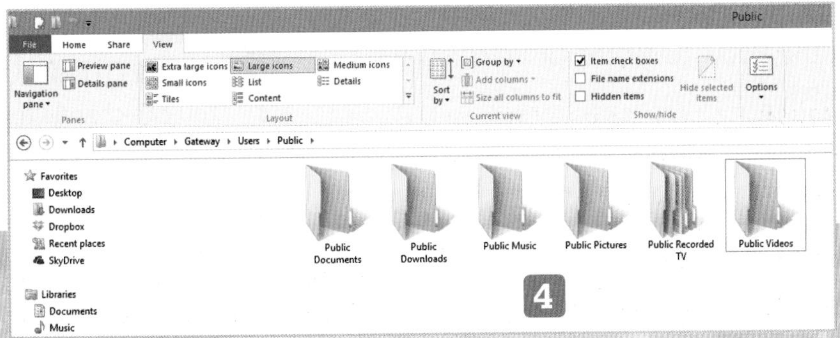

HOT TIP: If you share a laptop, save the data you want to share in Public folders for easy access by other users.

HOT TIP: Any time you want to share data with others on your network, move or copy it to these folders.

Share a personal folder

Sometimes you won't want to save, move or copy data into Public folders. Instead, you'll want to share data directly from a personal folder.

1. From File Explorer or the Desktop, locate the folder to share.
2. Right-click the folder and click Share with.

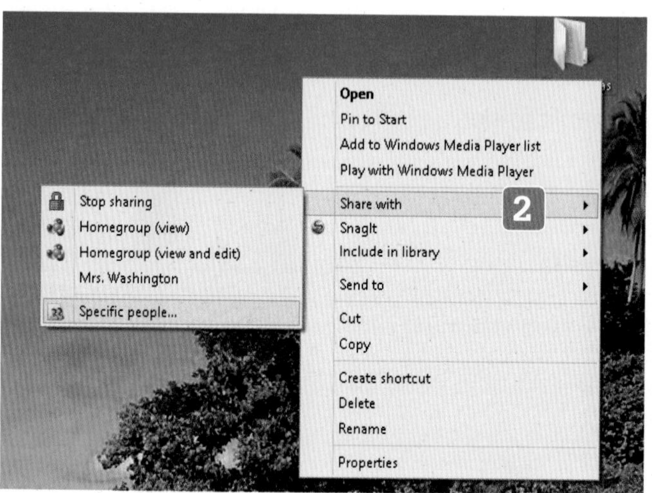

3. If you want to share with your homegroup or another user, select the appropriate option from the list. Follow any prompts to complete the process.
4. If you want to share with specific people who are not in a homegroup, choose Specific people, then:
   a. Click the arrow and choose with whom to share. (Everyone is an option.)
   b. Click Add.
   c. Click the arrow to set the permissions for the user.
   d. Click Share.

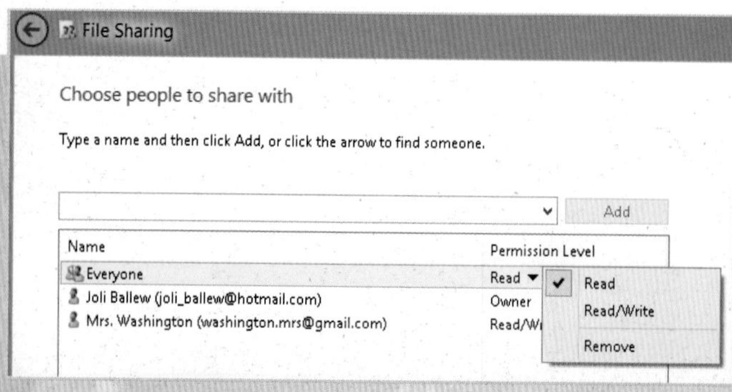

DID YOU KNOW?

You can change the sharing defaults in the Network and Sharing Center. Click Change advanced sharing settings to get started.

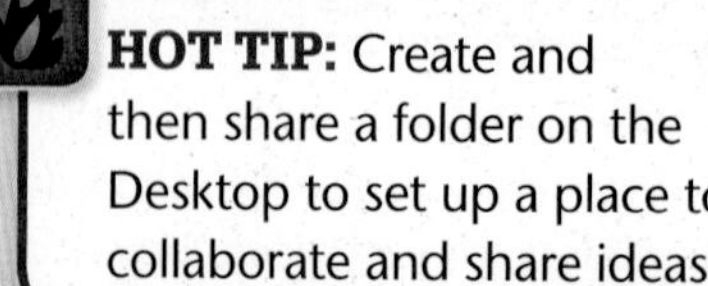

HOT TIP: Create and then share a folder on the Desktop to set up a place to collaborate and share ideas.

11 Explore media apps

Introduction

Windows 8 comes with three distinct media apps. There's a Photos app, a Music app and a Video app. You can use these apps to access and view your media in various ways. You can watch a slide show of your favourite photos, for instance. You can play a song or album that you've copied to your laptop or tablet. You can watch a movie or a TV programme, too, provided that the media is on your laptop or can be accessed from it. If you want to perform more complicated tasks though, such as editing photos, creating your own music CDs or accessing video and other media stored on shared, networked computers, you'll need to do that from the Desktop.

Navigate the Music app

The Music app, available from the Start screen, offers access to the music you have on your laptop or tablet. You can use this app to play music, add songs and albums to the 'now playing' list, and view information about an artist, among other things. If you have a Microsoft account, you can also access the Microsoft Store where you can purchase more music online.

1. From the Start screen, click the Music tile.

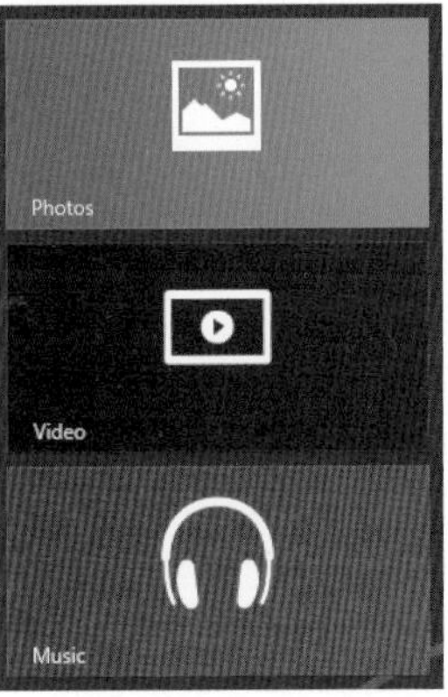

2. If you have music in your Music library, you'll see it under My Music. (Scroll to the left end of the app.)

3 Use the scroll bar, the scroll wheel on your mouse or flick with your finger to see the other Music options, including the ability to browse the Store for new releases.

HOT TIP: With the Music app open, use the key combination Windows + C to access the charms, and click Settings, then Preferences. From there you can configure options for the Music app.

HOT TIP: From the Music app, click xbox music store. Once inside, choose a song and click Preview to hear a sample.

ALERT: To purchase music from the Store, you'll have to set up an account.

Play a song with the Music app

If you have music in your Music library you can play it from the Music app. If you don't have any music, you can copy songs from CDs you own (provided your device has a CD drive). You'll learn how to do that later in this chapter.

1. Open the Music app and under My Music, click as necessary to locate a song to play.
2. Click the song and click Play.
3. Repeat. As you add songs, click Add to now playing.

4. Explore the playback options at the bottom of the screen (the control area). You may have to flick up or right-click to access these.

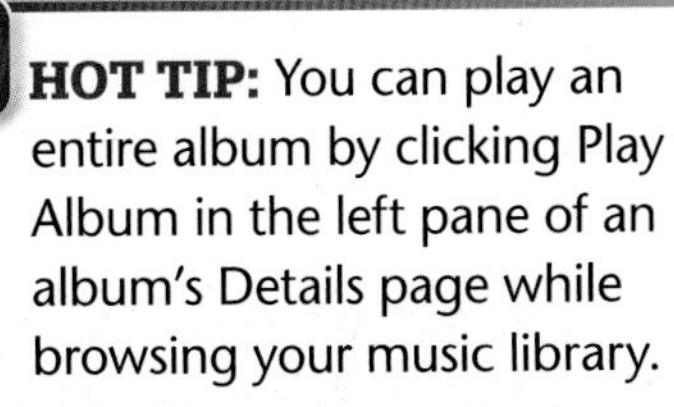

HOT TIP: You can play an entire album by clicking Play Album in the left pane of an album's Details page while browsing your music library.

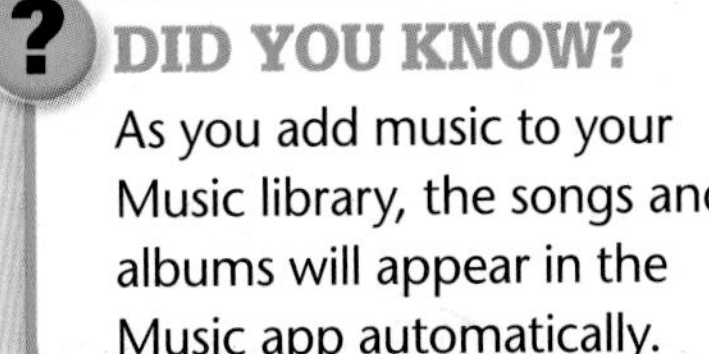

DID YOU KNOW?

As you add music to your Music library, the songs and albums will appear in the Music app automatically.

5 Click the album cover from the control area to view additional information. Click all the icons to see what they offer. Note the Back button.

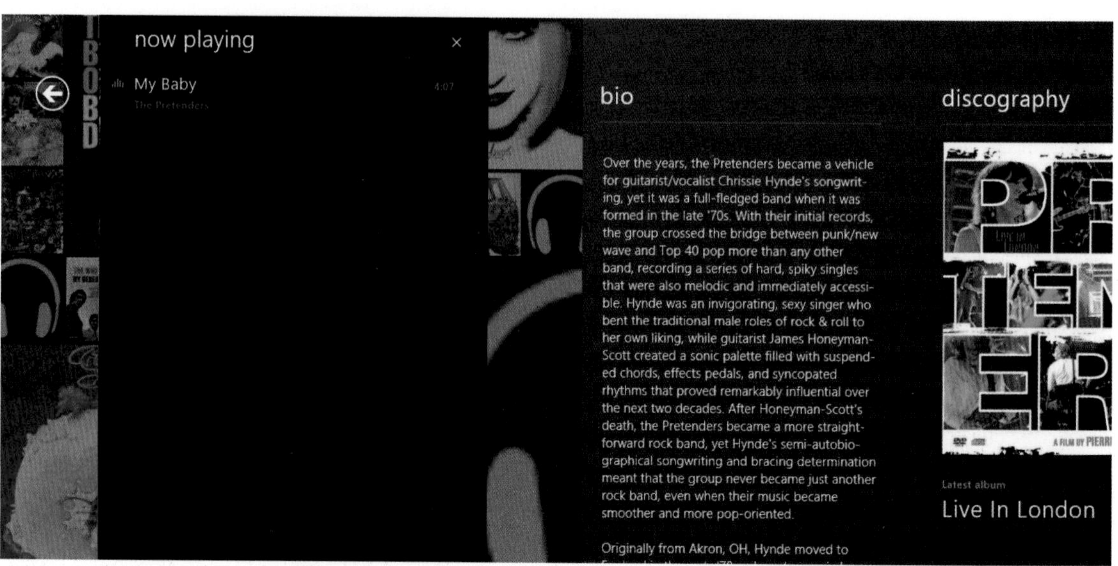

? DID YOU KNOW?

When you return to the Start screen after using the Music app for the first time, the tile will be live and will show a thumbnail of the song that is playing.

Navigate the Photos app

The Photos app, available from the Start screen, is the easiest place to view your photos. The app separates your photos by what's stored on your computer and what is stored in various places on the Internet. If you've created subfolders to organise your photos, those subfolders will appear, too.

1 From the Start screen, click Photos.

2 Note the folders that already appear. This is the landing page.

3 Click the Pictures library. (My Pictures library holds screenshots for this book!)

4 If you see subfolders, click them to access the pictures stored there.

5 Click or tap the screen and then the Back arrow to return to previous screens.

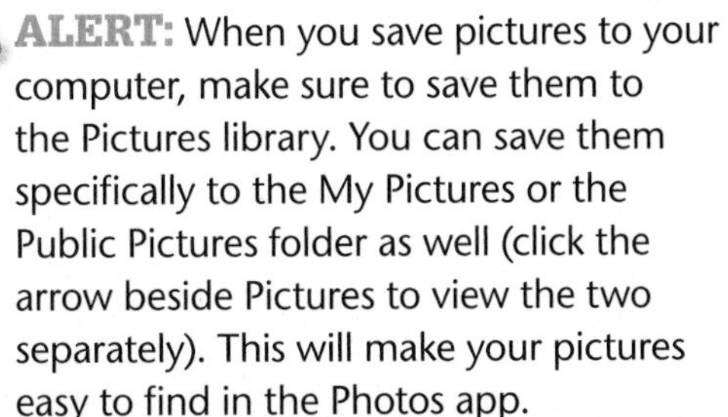

ALERT: When you save pictures to your computer, make sure to save them to the Pictures library. You can save them specifically to the My Pictures or the Public Pictures folder as well (click the arrow beside Pictures to view the two separately). This will make your pictures easy to find in the Photos app.

HOT TIP: You may not have any photos on your computer yet. If this is the case, skip forward to learn how to import pictures from a digital camera (or camera card) and then return here to view them.

View a photo

As you navigate the Photos app, clicking folders and subfolders, you'll see the photos you've stored on your laptop or are available from it. While in folders in subfolders, the photos are in Preview mode. You can view them this way or click them to view them in full-screen mode. We'll explore both here.

1. Open the Photos app from the Start screen.
2. Click the Pictures library.
3. If applicable, click any subfolder. You'll see photos in Preview mode.

4. Click any photo to view it in full-screen mode.
5. Use the arrow that appears in the middle of the left side, shown here, to move back one photo. Use the arrow that appears on the right (not shown) to move forward one photo.
6. Click once on the screen to show the Back arrow, shown here in the top left corner, to move back one folder. Repeat as necessary to return to the Photos landing page.

HOT TIP: While in Preview mode, flick or use the scroll wheel on your mouse to move through the photos quickly.

HOT TIP: At the Photos landing page, click SkyDrive photos, Facebook photos or Flickr photos to make the photos you have stored there appear in the Photos app.

Import pictures from a digital camera

You can put photos on your computer in lots of ways, but the easiest is to use the Photos app. The Photos landing page offers an option to add a device to *see* photos that are on it, but if you right-click while on that page, the option to *import* those photos appears.

1. Connect your camera, insert a memory card or connect an external drive that contains photos.
2. Open the Photos app and click any back buttons as necessary to access the landing page.
3. Right-click the landing page to access the toolbar.
4. Click Import.

5. By default, all the photos are selected as shown here, provided they have not already been imported. Right-click to deselect photos.

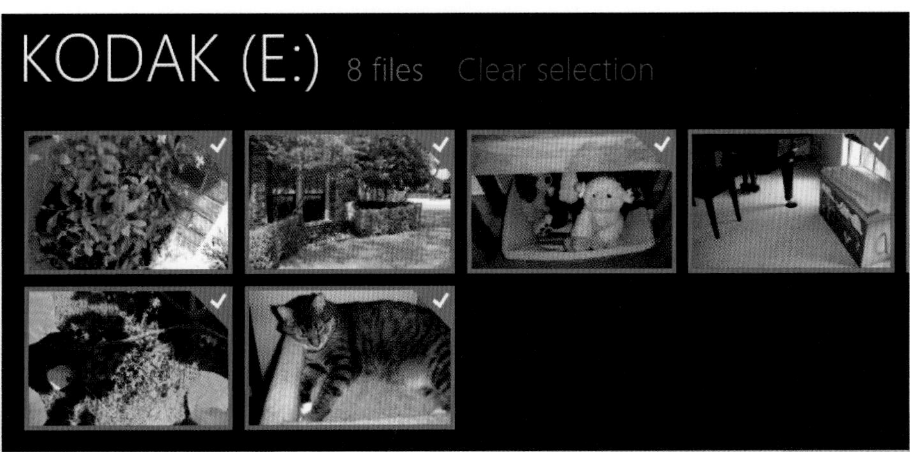

WHAT DOES THIS MEAN?

Import: when you import photos, you copy them to your laptop.

6 Type a name for the folder these pictures will be imported to and click Import.

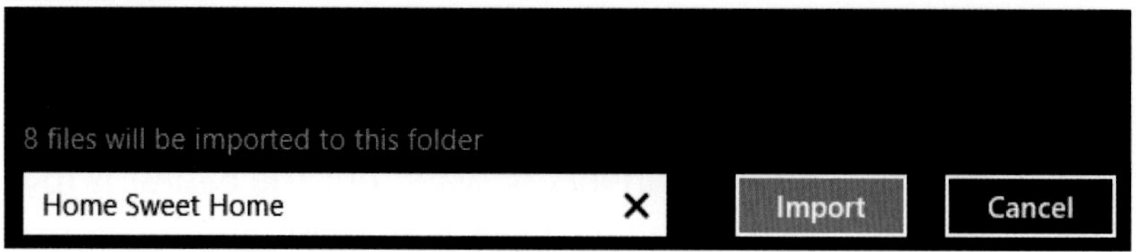

7 Click Open album (not shown) to view the photos.

HOT TIP: Create a descriptive name for the folder that will hold the imported photos; don't just accept the default name offered.

Play a slide show of photos

You can play a slide show of pictures in any folder. Once it starts to play, you can stop it in many ways: you can click Esc on the keyboard, right-click with a mouse, touch the screen and more.

1. Open the Photos app from the Start screen.
2. Navigate to any folder that contains photos.
3. Right-click and choose Slide show. (Remember, on a tablet you can swipe up.)
4. Stop the show using any method you choose.

HOT TIP: You can pause a slide show by tapping a key on the keyboard and start it again with a right-click of the mouse (you'll have to click Slide show again).

DID YOU KNOW?
You won't have any pictures available under SkyDrive, Facebook or Flickr until you click and log in with a compatible account.

Edit a photo

You can edit photos, but you'll need to use an editing program. To find out what your editing options are, from the Desktop, navigate to the Pictures library and then right-click any photo while inside File Explorer and choose Edit (shown here). Paint may open. Paint is a Desktop application included with Windows 8. Paint isn't a very good editing tool though. Consider the following instead.

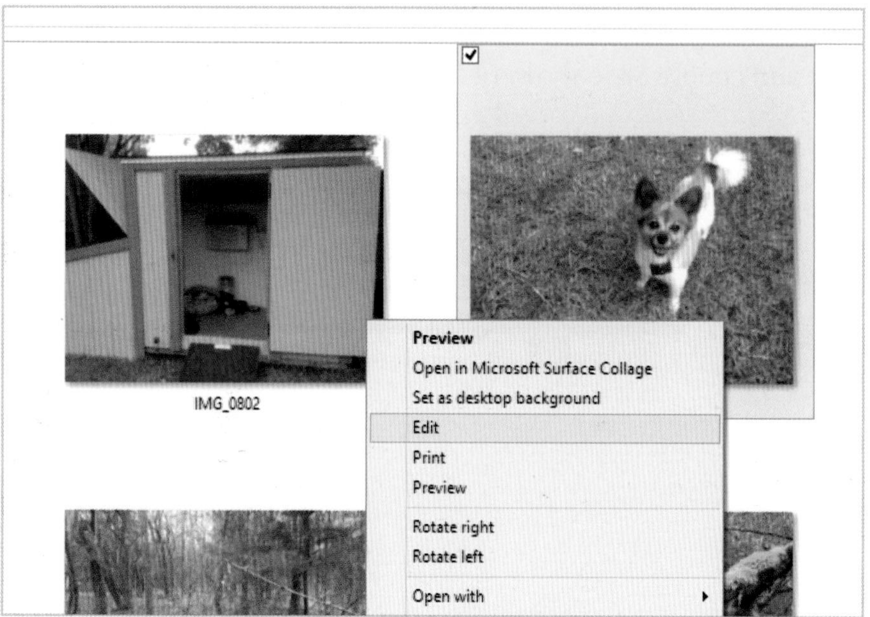

- Windows Live Photo Gallery – this is part of the free Windows Live Essentials suite. Like most editing programs, it enables you to fix red-eye, crop, adjust exposure and sharpness, and more. There are lots of automatic fixes to make it easy.
- Picasa – this is a free, digital photo organiser, so it might complicate locating and managing photos, but the editing tools that come with the program enable you to edit photos quickly and easily. Picasa offers the usual editing tools, including crop and various auto adjustments.

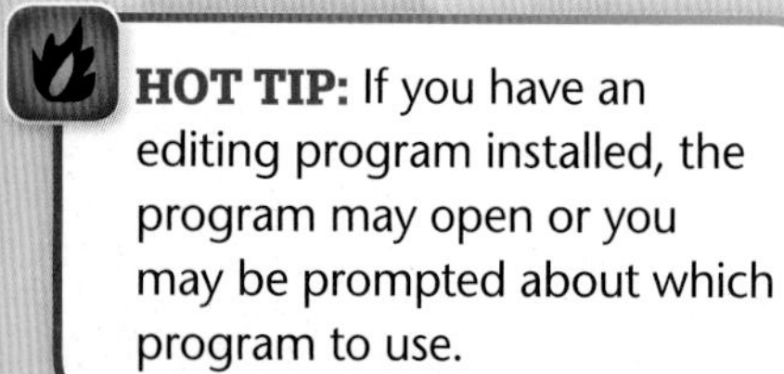

HOT TIP: If you have an editing program installed, the program may open or you may be prompted about which program to use.

HOT TIP: Try Windows Live Photo Gallery first. It's made by Microsoft so you know it will work well with Windows 8.

- Photoshop Elements – you'll have to pay for this program, but for what you get it's well worth the cost if you want to do some serious editing. The interface is user friendly and enables you to edit your photos in ways you never imagined.

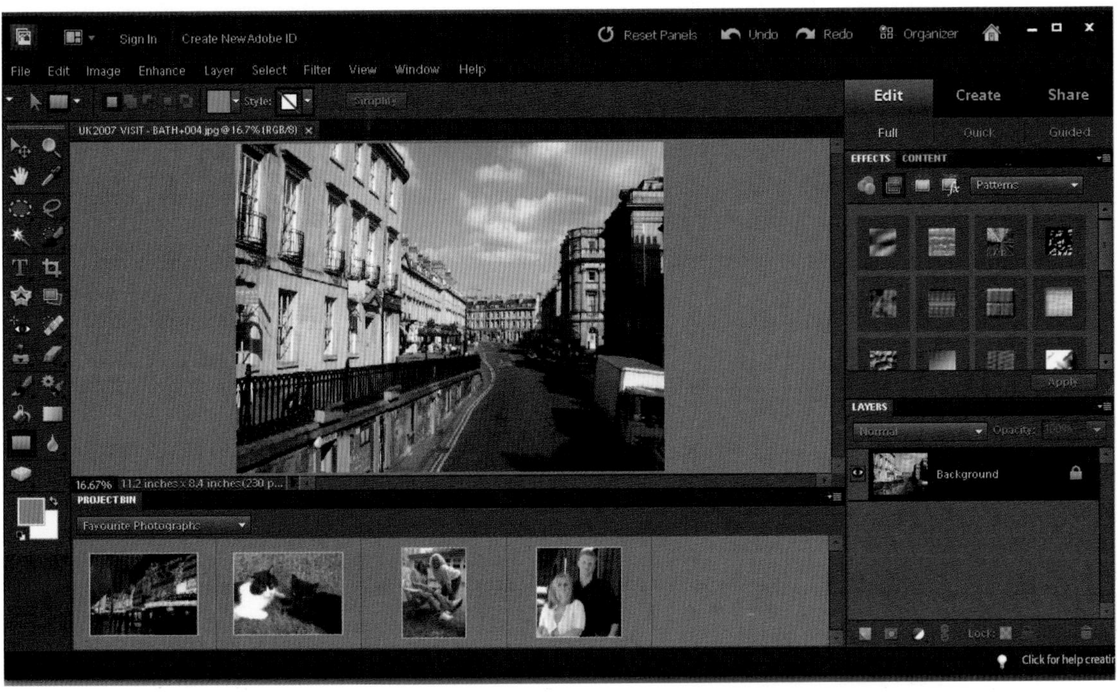

DID YOU KNOW?

When you right-click a picture in the Pictures library, the option to rotate them appears.

Play a video

The Video app is very similar to the Music app. It contains a My Videos section and offers access to the Store, where you can purchase movies and TV shows. If you have videos, perhaps something you've purchased or something you've taken yourself with a video camera, copy them to the Videos library before starting here.

1. From the Start screen, open the Video app.
2. If you have videos in your Video library, you'll see them under My Videos. (Scroll to the left side of the app to see this.)

3. Use the scroll bar, the scroll wheel on your mouse or flick with your finger to see the other video options, including options to purchase media.
4. To play a video in the Video app, click it once. The video will play and controls will become available on the screen. If the controls disappear, move your mouse on the screen to show them.

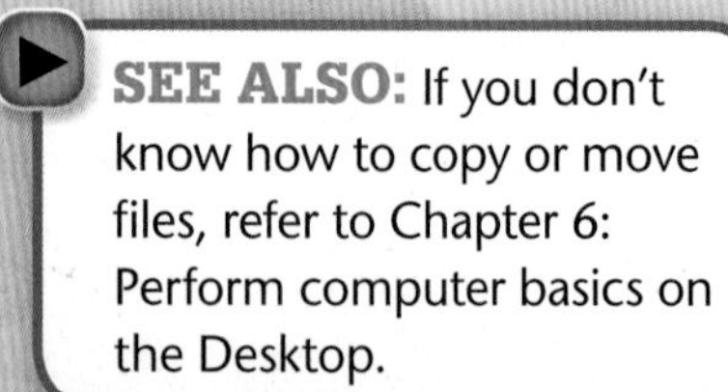

SEE ALSO: If you don't know how to copy or move files, refer to Chapter 6: Perform computer basics on the Desktop.

HOT TIP: As with other apps, you can use the default Settings charm to access the app's options.

Play a song in Media Player

Media Player isn't a Start screen app, it's a Desktop application and is much more powerful than the Music app you explored earlier. The best way to get to know Media Player is to play a song. Once the song is playing you can manage the media using the playback controls located at the bottom of the Media Player interface.

1 From the Start screen, type Media Player. Click Windows Media Player in the results. If prompted, opt to use the default options.

2 Click Music in the Navigation pane. (Note you can also click Artist, Album or Genre to locate a song.)

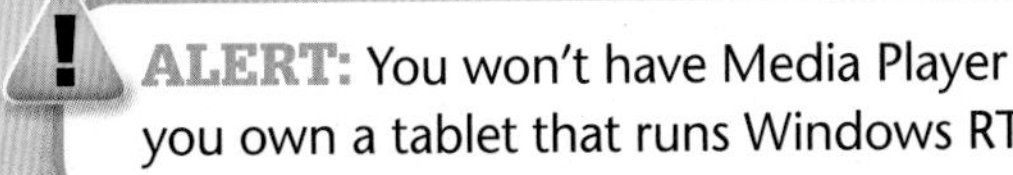

ALERT: You won't have Media Player if you own a tablet that runs Windows RT.

3 Double-click any song in the right pane to play it.

4 Use these media controls located at the bottom of the Media Player interface:

a. Shuffle – to let Windows Media Player choose what order to play the selected songs.
b. Repeat – to play the current song again.
c. Stop – to stop playback.
d. Previous – to play the previous song in the list, on the album and so on.
e. Play/Pause – to play and pause the song (and playlist).
f. Next – to play the next song in the list, on the album and so on.
g. Mute – to quickly mute the song.
h. Volume – to change the volume of the song.

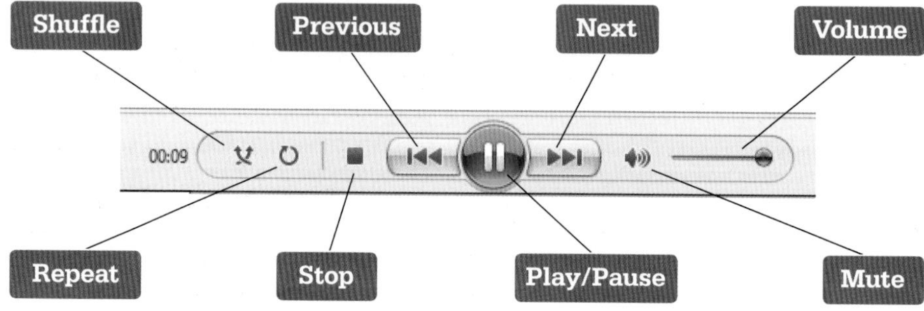

HOT TIP: While a song is playing, right-click any other song and choose Play Next, Play All or Play, as required.

DID YOU KNOW?
Media Player has Back and Forward buttons you can use to move around in its interface.

Copy a music CD you own

You can use Windows Media Player to copy CDs to your hard drive. This is called 'ripping'. To rip means to copy in media-speak. Once music is on your laptop, you can listen to it in the Music app and in Media Player, burn compilations of music to other CDs, and sync the music to a portable music player.

1. Insert the CD to copy into the CD drive.
2. Deselect any songs you do not want to copy to your computer.
3. In Windows Media Player, click the Rip CD button.

HOT TIP: Right-click any album cover and click Find Album Info, and Windows Media Player will look online for the album cover, track list and other information.

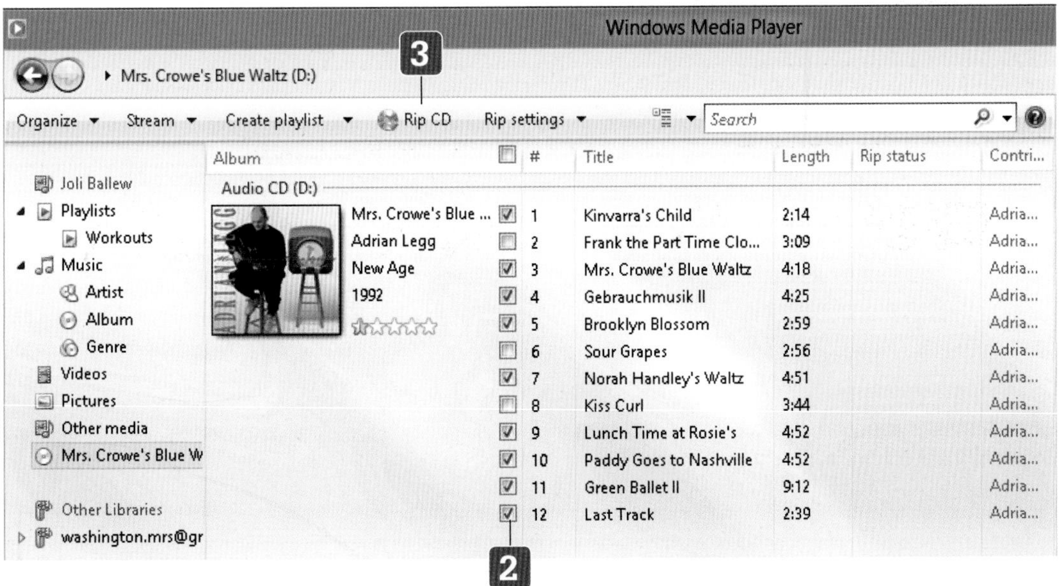

DID YOU KNOW?

You have the right to rip any CD you own to your computer for no extra cost and without breaking any laws.

HOT TIP: Click the arrow beside Organize and click Options to change the settings configured by default, such as what format you use when you rip a CD. (You'll want to choose MP3 if you plan to copy the music to a portable player, for instance.)

Create your own music CD

Although you can take your laptop with you, it's unwieldy if you just want to listen to music. There are two additional ways to take music with you when you are on the road or on the go. You can copy the music to a portable device (music player, tablet or phone) or you can create your own CDs, choosing the songs to copy and placing them on the CD in the desired order. Here you'll learn how to create a music CD. (To copy songs to a portable player, use the Sync tab instead of the Burn tab.)

1. Open Media Player.
2. Insert a blank CD and click the Burn tab.
3. Click any song or album to add and drag it to the List pane, shown here. You can drag any song to move it to a new position in the Burn list.
4. When you've added the songs you want, click Start burn.

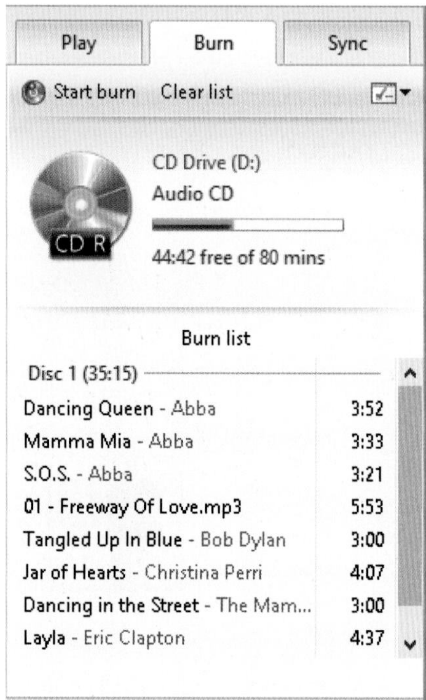

DID YOU KNOW?
Look at the slider in the List pane to see how much room is left on the CD. A typical CD can hold about 80 minutes of music.

HOT TIP: Click the arrow beside Organize and click Options to change the settings configured by default, including whether or not to use 'volume levelling' when burning CDs or if you want to burn the CD without any gaps between tracks.

WHAT DOES THIS MEAN?
Burn: a term used to describe the process of copying music from a computer to a CD.

Access media on networked devices

If you have a network at home, you can share the media on your laptop with other computers that are members of the network. Likewise, you can share media from networked computers and access that media from your laptop. Sharing allows you to keep only one copy of media (music, videos, pictures) on one computer, while sharing it with other computers, laptops, some tablet computers, various media extenders and Microsoft's Xbox 360.

ALERT: Sharing is limited on Windows RT tablets.

1. Open Windows Media Player and click the Stream button.
2. Choose the streaming options you require.

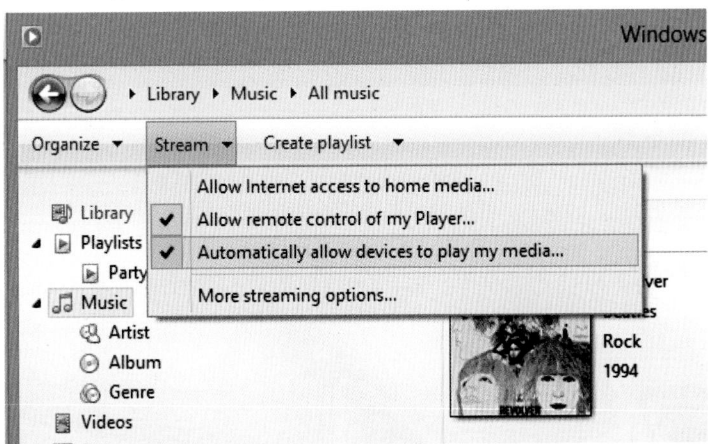

3. To see additional options, click the Stream button again and choose More streaming options.
4. Configure options as you wish and click OK when you've finished.

ALERT: The Windows 8 computer that stores the media you want to share must be connected to your home network and turned on for others to access it. The network must be private as well.

HOT TIP: You must repeat this task on other Windows computers on your network in order for streaming to work effectively.

12 Stay in touch with others

Introduction

Windows 8 offers two apps to help you keep in touch with your contacts. One is Messaging, the other is People.

Messaging lets you chat using instant messages with friends who use compatible messaging services like those offered by Facebook, as well as others who use the Windows 8 Messaging app on their own Windows 8 devices. The Messaging app also offers app commands on a toolbar that let you invite others and manage conversations easily.

The People app holds the contact information you keep about others and offers access to your friends' social networking updates. Like Messaging, there are commands that enable you to configure the app to suit your preferences.

Skype is another messaging option. You can download Skype from the Store and use it to video chat with other Skype users. You'll learn how to use all three in this chapter.

Add social network information to the Messaging app

You'll need contacts that use compatible messaging services to use the Messaging app, and you'll need at least one person you can message with to get started. One way to populate your computer with contacts is to add social networking information, such as your Facebook user name and password, to the apps you use. When you do, you can easily communicate with those who also use compatible services and are your contacts there.

1. Open the Messaging app from the Start screen.

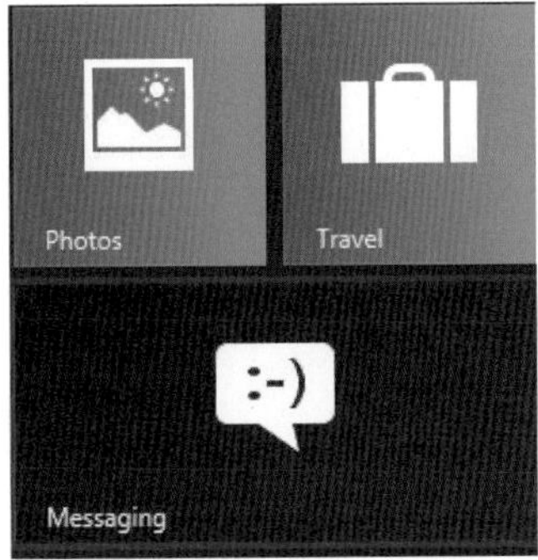

2. While inside the Messaging app, access the default charms (Windows key + C or flick inwards from the right side of the screen).
3. Click the Settings charm and then click Accounts.
4. Click Add an account.

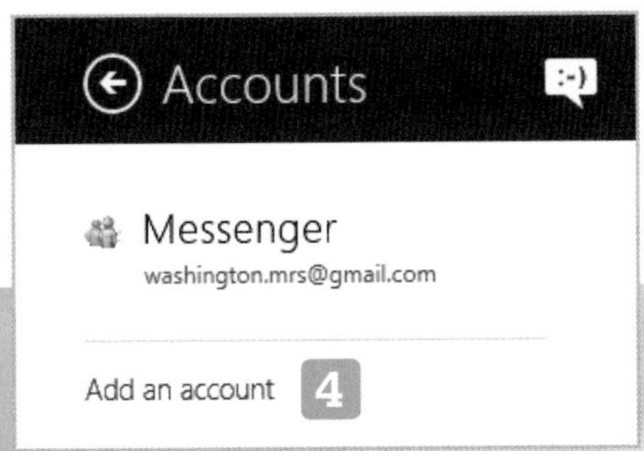

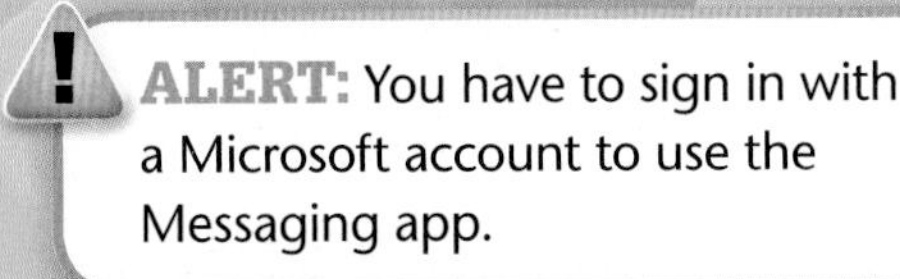

ALERT: You have to sign in with a Microsoft account to use the Messaging app.

5 Choose the account from the resulting list.

6 Click Connect and input the required information.

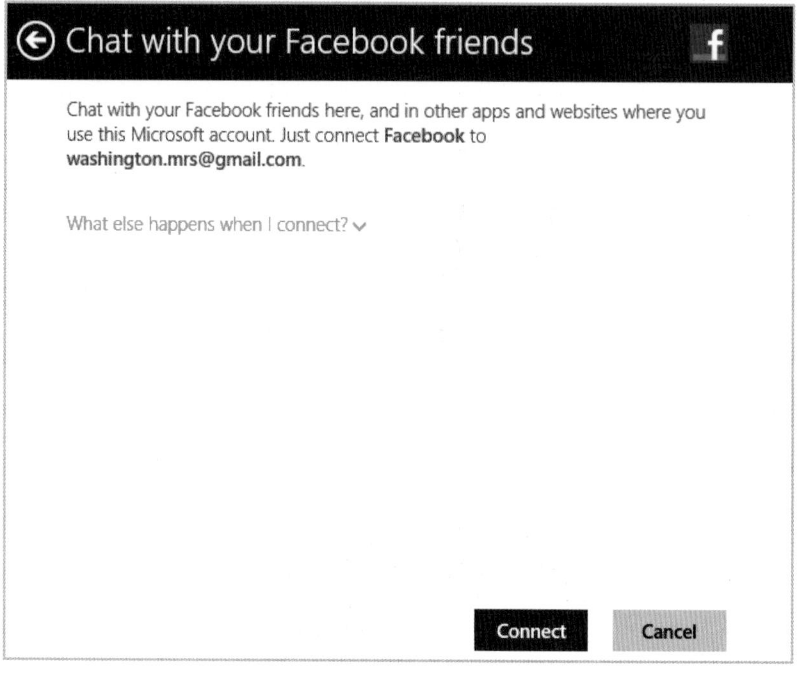

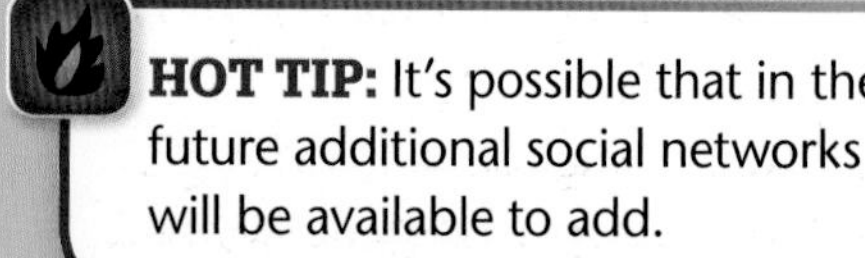

HOT TIP: It's possible that in the future additional social networks will be available to add.

Send a message

Once you have a few contacts, you can start a conversation with one of them. To start a new conversation (also called a 'thread') with someone, follow these steps.

1. With the Messaging app open, click the + sign to start a new message.

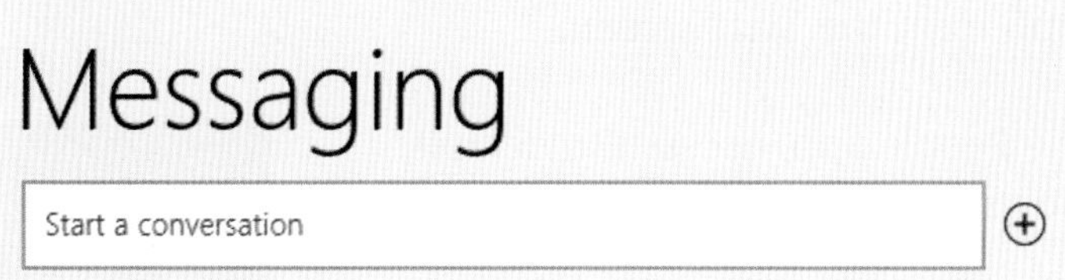

2. The People app will open. Choose the desired contact and click Choose.

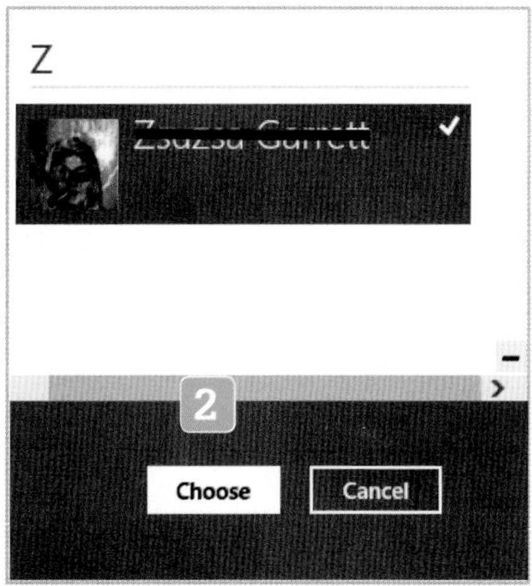

3. Type your message in the text message window and press Enter. Your message will appear at the top of the page.

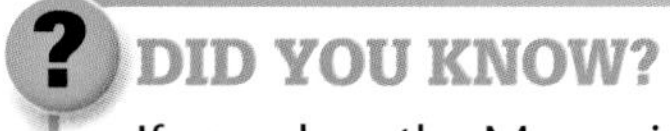

DID YOU KNOW?

If you close the Messaging app and reopen it later, it will be just as you left it.

HOT TIP: Add all your contacts to the People app, especially those you communicate with via social networks like Facebook, and it will be easier to communicate with them.

ALERT: An instant message is not the same thing as a text message. Instant messages are generally sent from computer to computer, or device to device, while simple texts are sent using mobile phones.

Add a social network to the People app

Like the Messaging app, you can add information about the social networks you belong to while inside the People app. When you do, you can see their status updates, access their contact information, send them email and messages, and more. To get started, open the People app from the Start screen.

1. While inside the People app, access the default charms (Windows + C or flick inwards).
2. Click the Settings charm and then click Accounts.
3. Click Add an account.
4. Choose the account from the resulting list.
5. Click Connect and input the required information.

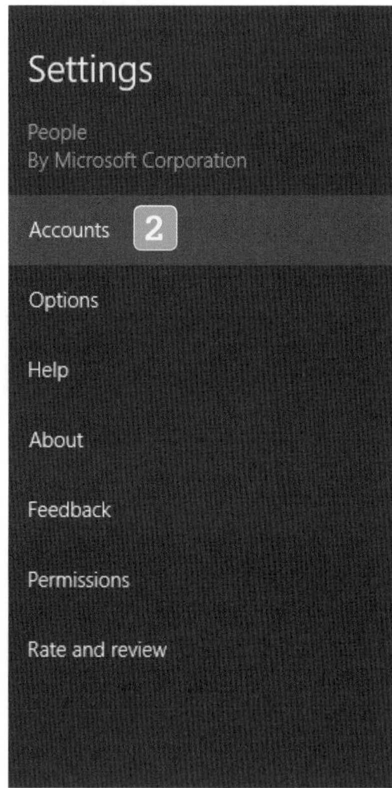

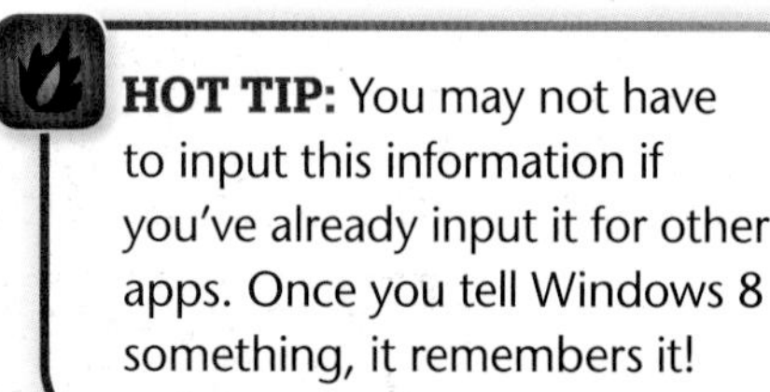

HOT TIP: You may not have to input this information if you've already input it for other apps. Once you tell Windows 8 something, it remembers it!

? DID YOU KNOW?

If you position your mouse in the bottom right corner of the People app and click the – sign that appears, the screen will change from the large tiles you currently see for your contacts to small, alphabetic tiles you can use to go directly to groups of contacts. Click any tile to return to the default view.

Edit a contact

The information you have for a contact may need to be updated manually if a person changes their phone number or email account, moves to a new address or gets a new job, among other things.

1. Locate the contact to edit in the People app.
2. Click the name of the contact so that it appears in its own screen (possibly with a social networking update to the right of it).

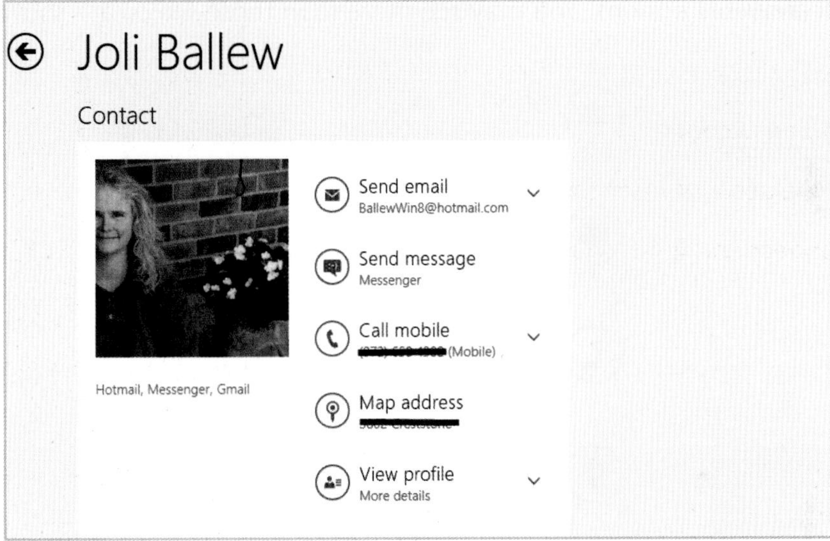

3. Right-click or flick upwards and click Edit.
4. Replace or add data as you wish and click Save.

DID YOU KNOW?

Changes made by a contact may automatically populate in the People app if the contact makes those changes from a compatible social network you also belong to (and have added to the People app).

Communicate with a contact

There are so many ways to communicate with a contact it would be difficult to try to describe them all. You can send an instant message or an email, call them on the phone, visit them in person and so on. The People app puts all compatible options in one place.

1. Open the People app.
2. Locate the contact and click the contact name once.
3. Note the available options. You may see more than those which are shown here.

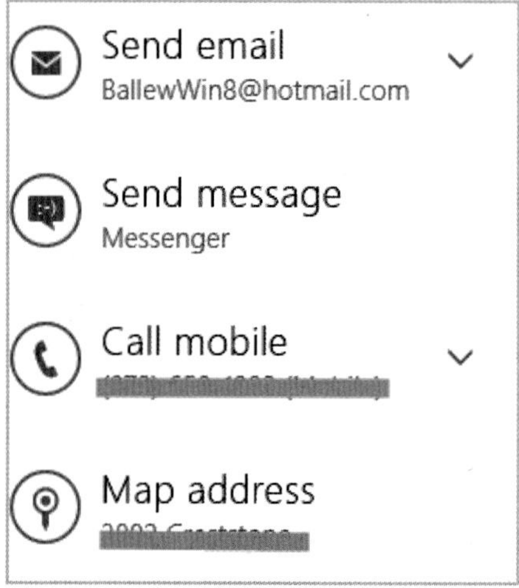

4. Click the contact option to use and continue as necessary.

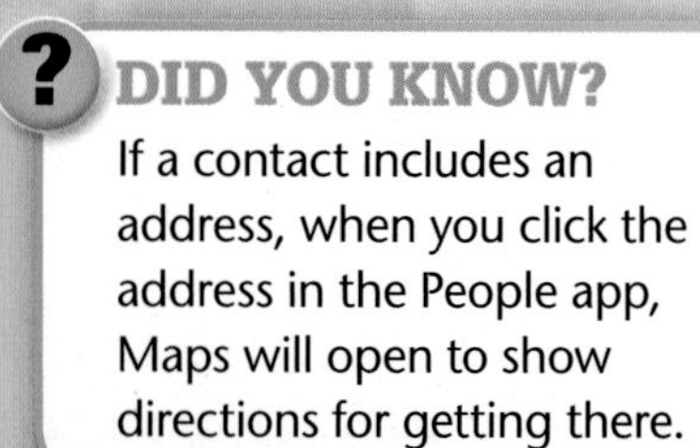

DID YOU KNOW?
If a contact includes an address, when you click the address in the People app, Maps will open to show directions for getting there.

HOT TIP: If you want to 'call' someone from the People app using your laptop or tablet, you'll have to get the Skype app.

Update your status

You can update your Facebook status and compose a tweet (using Twitter, another social networking technology) from inside the People app.

1. Open the People app and click Me. You may have to click a Back arrow or scroll left.
2. Click the arrow available under the What's new section (if applicable).

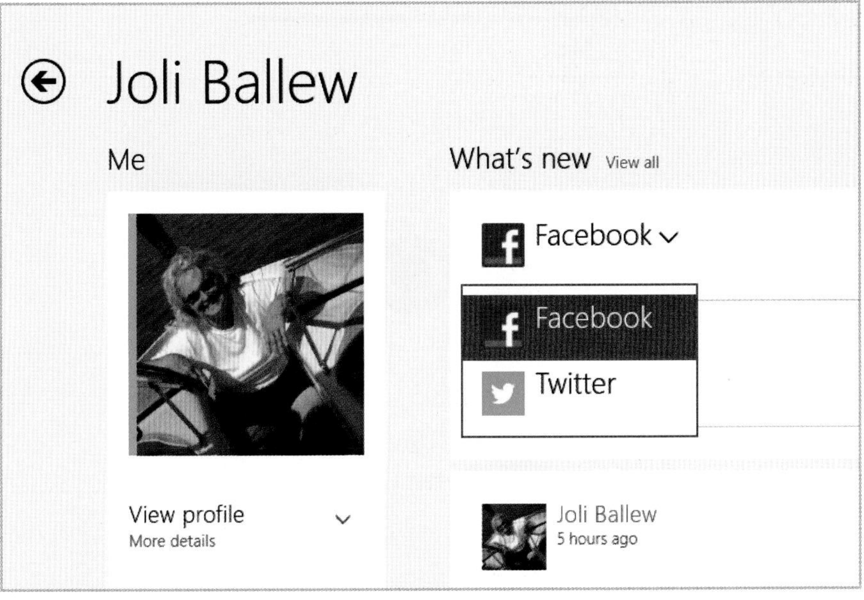

3. Select Facebook, Twitter or another available option.
4. Type your update or tweet as applicable.

HOT TIP: You can 'like' and comment on Facebook posts, and retweet and reply to Twitter entries, from inside the People app.

View others' updates

You view others' updates, posts and tweets from the What's new option (available under the Me option you just explored). You can click any option available under an entry to reply, like or respond to it, as applicable. If you have signed in with multiple social networks, you can filter what you see from the toolbar.

1 Open the People app and click the What's new tab.

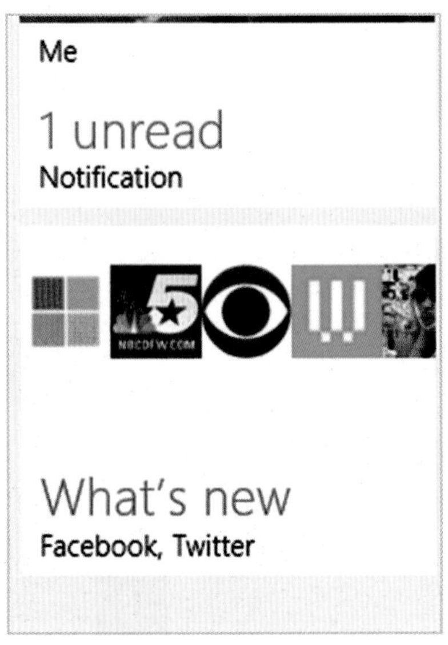

2 Use your finger to flick left and right, or use the scroll wheel on your mouse to move through the posts. (There's a scroll bar at the bottom of the screen as well.)

3 Notice the options under each post or tweet. Click to respond as you wish.

4 Right-click or flick upwards and click Filter.

5 Choose which social network(s) you'd like to view.

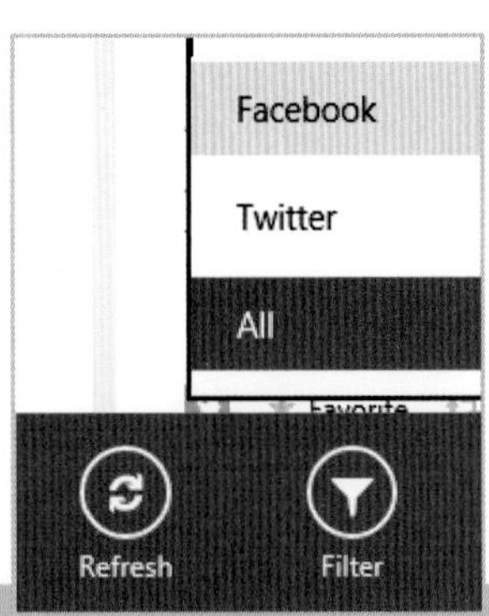

DID YOU KNOW?

The Refresh button, available next to Filter on the People toolbar, will refresh the information shown under What's new.

HOT TIP: To filter your contacts list by certain social networks, from the Settings charm, click Options and review the settings.

Get Skype

Skype is an app that lets you hold video conversations with others who also use Skype. You'll need to get Skype if you don't already have it and then contact those who also use Skype to become a contact.

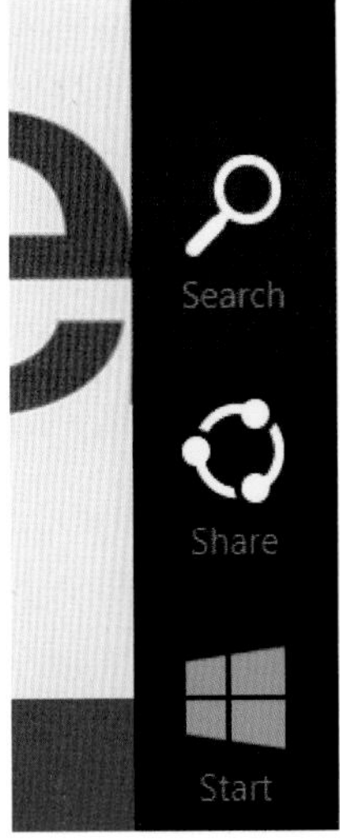

1. From the Start screen, type and then click Store.
2. Use the Windows key + C to access the charms and click Search.
3. Type Skype in the search box. Click Skype (shown second in the list here).

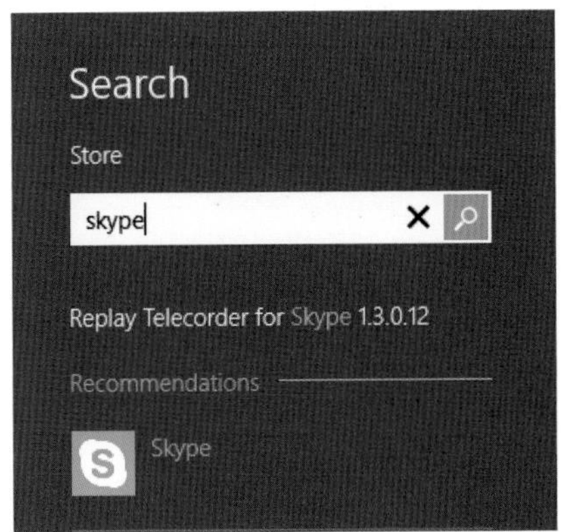

4. Click Install.
5. Click Install and type your Microsoft account and password if prompted.
6. From the Start screen, click Skype to open it.

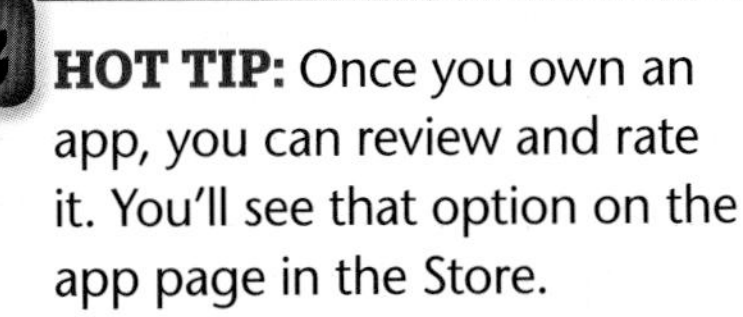

HOT TIP: Once you own an app, you can review and rate it. You'll see that option on the app page in the Store.

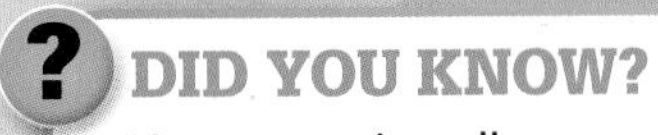

DID YOU KNOW?
You can uninstall any app you don't like from the Start screen's toolbar.

Use Skype to video chat

You will need to have at least one contact who also uses Skype if you want to try it out. You can right-click the Skype interface and click Add contact if you want to try to add contacts from your People app. Or you can tell others your Skype name and ask them to add you. Whatever the case, once you have a Skype friend, you can call them.

1. Open Skype from the Start screen.
2. Click any contact you'd like to Skype with.
3. Note the options available:
   a. Video chat.
   b. Phone call.
   c. Add others to the conversation.
   d. Instant message.

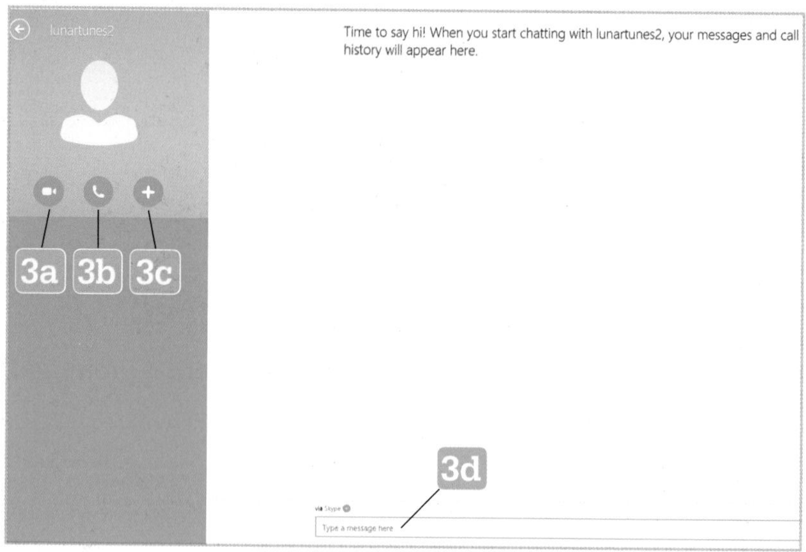

4. Click any option and follow any prompts to get started.

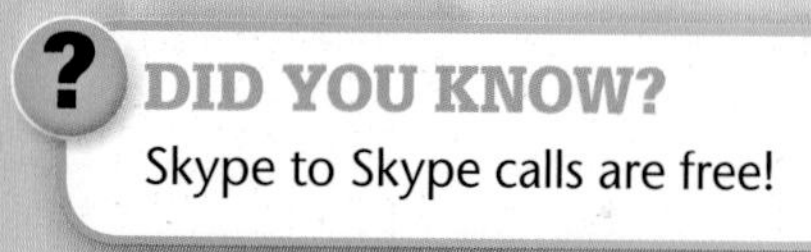

DID YOU KNOW?
Skype to Skype calls are free!

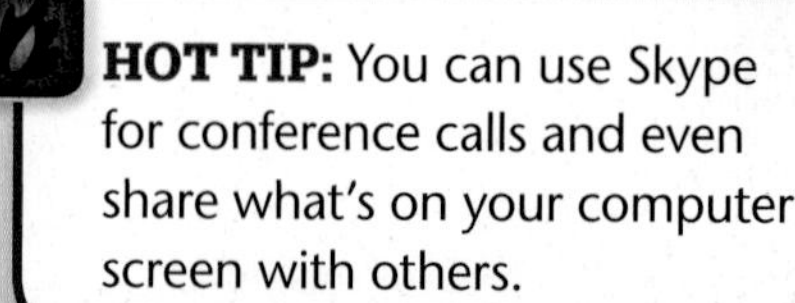

HOT TIP: You can use Skype for conference calls and even share what's on your computer screen with others.

13 Access and use online stores

Introduction

Microsoft offers various 'stores' where you can purchase media. You can rent a movie, for instance, or buy the latest album by your favourite artist. You can purchase a game, such as Cut the Rope or Angry Birds. You can get free stuff, too – there are free apps that help you count calories, communicate with friends, video chat and more.

Although these stores and the items in them are useful for all Windows 8 users, they are especially suitable for those with laptops and tablets. One of the best things about having a mobile device is that you can take your media with you. You can watch the movies you acquire on the plane, play games while waiting for a bus, join meetings from a hotel room, make video calls to your kids at university, listen to audiobooks, and much, much more from wherever you are.

There are a few things to keep in mind before you start, though. You'll need a Microsoft account to access any store, so if you don't have one, refer to Chapter 2: Learn Windows 8 Essentials to find out how to get one. You'll need to input credit information the first time you make a purchase from any store. Finally, you'll need an Internet connection, preferably Wi-Fi.

Explore the default Store

There is a Store tile on the Start screen. This tile takes you to the default Store, where you can get free apps or buy others.

1. From the Start screen, click or tap Store. Log in with a Microsoft account if prompted.

2. Scroll through the categories and titles.
3. Click or tap a category title that interests you, such as Games, Entertainment, or News & Weather.

4 Note the options to filter what is shown. Filter and browse as you wish. (Note the Back arrow.)

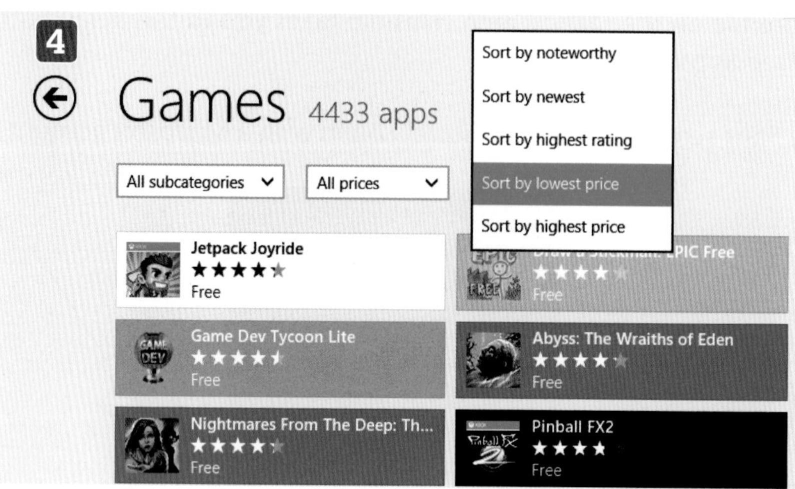

DID YOU KNOW?
If you click or tap an app tile, its details page appears. From there you can buy or install an app, read reviews, get a description and more.

HOT TIP: The Spotlight category offers access to Top paid, Top free and New releases.

DID YOU KNOW?
A number on the Store tile means some of your apps have updates available.

Get a free app

There are thousands of free apps. Here you'll learn how to get one.

1 From the Start screen, click or tap Store.

2 Under Spotlight, click Top free.

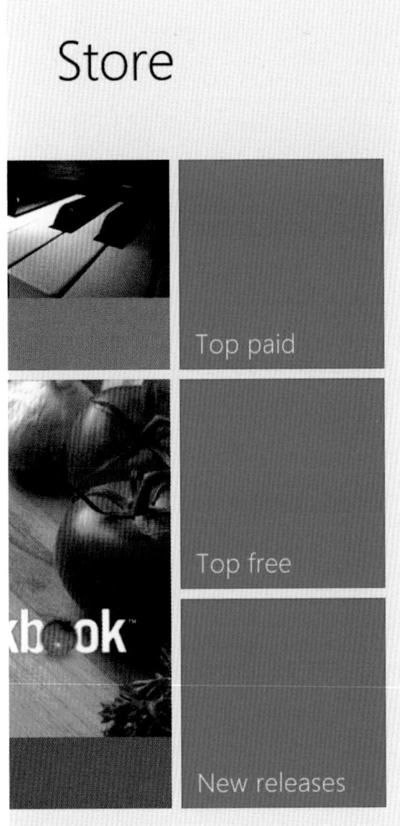

3 Click any app that interests you. These are all very popular.

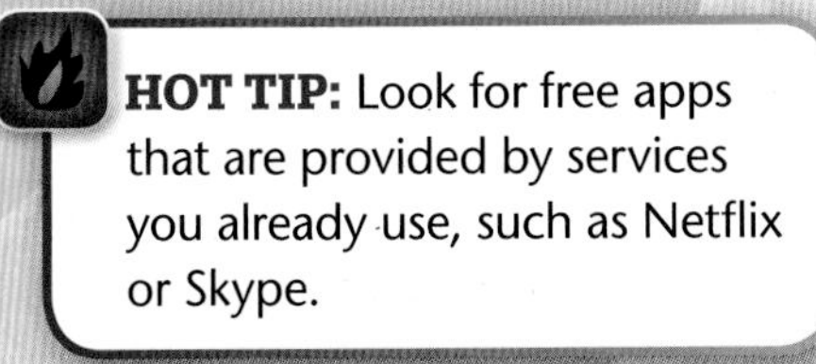

HOT TIP: Look for free apps that are provided by services you already use, such as Netflix or Skype.

4 Click Install.

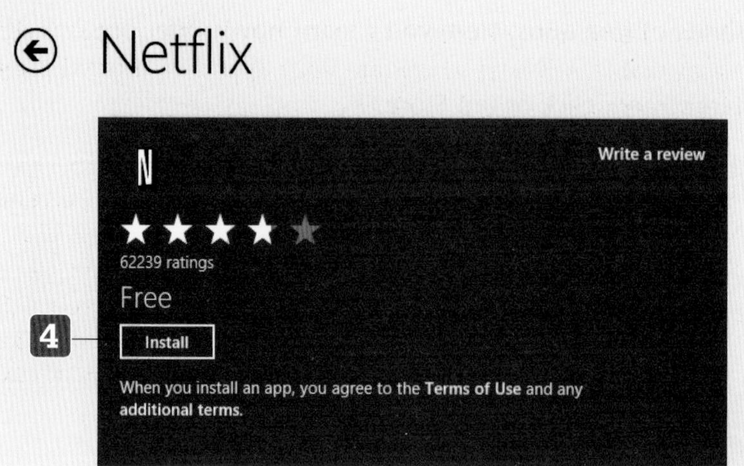

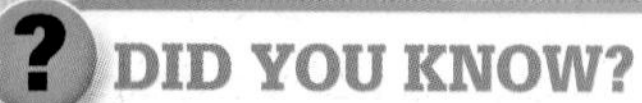

DID YOU KNOW?
You can read reviews and learn more about any app from its details page.

HOT TIP: It's okay to try any free app – you can easily uninstall it if you don't like it.

Get app updates

The Store tile is a live tile. When you see a number on the tile it means updates for apps you own are available. It's best to update your apps when notified because updates often fix problems with the app or add features.

1. From the Start screen, look at the Store tile.
2. If the Store tile has a number on it, click the tile.

HOT TIP: It's best to install updates for apps you use, make a note of the apps you see in the list that you don't use, and then uninstall those apps.

3. In the top right corner of the Store interface, click Updates.
4. Right-click to deselect any app update.
5. Click Install (not shown).

Updates (15)

DID YOU KNOW?
You can continue to work or browse while the updates are installing.

ALERT: The Music & Video category of the default Store doesn't offer albums, movies and the like. It offers apps that have to do with music and video, such as YouTube Player, iHeart Radio, Play Guitar! and so on. If you want to buy music and videos, you'll have to access the related Xbox store, detailed next.

Explore the Xbox Music Store

The Xbox Music Store offers a place to purchase music. You access it from the Music app.

1. From the Start screen, click or tap Music.
2. In the top right corner of the interface, if applicable, click Sign In. Input your Microsoft account credentials.

3. Scroll right and click All music.

4. Choose a category on the left and select a song on the right.

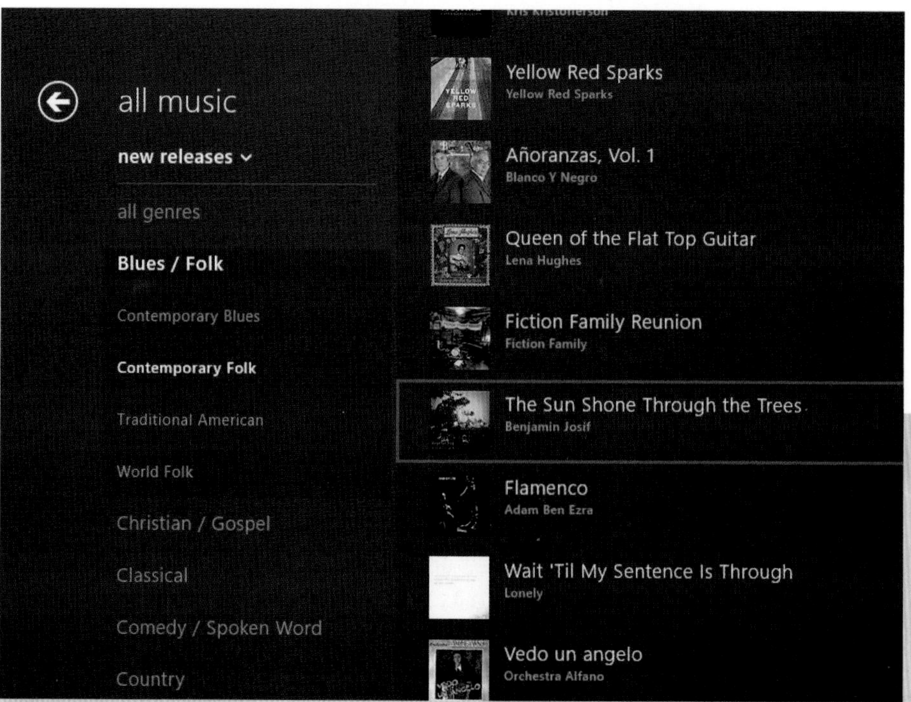

5 Note the options, including the option to buy the music.

6 Right-click while a song plays to view the controls.

HOT TIP: If you decide to make a purchase, follow the prompts provided to complete the transaction.

Explore the Xbox Video Store

The Xbox Video Store offers a place to purchase video media. You access it from the Video app.

1. From the Start screen, click or tap Video.
2. In the top right corner of the interface, if applicable, click Sign In. Input your Microsoft account credentials.
3. Scroll right to view the movies store and the television store.

4. Click either option and browse the titles. Click any title to learn more.

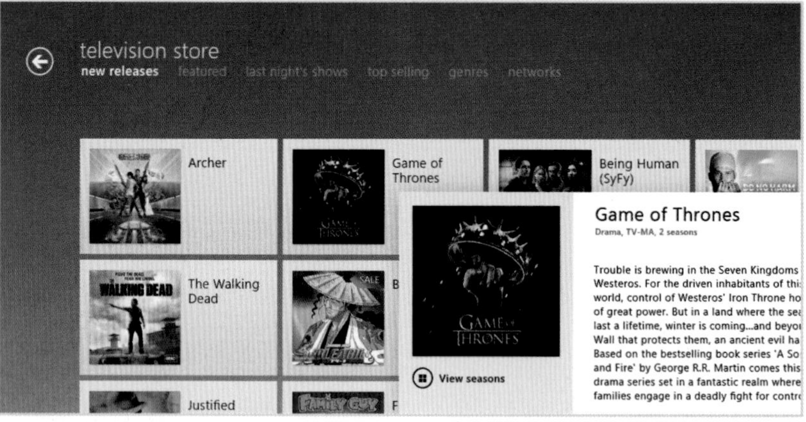

5. If you want to make a purchase, you may have to select a season to view the purchasing options. If you select a movie, you can buy or rent it as applicable.

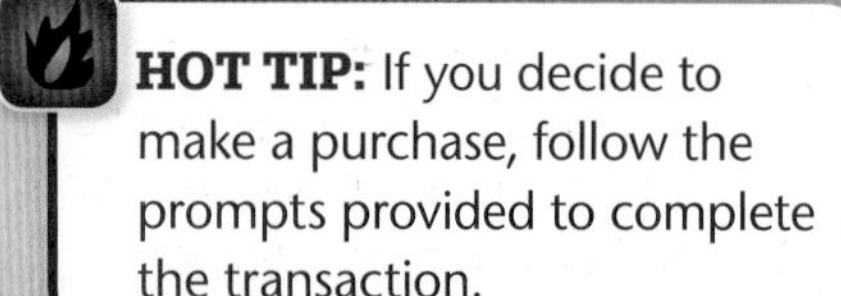

HOT TIP: If you decide to make a purchase, follow the prompts provided to complete the transaction.

Search across stores

Sometimes you may not know exactly what you want but you have an idea. When this happens you can search across multiple stores easily.

1. Use Windows + C to access the charms and click Search.
2. Type a keyword.
3. Click Store, then Music, then Video. Note the results for each. Video is shown here.

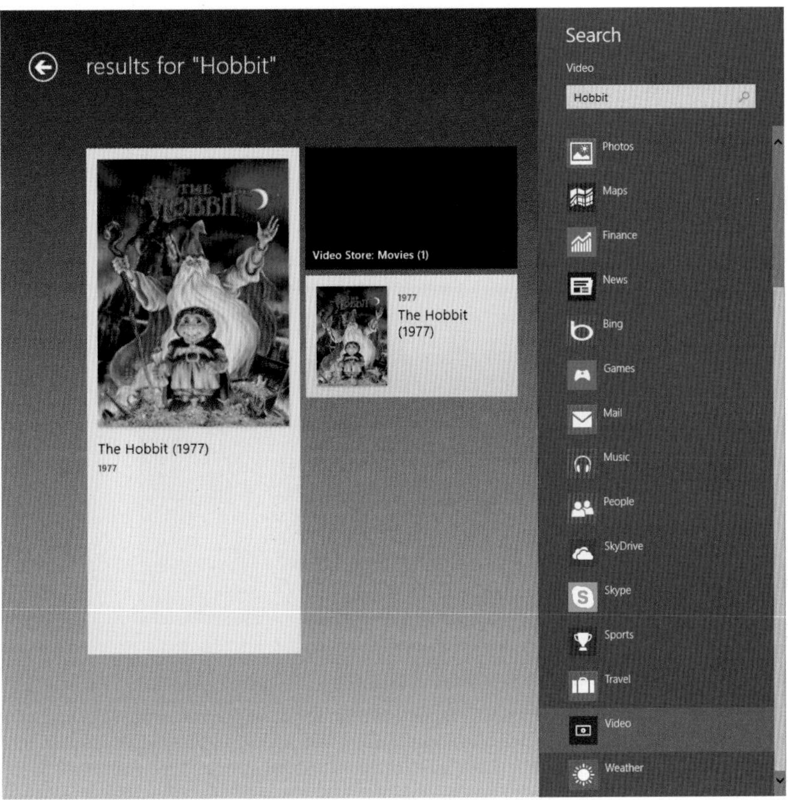

4. Click any result to see it in the applicable store.

DID YOU KNOW?
You can search across more than stores. You can type, say, Coffee in the Search window and then click Maps to find coffee places near you, News to learn more about coffee, Finance to see the current price for coffee, and so on.

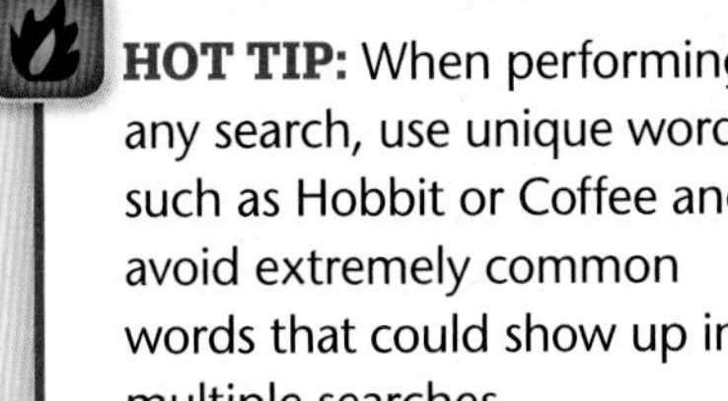

HOT TIP: When performing any search, use unique words such as Hobbit or Coffee and avoid extremely common words that could show up in multiple searches.

Remove or uninstall unwanted apps

After you've acquired a good number of apps from the Store, you'll need to uninstall the ones you've decided you don't like or won't use. You do this from the Start screen. If you want to keep the app but don't want it on the Start screen, you can remove it.

1. Locate the app on the Start screen. (If you don't see it there, right-click and click All apps.)
2. Right-click the app to uninstall.
3. Click Uninstall.
4. If you like the app and want to keep it but want to remove it from the Start screen, click Unpin from Start instead of Uninstall.

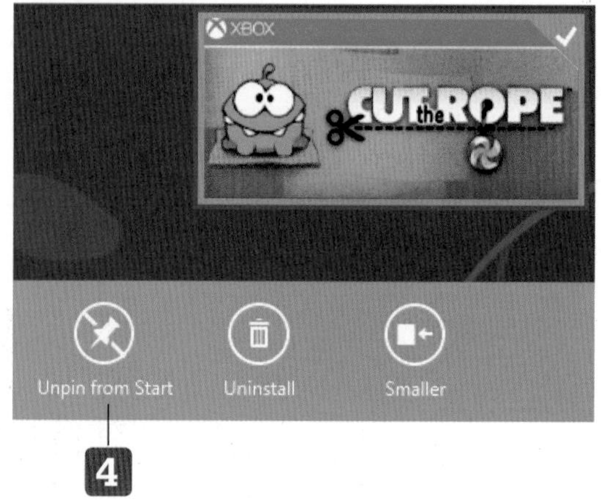

HOT TIP: If you use an app often and get tired of scrolling right to access it, leave it on the Start screen but move it (by dragging) to a better location.

ALERT: You can't pin apps like these to the Desktop's taskbar.

Delete unwanted media

You may acquire media you watch or listen to and either don't like or for whatever reason no longer want. Since media takes up quite a bit of hard drive space, you should delete anything you don't want to keep.

1. Use Windows + D to access the Desktop.
2. Click File Explorer.
3. Restore the window so that you can also see the Recycle Bin.

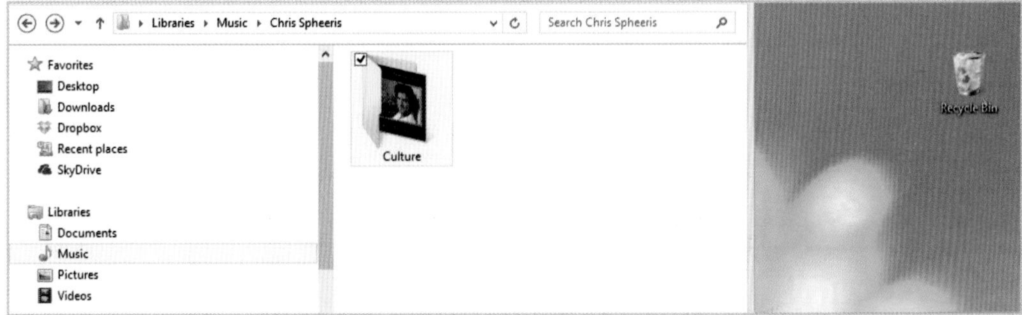

4. Locate the folder, song, movie or item to delete.
5. Drag the item to the Recycle Bin.

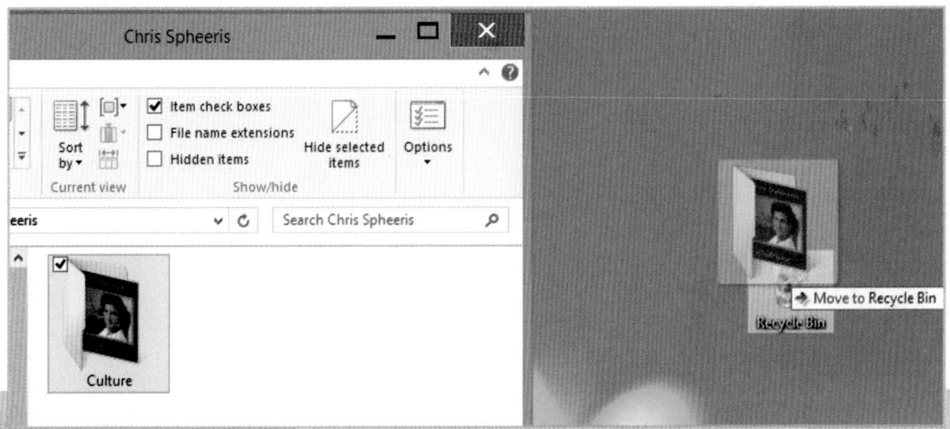

DID YOU KNOW?
If you accidently delete something you want to keep, you can restore it from the Recycle Bin (at least until you empty the Recycle Bin).

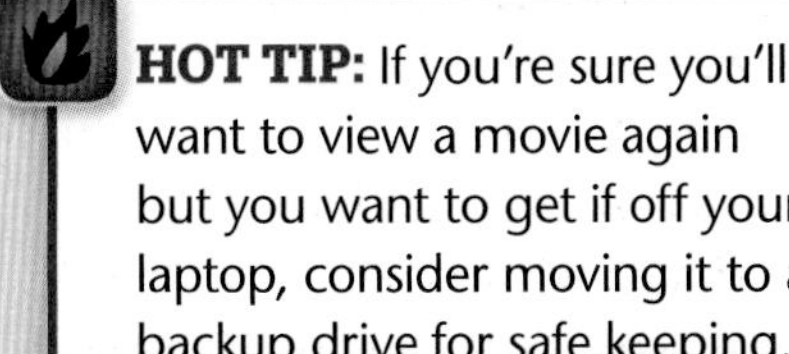

HOT TIP: If you're sure you'll want to view a movie again but you want to get if off your laptop, consider moving it to a backup drive for safe keeping.

14 Manage, protect, secure and restore your device

Introduction

Mobile devices like laptops and tablets require a certain amount of extra attention when it comes to protecting and securing them. They need a protective case and a physical lock, they should be configured with passwords, and they should be backed up regularly in case the device goes missing. In addition to this, mobile users (like yourself) should know how to choose a power plan to lengthen battery life and how to store data in the cloud so it can be accessed from other places, among other things. Of course, you need to know how to reset or restore your laptop or tablet if things go really wrong. This chapter contains all of this and more.

Configure a password-protected screensaver

Your computer will automatically lock after a specific amount of idle time (requiring you to input your password when you're ready to use the computer again), but you can configure a screen saver to engage after as little as one minute of inactivity. You can also configure your computer to display the logon screen when you are ready to access the computer again.

1. At the Start screen, type Change screen saver and click Settings. Click Change screen saver in the results.
2. Select a screen saver, choose how long to wait and tick On resume, display logon screen.
3. Click OK.

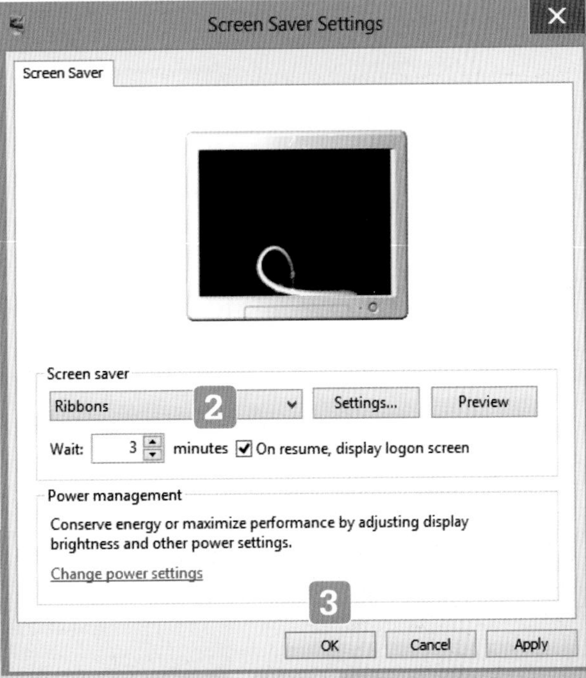

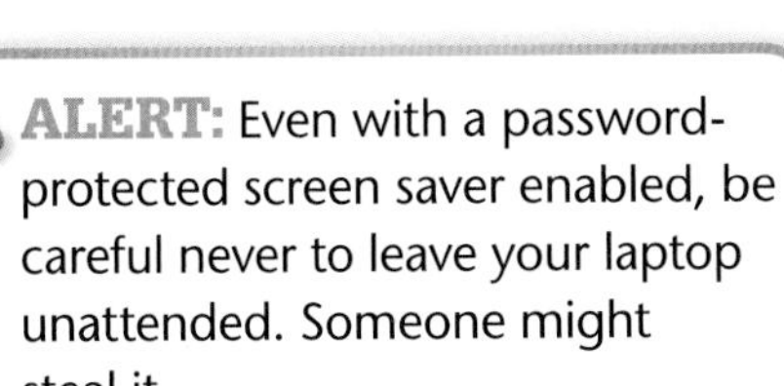

ALERT: Even with a password-protected screen saver enabled, be careful never to leave your laptop unattended. Someone might steal it.

ALERT: The Bubble screen saver is see-through – even when it's engaged you can still see what's on the screen. Select something else if you're looking for privacy.

Choose the proper power plan

All Windows 8 computers are set to use a specific power plan. This means that after a predetermined period of time, the display will dim and the hard drive will sleep. (There are two groups of settings: one for when the device is plugged in and one for when it is running on batteries.) In addition, some power plans restrict specific resources more than others to lengthen battery life. If you aren't happy with your computer's performance or you feel your battery is being drained too quickly, you can change this behaviour.

HOT TIP: One simple way to get longer battery life while maintaining a workable laptop is to choose the Power Saver plan, lower the brightness and keep the other default settings.

1. From the Start screen, type Power.
2. Click Settings, and click Power Options.
3. Next to the selected plan (or any other), click Change plan settings.

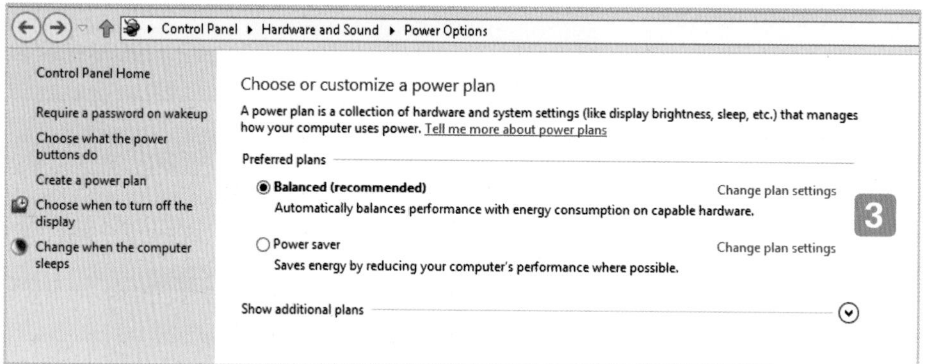

4. Use the drop-down lists to make changes you wish to make.
5. Click Save changes.

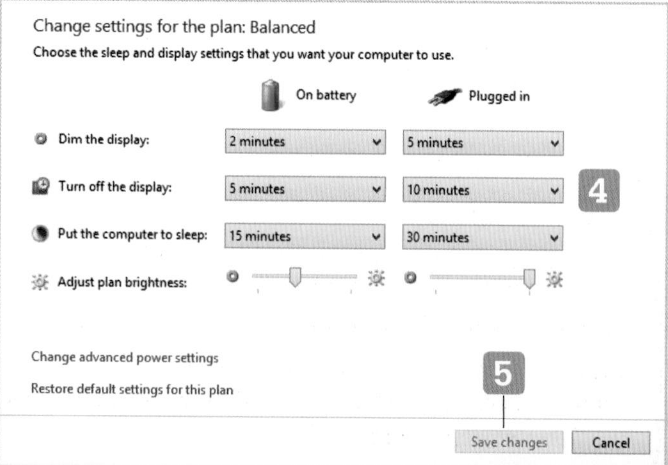

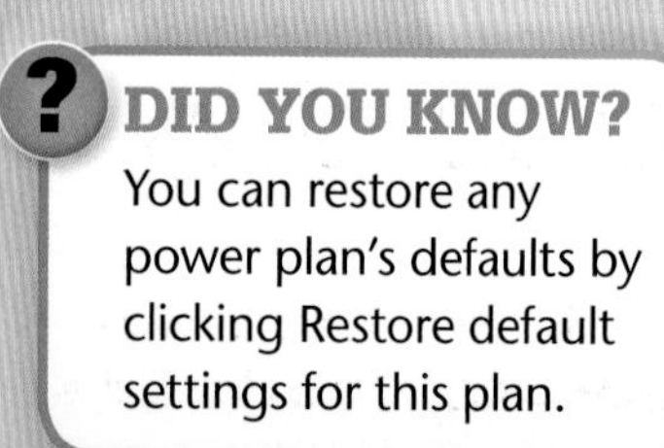

DID YOU KNOW?

You can restore any power plan's defaults by clicking Restore default settings for this plan.

Store data in SkyDrive

When you set up a Microsoft account you are given some free space on Microsoft's Internet servers to store some of your files, pictures and other data. This space is called SkyDrive. If you save your data to SkyDrive when you work from your laptop or tablet, when you get back home or to the office you can use that copy of the file to work with (and then resave it to SkyDrive when you have finished there). When you do this, you always have access to the most up-to-date version of the file, no matter where you are or how you work.

1. From the Start screen, click SkyDrive. If applicable, type your Microsoft account and password.
2. If you've used SkyDrive before, it will already be personalised, as shown here. (If not, you'll see only the default folders.)

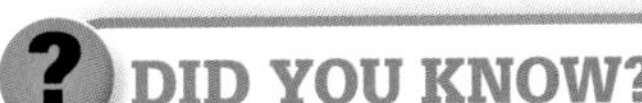

DID YOU KNOW?

You can access data you've saved to SkyDrive from any Internet-enabled computer. It does not have to be a Windows 8 computer.

3. Click any category to see what's inside. If subfolders exist, explore those, too.

DID YOU KNOW?

It's easy to save files to SkyDrive from Microsoft Office 2013 applications on tablets: it is the default!

HOT TIP: When you save a file in any program, in the Save as dialogue box, look for SkyDrive in the left pane, under Favorites.

WHAT DOES THIS MEAN?

SkyDrive: means you have access to a *drive* (like a hard drive) in the *sky* (which is actually the Internet). Because the Internet is often represented in technical documentation as a cloud, the word sky really fits here.

Enable Airplane mode

During aircraft takeoff and landing, you are prompted to turn off all electronic devices. However, once you have the go-ahead that it's okay to use 'approved electronic devices' you can turn on your laptop or tablet and use it, provided you enable Airplane mode.

1. Click Windows key + I.
2. Click the Network icon.
3. Move the slider for Airplane mode from Off to On.

HOT TIP: Another way to enable Airplane mode is to type Airplane at the Start screen, click Settings and then click Turn airplane mode on or off.

WHAT DOES THIS MEAN?

Airplane mode: shuts down all network communications as well as mobile connections, theoretically so that your transmissions won't interfere with the plane's transmissions.

Use ReadyBoost

ReadyBoost is a technology that enables you to use a USB flash drive or a secure digital memory card as cache (a place where data is stored temporarily and accessed when needed) to increase computer performance. Cache works like RAM, and more is certainly better!

1. Insert a USB flash drive, thumb drive or memory card into an available slot on the outside of your laptop or tablet.
2. When prompted in the upper right corner, click to view your options.
3. Choose Speed up my system, Windows ReadyBoost.

HOT TIP: Only newer and larger USB keys will work for ReadyBoost.

4. Choose to dedicate the device to ReadyBoost and click OK (not shown).

ALERT: USB keys must be at least USB 2.0 and meet other requirements, but don't worry about that, you'll be told if the hardware isn't up to par.

HOT TIP: ReadyBoost offers a quick way to enhance performance on laptops and tablets when opening the device and physically adding more RAM is impossible.

WHAT DOES THIS MEAN?

RAM: random access memory is where information is stored temporarily so the operating system has quick access to it. The more RAM you have, the better your computer should perform.

Cache: a temporary storage area similar to RAM.

Enable File History

File History saves copies of your files regularly so you can get them back if they're lost or damaged. While most of the security features in Windows 8 are enabled by default (such as the Firewall and Windows Defender), File History is not: you must manually enable it. You'll need a large-capacity external drive for File History for it to be effective, so it's best to run backups when you have your laptop at home or at work.

1. Connect an external drive or make sure a network drive is available.
2. From the Start screen, type File History.
3. Click Settings, then click File History.
4. In the File History window, click Turn on.
5. Wait while File History copies your files for the first time. You can always return here and click Run now, if you want to.

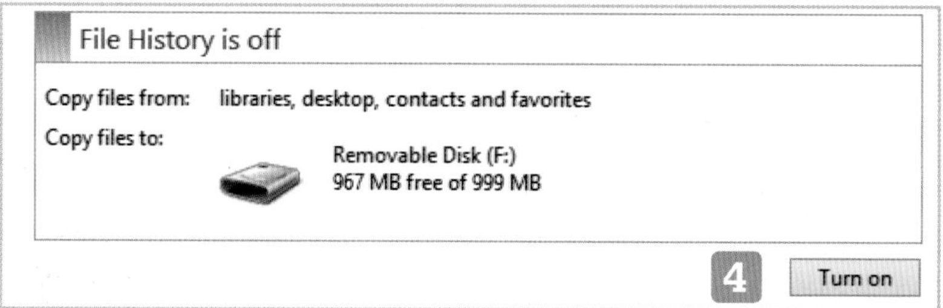

HOT TIP: Click Advanced Settings to change how often File History makes copies of files once the initial backup is created. Every hour is the default.

ALERT: If you ever need to restore files using File History, open the File History window and click Restore personal files.

Consider a physical lock

Almost all newer laptops come with a slot on the outside for connecting a physical lock. The most popular of these is called a Kensington slot, which uses a Kensington lock.

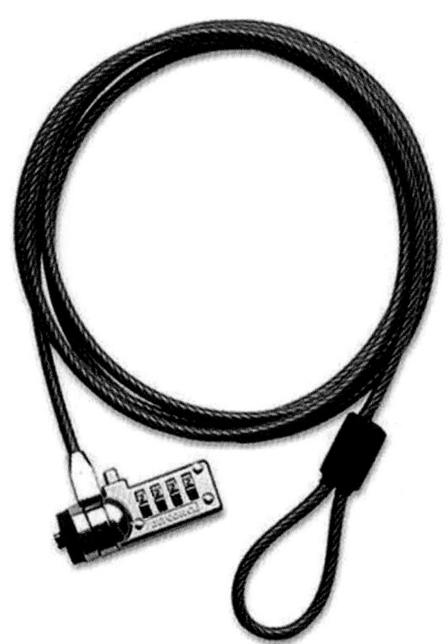

Use this lock when you leave your laptop:

- unattended while giving a presentation
- in a hotel room
- in your office at work
- in your office at home.

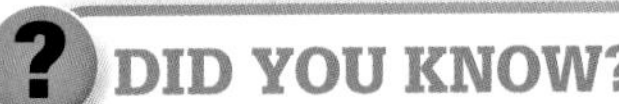

DID YOU KNOW?
A lock slot on the outside of your laptop is a small rectangular slot.

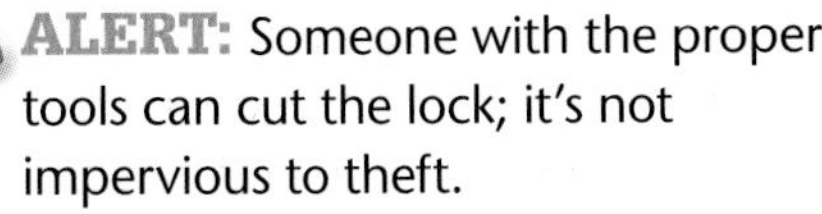

ALERT: Someone with the proper tools can cut the lock; it's not impervious to theft.

DID YOU KNOW?
You may also find lock slots on gaming consoles, video projectors and computer monitors, among other things.

Install hardware

Although you probably won't carry around a printer when you travel with your laptop, you may want to access a printer while at home or work. Printers are hardware and must be installed. Likewise, you must install other hardware such as digital cameras, USB drives, external monitors, external hard drives, card readers and so on.

1. Connect the device to a wall outlet if applicable.
2. Connect the device to your laptop using the cable.
3. Insert the CD for the device if you have it.
4. Wait while the hardware installs.
5. If applicable, work through any set-up processes.
6. From the Start screen, type Devices, then Settings. Click Devices in the results.

7. Verify that the device was installed.

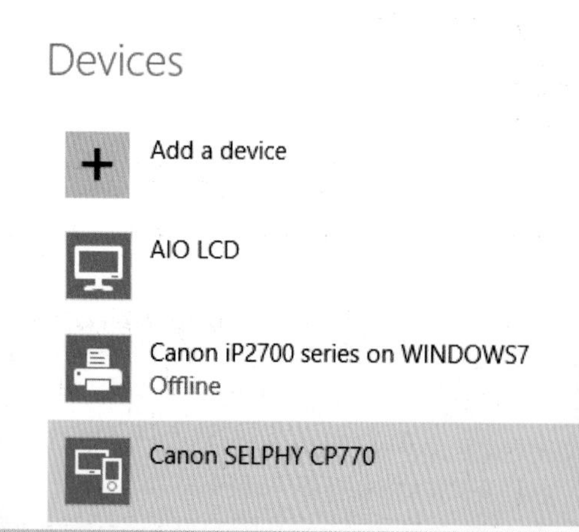

HOT TIP: If you have a small screen on your laptop, when at your desk, connect to a larger external monitor.

SEE ALSO: Install software, next.

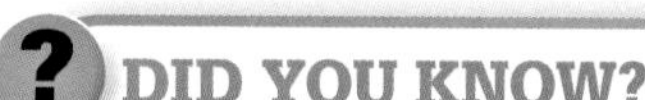

DID YOU KNOW? Most of the time all you have to do is connect the new hardware and wait for it to be installed automatically.

ALERT: Read the directions that come with each new device you acquire. If there are specific instructions for installation, follow those directions, not the generic directions offered here.

Install software

As with installing hardware, software installation almost always goes smoothly. Just make sure you get your software from a reliable source, such as Amazon, Microsoft's website, Apple's website (think iTunes, not software for Macs only) or a retail store.

1. Download the installation file from the Internet and skip to Step 4,or insert the CD or DVD in the appropriate drive and proceed to Step 2.
2. Click the prompt that appears in the top right corner to see your options.

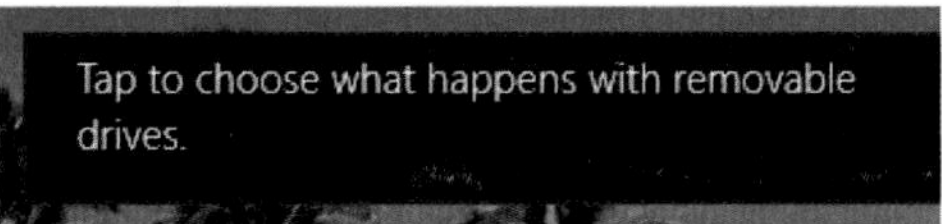

ALERT: If you have a tablet that runs Windows 8 RT, you'll have to get any software you want from the app Store, available on the Start screen.

3. If you are not prompted or you miss the prompt:
   a. Open the Computer window. (You can type Computer at the Start screen.)
   b. Double-click the CD or DVD drive.
4. Double-click the application file or do whatever else is necessary to start the installation.
5. Work through the installation wizard.

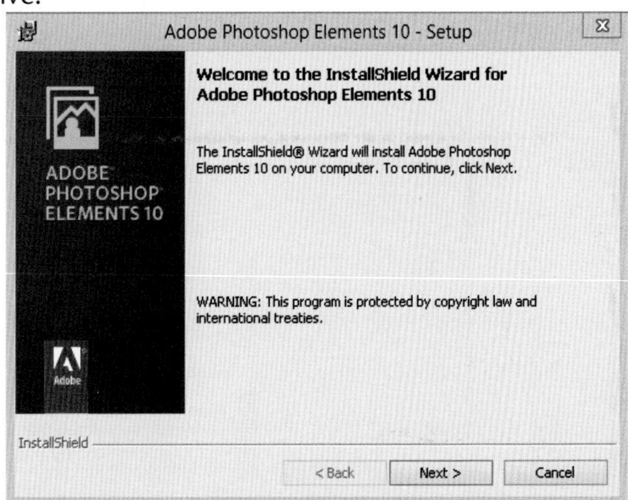

Adobe screenshot reprinted with permission from Adobe Systems Incorporated.

HOT TIP: If you download software from the Internet, copy the installation files to a CD or DVD for safe keeping and write the product ID or key on it.

ALERT: To install software you must locate the application file or the executable file. Often this is named Setup, Install or something similar. If you receive a message that the file can't be opened, you've chosen the wrong file.

Use the Action Center

Windows 8 tries hard to take care of your device and your data. You'll be informed if you don't have the proper security settings configured or if Windows Update or the Firewall is disabled. You can resolve these issues in the Action Center, a Desktop application.

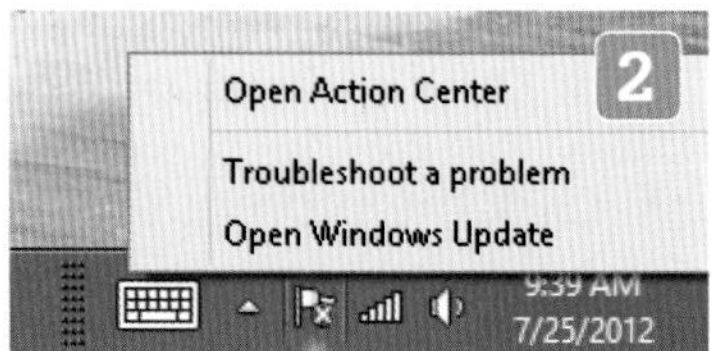

1. From the Desktop, on the taskbar, locate the Action Center flag.
2. Right-click the flag icon and then click Open Action Center.
3. If there's anything in red, click the down arrow (if necessary) to see the problem and resolve it.
4. Click the button that offers the suggestion to the problem to view the option and resolve it.
5. If there's anything in yellow, click the down arrow to see the problem and solution.
6. Close the Action Center when all problems have been resolved.

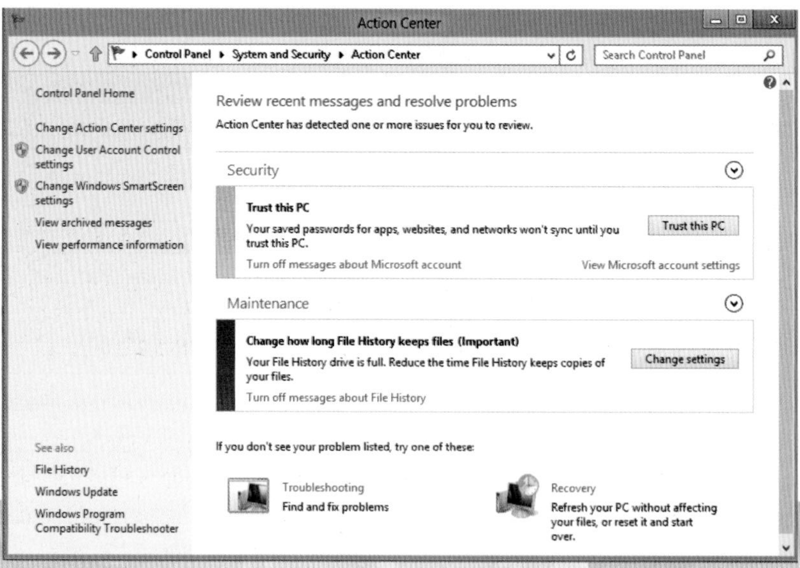

ALERT: When you see alerts, pay attention! You'll want to resolve them.

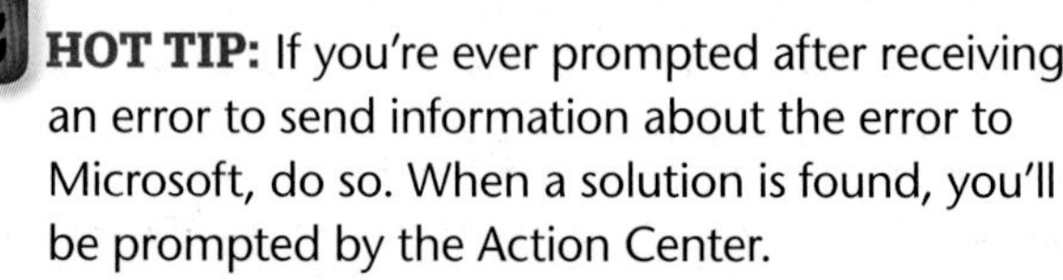

HOT TIP: If you're ever prompted after receiving an error to send information about the error to Microsoft, do so. When a solution is found, you'll be prompted by the Action Center.

Scan for malware with Windows Defender

You don't have to do much with Windows Defender except understand that it offers protection against some of the more common Internet threats. It's enabled by default and it runs in the background. However, if you ever think your computer has been attacked by an Internet threat (adware, worm, malware, etc.) you can run a manual scan here. Windows Defender may be able to get rid of it.

1. Open Windows Defender. (You can search for it from the Start screen.)
2. Verify that Windows Defender is enabled and note the option to run a scan if desired.
3. Click the X in the top right corner to close the Windows Defender window.

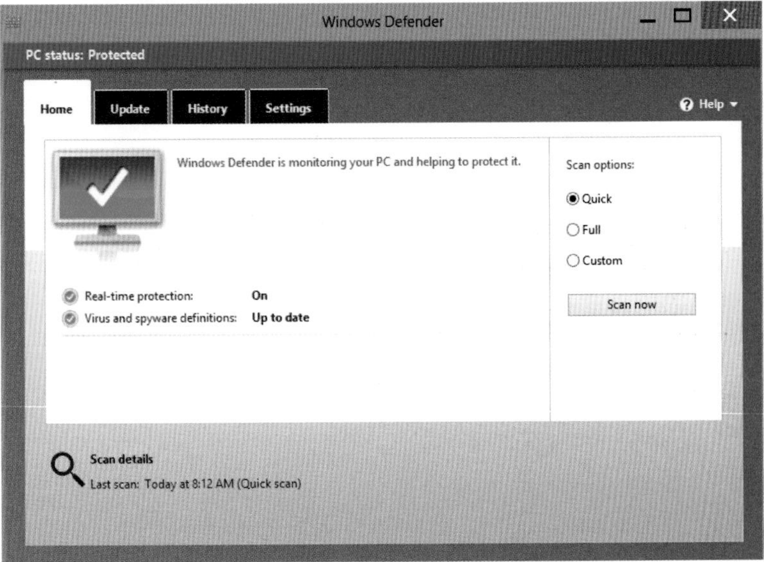

HOT TIP: Click each tab available from Windows Defender to explore all the options.

ALERT: Windows Defender and Windows Firewall will probably be disabled if you've purchased and installed a third-party anti-virus, anti-malware tool. Do not enable it if this is the case.

WHAT DOES THIS MEAN?

Malware: stands for malicious software. Malware includes adware, worms, spyware, etc.

Enable the Firewall

Windows Firewall is a software program that checks the data that comes in from the Internet (or a local network) and then decides whether it's good data or bad. If it deems the data harmless, it will allow it to come through the Firewall; if not, it's blocked.

1. Open Windows Firewall. (Type Firewall at the Start screen and click Settings to find it.)
2. Verify that the firewall is on. If not, select Turn Windows Firewall on or off, enable it and click OK.
3. Review the other settings.

DID YOU KNOW?

The first time you use a program that is blocked by Windows Firewall by default, you'll be prompted to 'unblock' the program. This is a safety feature to protect rogue programs from gaining unwanted access to your computer.

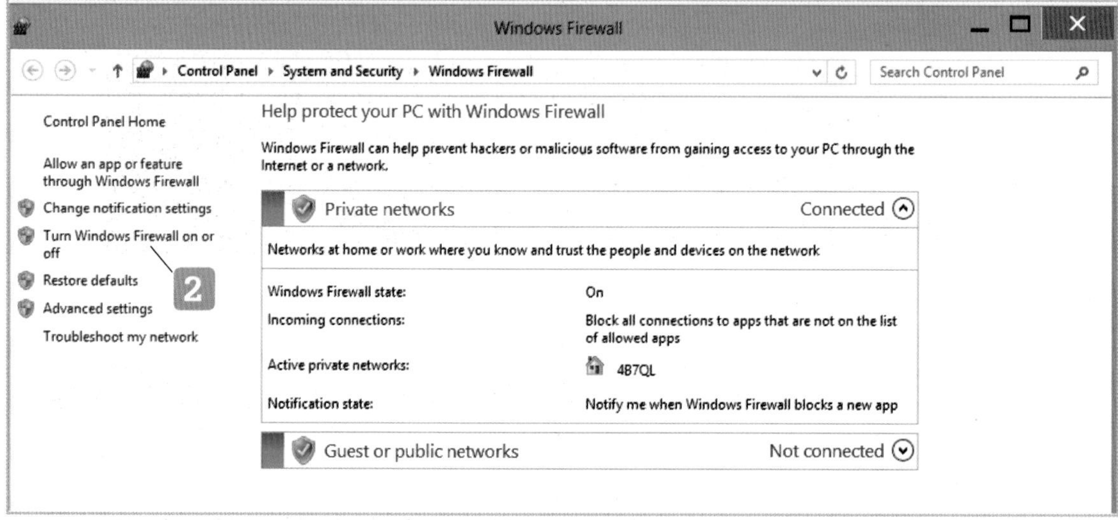

ALERT: You have to have a firewall (either Windows Firewall or a third-party firewall) to keep hackers from getting access to your computer and to help prevent it from sending out malicious code if it is ever attacked by a virus or worm.

Locate the Help wizards

If you encounter a problem you can't resolve on your own, you can use the available Help wizards to assist you in finding a solution. These wizards walk you through the required processes to find a solution.

1. At the Start screen, type Help.
2. Click Settings, then click Find and fix problems.

3. Use the options to find what you need help with.

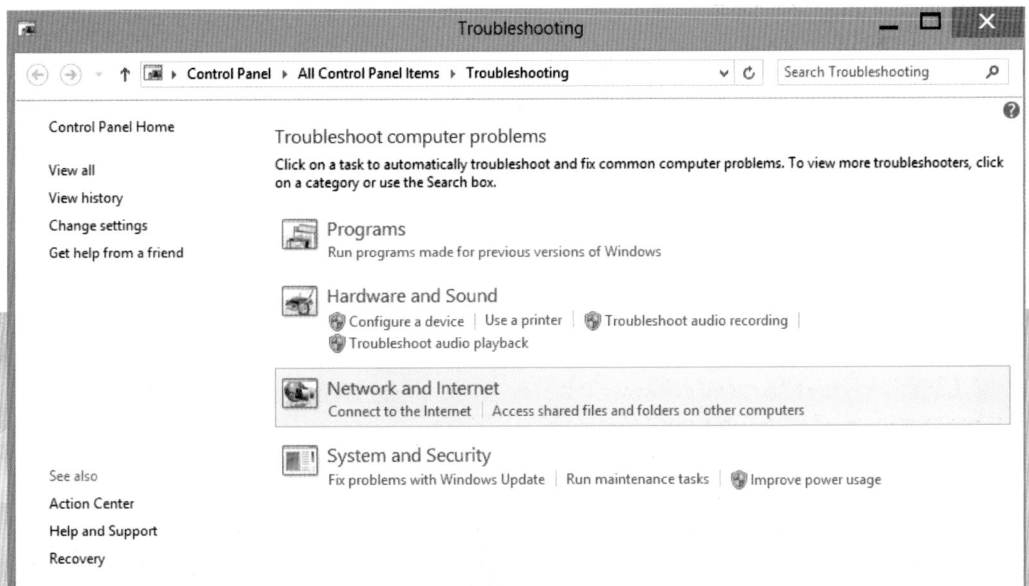

4 Work through the wizard.

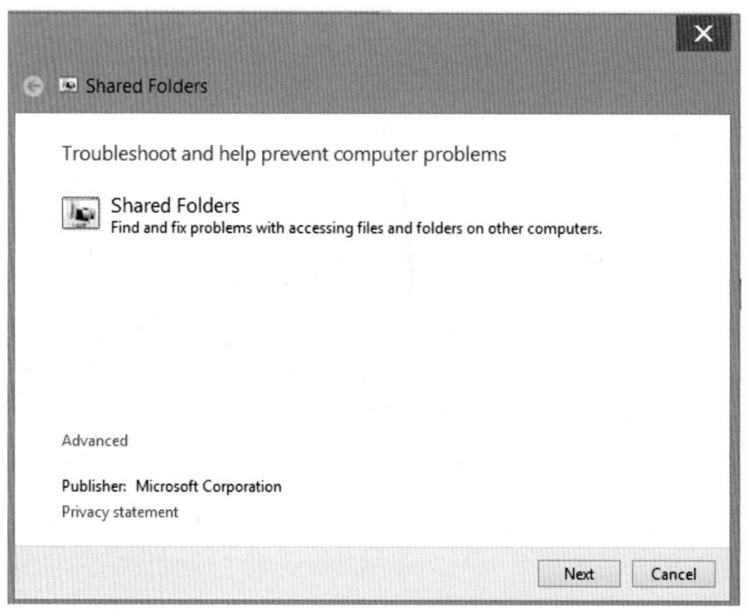

ALERT: Although most of these wizards can resolve simple problems, they can't resolve all of them. If a wizard can't find a solution, you may have to look online for the answer.

HOT TIP: Before you troubleshoot any hardware, turn off the device, turn it back on and disconnect and reconnect it to your laptop. If it's internal hardware, restart your computer.

Use System Restore

System Restore regularly creates and saves restore points that contain information about your laptop that Windows uses to work properly. If your laptop starts acting up, you can use System Restore to restore it to a time when the laptop was working properly. Before you start, connect your laptop to an electrical outlet.

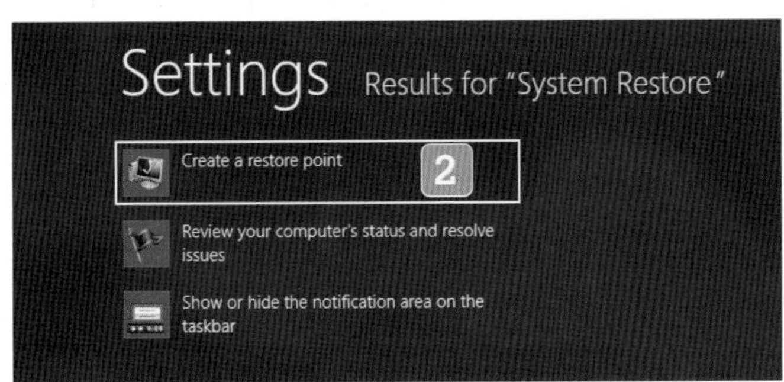

1. At the Start screen, type System Restore.
2. Click Settings, then click Create a restore point.
3. Click System Restore.
4. Click Next to accept and apply the recommended restore point.
5. Click Finish.
6. Wait patiently while the process completes.

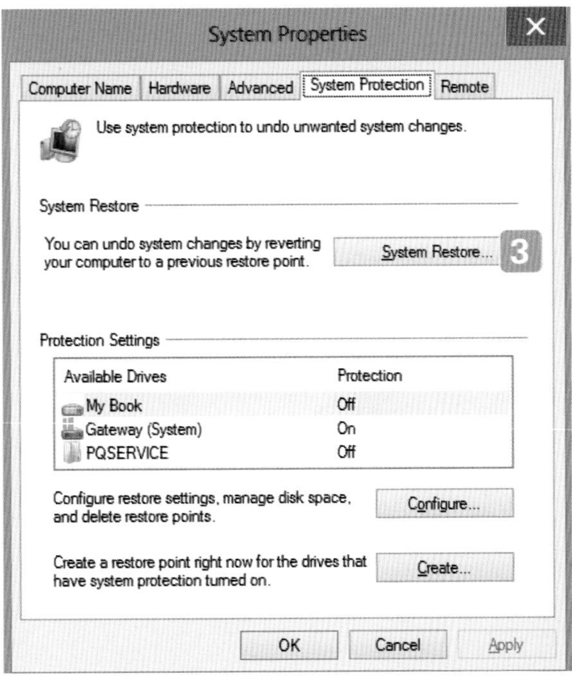

ALERT: If you're running System Restore on a laptop or tablet, make sure it's plugged in. System Restore should never be interrupted.

DID YOU KNOW?

System Restore works only with its own system files, so running System Restore will not affect any of your personal data. Your pictures, email, documents, music, etc. will not be deleted or changed.

WHAT DOES THIS MEAN?

Restore point: a snapshot of a computer's previous state that can be applied in place of the current state, to make an unstable computer stable again.

Refresh your laptop or tablet

If your device isn't running well and you've already tried the various troubleshooting options, including System Restore, you may need to refresh it. When you do, all third-party programs you've installed from disks or websites are removed and your computer settings are returned to their defaults. This resolves almost all problems most users will encounter. Apps from the Windows Store will remain, as will your photos, music, videos and other personal files, so you won't have to start from scratch once the restore is complete.

1. Access the Settings charm.
2. Click Change PC settings.
3. Click the General tab.
4. Scroll to locate Refresh your PC without affecting your files.
5. Click Get started.

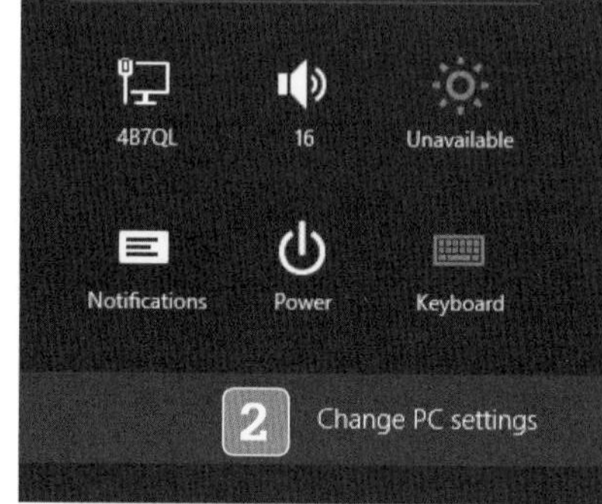

6. Read the information offered, click Next and work through the refresh process.

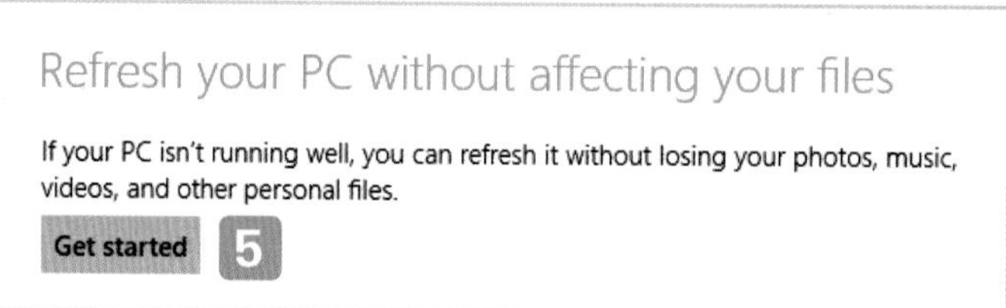

HOT TIP: Refresh your device only if other options have failed to fix the problem.

ALERT: Before you refresh your device, locate the product codes you'll need to reinstall third-party programs.

Reset your laptop or tablet

If refreshing your device doesn't resolve your existing problems, you'll have to reset it and start again. When you do, everything will be deleted, including all your apps, applications, settings and personal files. You'll need to back up these files before continuing here. This is a drastic step, so be sure this is what you want to do before you do it.

1. Access the Settings charm.
2. Click Change PC Settings.
3. Click the General tab.
4. Scroll to locate Remove everything and reinstall Windows.
5. Click Get started.

HOT TIP: Reset your laptop or tablet before you sell it or give it away.

Remove everything and reinstall Windows

If you want to recycle your PC or start over completely, you can reset it to its factory settings.

Get started 

ALERT: If you reset your device, when it starts again it will perform, act and look just like it did the day you brought it home.

HOT TIP: The option under Remove everything and reinstall Windows is Advanced Startup. Choose this option to boot from a USB or DVD, change Windows Start settings, restore from a system image, and more.

15 Tips for tablet users

Introduction

If you have a tablet and do not want to purchase and carry around a Bluetooth keyboard or keyboard dock, and if you also opt not to add a USB or Bluetooth mouse (or can't), you'll have to rely solely on touch to navigate your device. In this chapter you'll learn how to use the various touch techniques for doing so. Beyond getting the most from touch, you can make your tablet easier to use by configuring a login PIN and learning to get more life out of your battery, among other things.

Understand the limitations of Windows RT

Tablet computers come installed with either a full version of Windows 8 like you see on laptop computers or something called Windows RT. You can determine which operating system you have installed from Control Panel, under System and Security, System, as shown here. If you see Windows RT, you'll want to read this section.

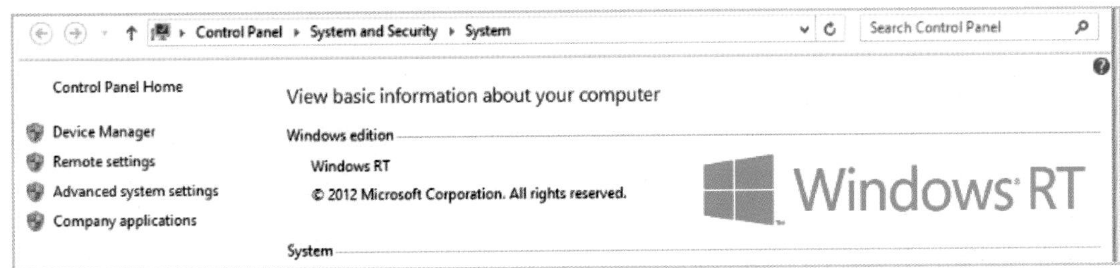

Windows RT differs from the full version of Windows 8 in many ways. To name only a few, Windows RT:

- comes preinstalled with the Microsoft Office 2013 Home and Student suite of applications
- supports touch, offers a long battery life and great performance
- does not include Windows Media Player, but is compatible with many media apps available in the Store, such as Netflix, Xbox Music and so on
- does not support Windows 7 or earlier Desktop applications, or those you install yourself, such as Photoshop, iTunes or Google Chrome.

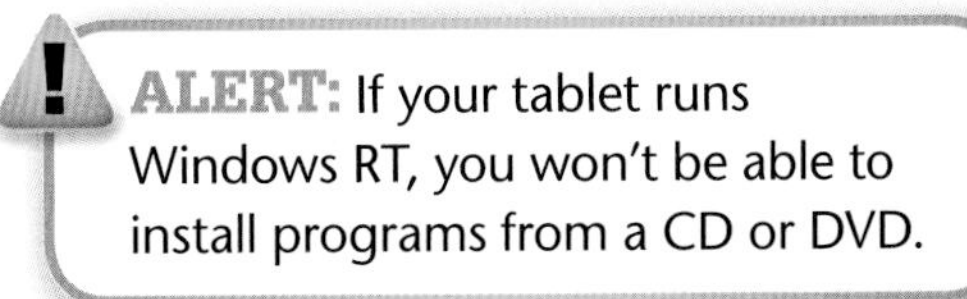

ALERT: If your tablet runs Windows RT, you won't be able to install programs from a CD or DVD.

HOT TIP: Every day, more and more apps become available from the Store. It's highly likely you can find apps there that will replace any you feel you are missing from Windows 7 and onwards.

ALERT: In this chapter, and throughout this book, we assume you are not running Windows RT.

Use tap and double-tap

The two most common touch techniques are tap and double-tap. For the most part, a single tap is like a left mouse click. A double-tap is like a double left mouse click. Here are a few things to try if you would like to experiment with these techniques.

- From the Start screen, tap any tile to open its related app.
- From the Desktop, double-tap the Recycle Bin to open it.
- Use a single tap to type a key on the onscreen keyboard.
- From File Explorer, double-tap to open any folder.
- While in a folder, tap once to select an item. Then tap once on the Home tab to view editing options such as Cut, Copy, Paste, Move and so on. Tap any command once to engage it.

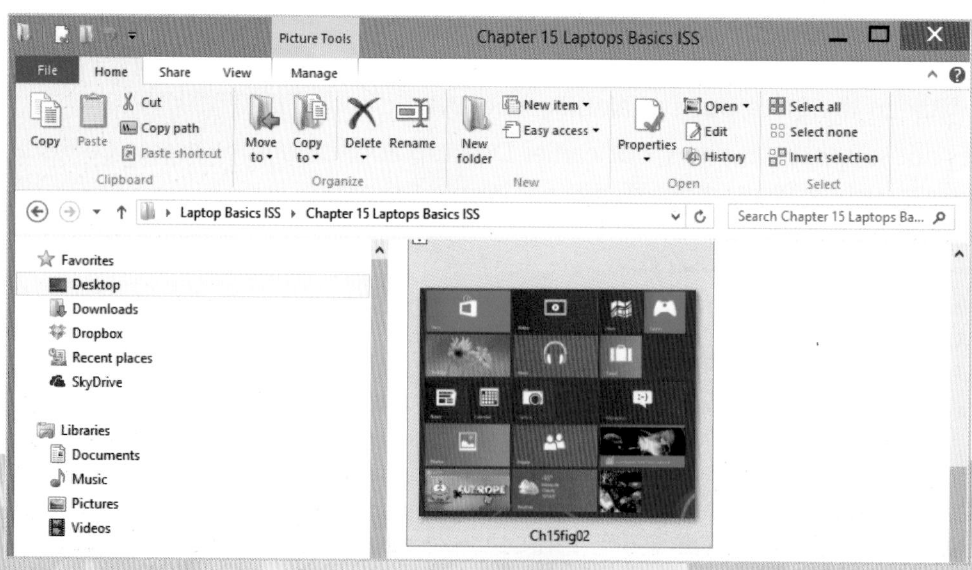

DID YOU KNOW?
When an item is selected, a tick appears beside it.

HOT TIP: Purchase a 'pen' or stylus for your touch device. You can use it instead of your finger to tap the screen.

Use a long tap

A long tap is generally equivalent to a right-click on a traditional mouse. You will use a long tap to view contextual menus or access app toolbars, for the most part.

- Use a long tap on an empty area of the Desktop to access personalisation options, among other things.

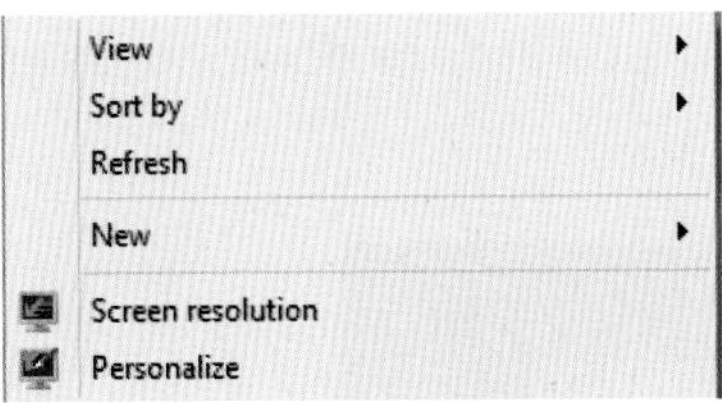

- Use a long tap on a picture to rotate it, among other things.
- Long tap an item on the taskbar to see its related jump list.

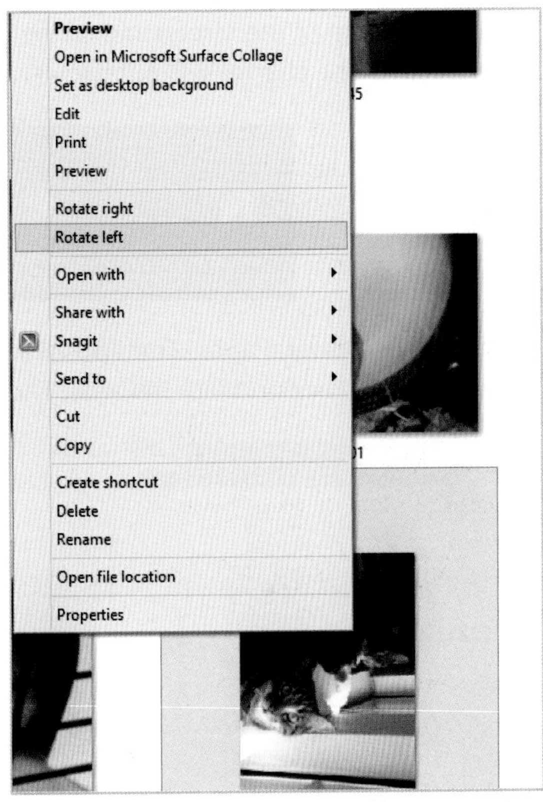

? DID YOU KNOW?

When you successfully perform a long tap, a square or tick generally appears on the screen.

? DID YOU KNOW?

Most of the time after performing a long tap you then perform a single tap to make a choice from the resulting list.

WHAT DOES THIS MEAN?

Jump list: the list that appears when you long tap an icon on the Desktop's taskbar. It generally offers things like a list of recently accessed websites, documents, images, or whatever else you've recently done with that particular application.

Flick, swipe and pinch

There are three more touch techniques to explore: flick, swipe and pinch. Flick and swipe are basically the same movement, but it's best to include both terms here. These techniques were explained in a short tutorial when you first set up your tablet, but you may have forgotten them.

- Open any app. Try Mail, Maps, Calendar, News or others. Position a finger at the top or bottom of the screen and swipe or flick slowly upwards or downwards as applicable. The charms will appear.

- Tap to open several apps. Then position your left thumb in the middle of the far left side of the screen and flick inwards. The last used app will appear.

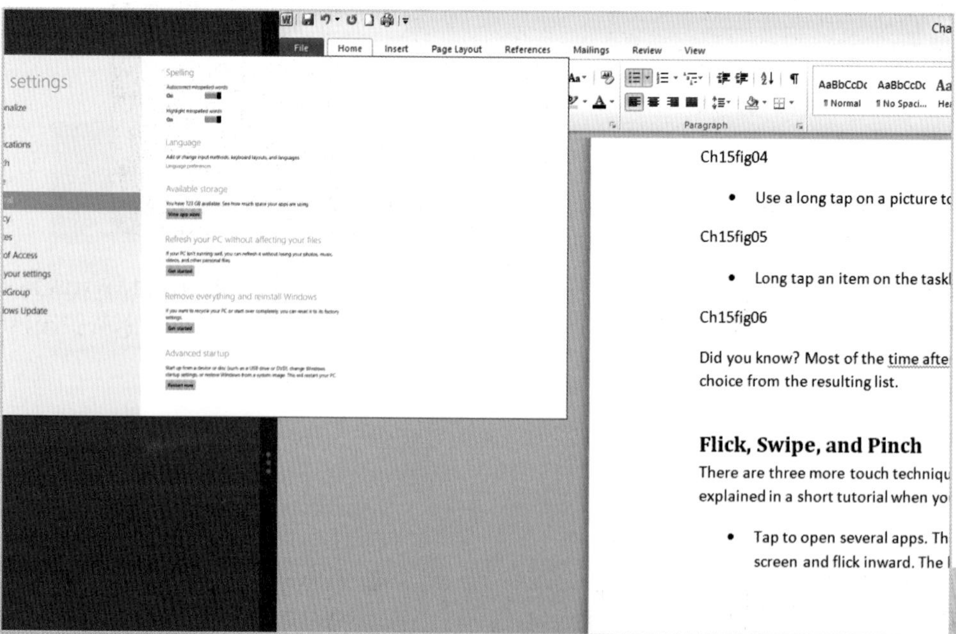

DID YOU KNOW?

You can close an app by dragging (swiping) slowly from the top of the app to the bottom and drag it off the screen.

HOT TIP: Sometimes on webpages that offer a slide show of photos, you can swipe to move from one to the next.

- Position a finger or thumb in the middle of the right side of the screen and flick inwards to access the charms.
- Open Maps and find your current location. Use a pinching motion with your thumb and forefinger, pinch in and out to zoom.
- On the Start screen, pinch inwards to make the tiles very small.

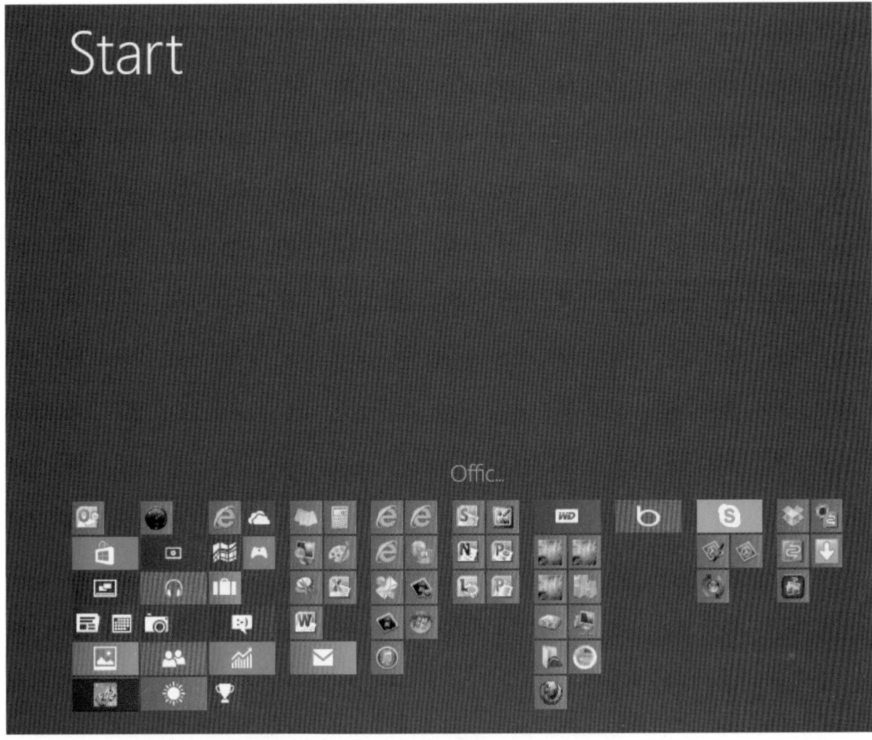

- Some third-party apps allow for rotation of certain elements. To use the rotation option, use two fingers and move them in a circle. Very few apps support this feature at the moment.

HOT TIP: From anywhere, flick inwards from the right side of the screen and tap Start to get to the Start screen.

DID YOU KNOW?

You can zoom in and out on almost anything. Try it on the Start screen. While there, tap and drag downwards on any group of apps. Note the new option that appears to name the group of tiles.

Use tap, hold and drag

You can tap, hold and drag to move a tile to a new location on the Start screen. You can tap, hold and drag downwards to select an item, too. Practise these two techniques now.

1. Access the Start screen.
2. Tap any tile, hold it for a second, drag the tile downwards just a little and then drag it to a new location on the Start screen.
3. Drop it there.

DID YOU KNOW?

You can select multiple items on the Start screen, but when you do, some of the options, such as Larger or Smaller, will disappear.

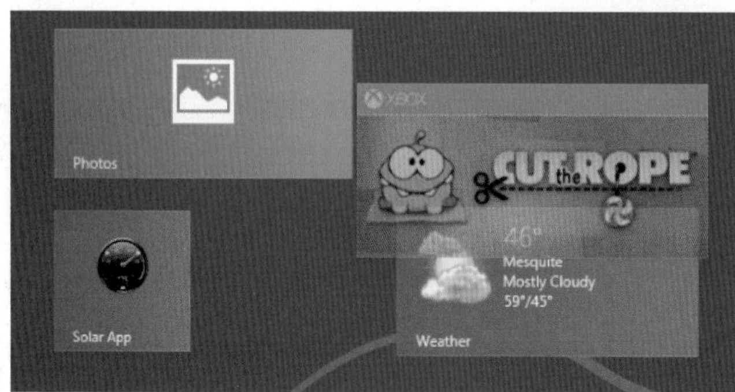

4. Tap any tile, hold it for a second and drag it downwards just a little until a tick appears.
5. Let go. Note the options that appear.
6. Repeat Step 4 to deselect an item. The tick will disappear.

DID YOU KNOW?

If you select multiple tiles on the Start screen, a new option, Clear selection, appears.

HOT TIP: To reposition a window on the Desktop, tap and drag from its title bar.

Type at the Start screen

If you don't have a keyboard, typing at the Start screen after logging in can be a bit trying. Here are a few tips to help you get started.

- Flick inwards, tap Settings, tap Keyboard, then tap Touch keyboard and handwriting panel (the second option). A keyboard will appear on the Start screen.

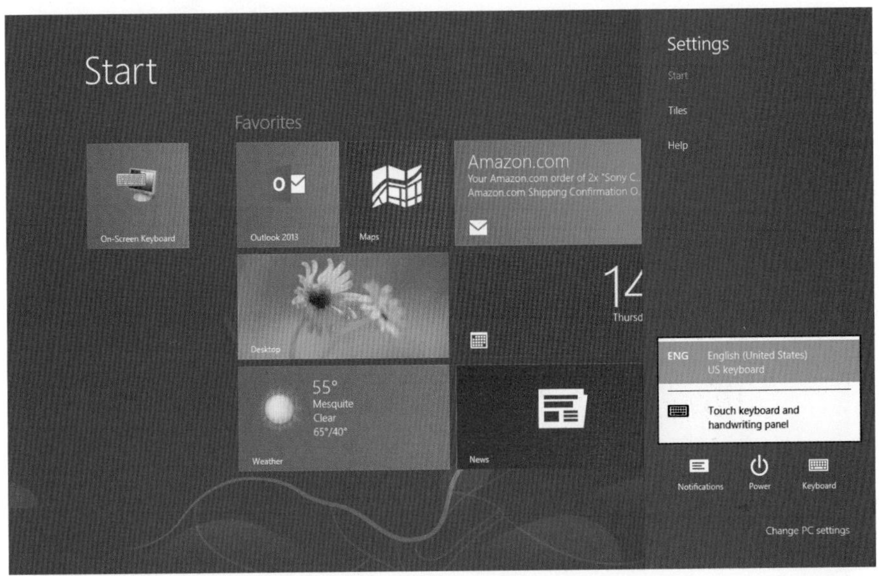

- Access the Search charm and type OSK. From the results, tap On-Screen Keyboard. Tap the Windows key to return to the Start screen.

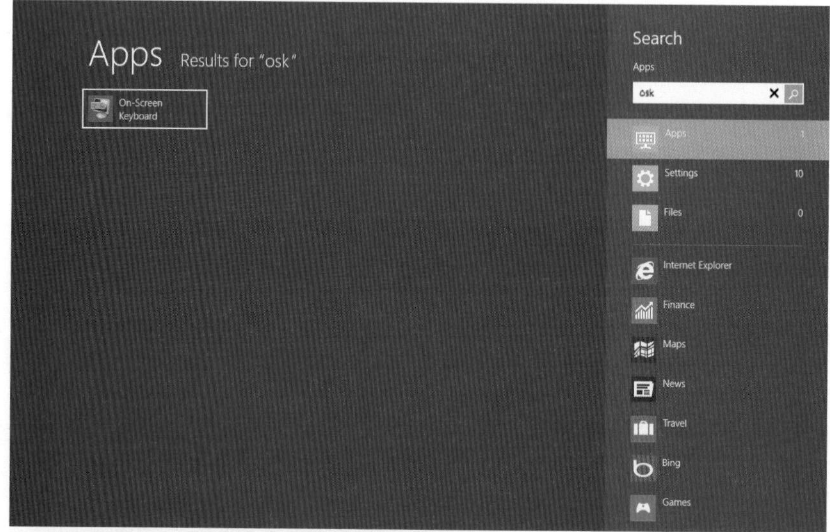

- Right-click, tap All apps, tap On-Screen Keyboard, then tap the Windows key.

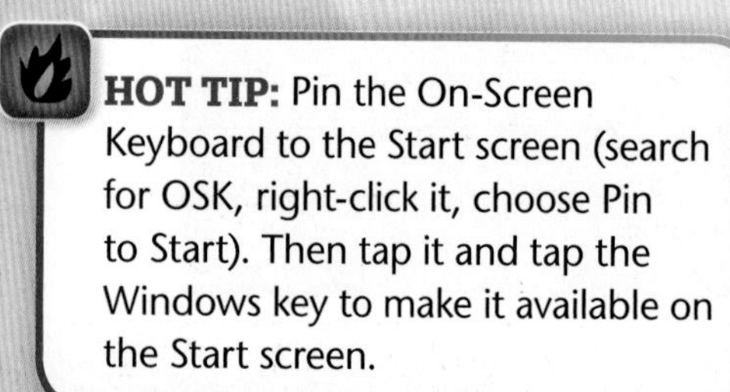

HOT TIP: Pin the On-Screen Keyboard to the Start screen (search for OSK, right-click it, choose Pin to Start). Then tap it and tap the Windows key to make it available on the Start screen.

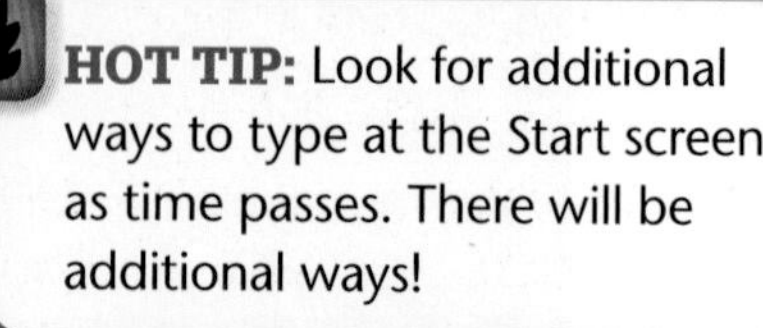

HOT TIP: Look for additional ways to type at the Start screen as time passes. There will be additional ways!

Change Pen and Touch settings

If you don't like the way tap or double-tap works, you can change the settings.

1. From the Start screen, flick in from the right side to access the charms.
2. Tap Settings, Keyboard, then Touch, Keyboard and Handwriting Panel.
3. Type Pen and Touch.
4. Tap Settings and tap Pen and Touch.

5. In the Pen and Touch window, select either Double-tap or Press and hold, and tap Settings.
6. Configure the settings as you choose and tap OK.
7. Tap OK to close the Pen and Touch dialogue box.

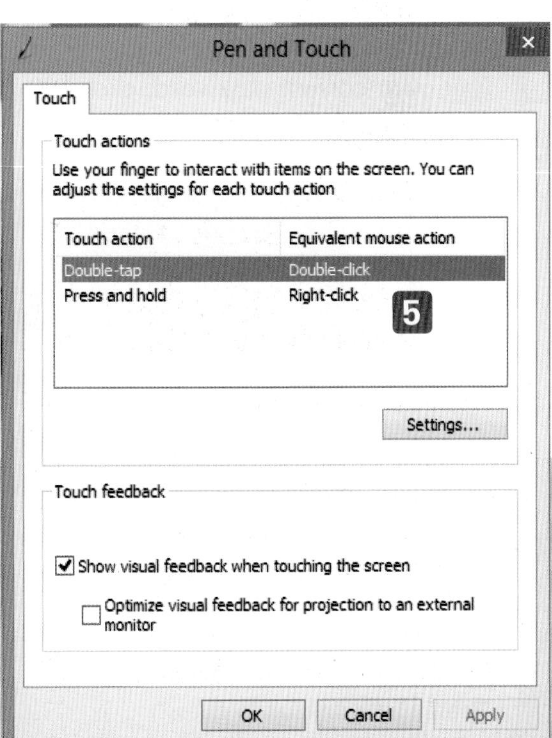

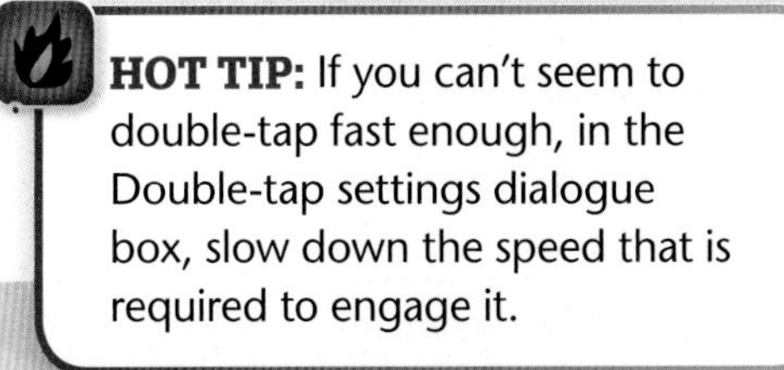

HOT TIP: If you can't seem to double-tap fast enough, in the Double-tap settings dialogue box, slow down the speed that is required to engage it.

HOT TIP: If you don't like the tap and hold feature, you can disable it from the Press and hold settings dialogue box.

Configure a PIN

It's difficult to type a long and complicated password at the Start screen, especially when you're tapping it out. Switch to a PIN for an easier life.

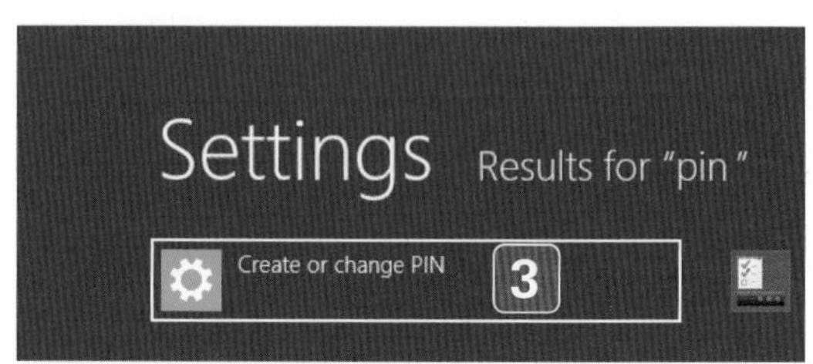

1 At the Start screen, access the charms, tap Search and type PIN.

2 On the right side of the screen, click Settings.

3 Tap Create or change PIN.

4 Tap Create a PIN.

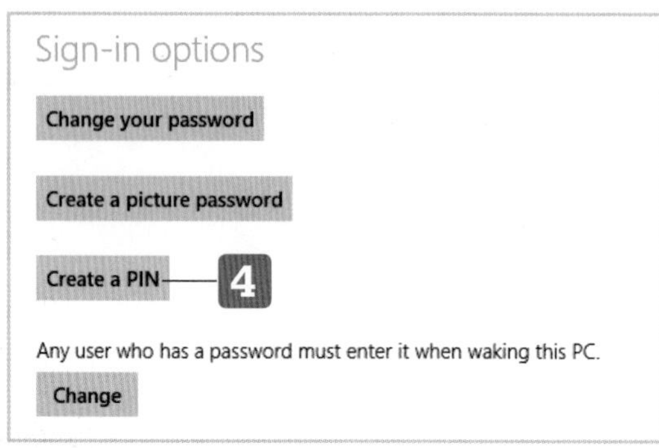

5 Type your current password, click OK, then enter the desired PIN twice.

6 Tap Finish.

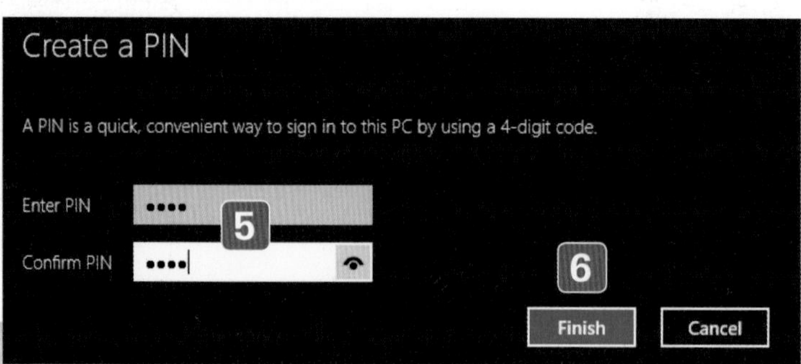

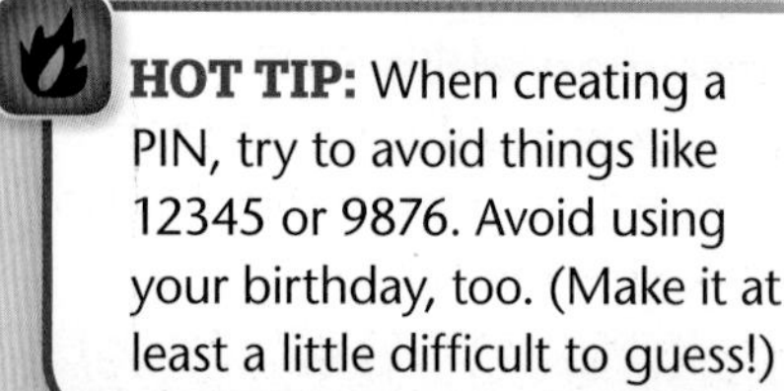

HOT TIP: When creating a PIN, try to avoid things like 12345 or 9876. Avoid using your birthday, too. (Make it at least a little difficult to guess!)

HOT TIP: You create a PIN in PC Settings. You can use this same interface to configure many of the personalisation tasks you'll find in this chapter and others.

Lengthen battery life

There are lots of ways to enhance battery life. You can lower the screen brightness, turn off Bluetooth, and more.

- In the PC Settings hub, tap Wireless. Turn off Bluetooth if you don't need it. (You can also turn off Wi-Fi.)

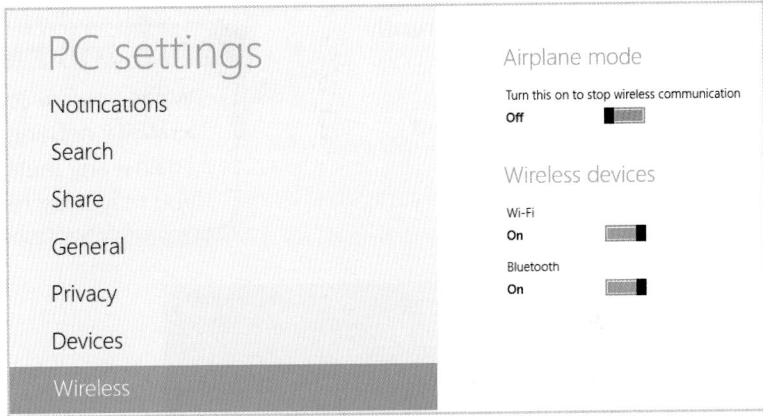

- From the Settings charm, move the slider for Brightness down.
- From the Settings charm, tap Power and tap Sleep to put your tablet to sleep at anytime.

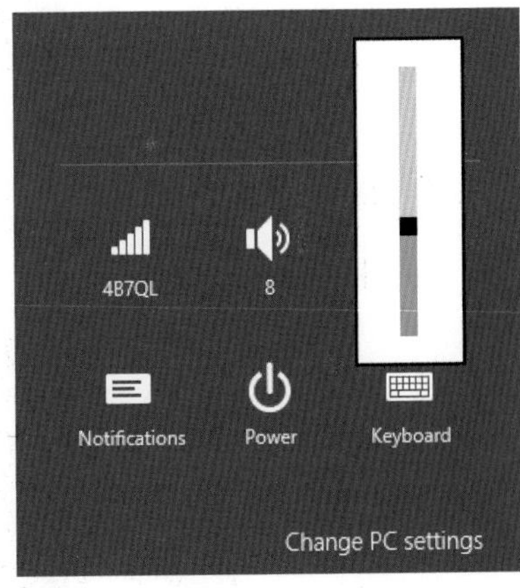

- Visit the manufacturer's website to learn more.

DID YOU KNOW? It is possible to access advanced power settings from the Power Options window. You may be able to enhance battery performance there.

ALERT: Your tablet is always seeking out available Wi-Fi networks. If you know you don't need to be connected, you can disable Wi-Fi to extend your battery life.

Remember Wi-Fi networks

When you connect to a new Wi-Fi network, you are prompted to remember it (or not). It's best to remember all Wi-Fi networks so you'll be automatically connected the next time you are near one.

1. From the Settings charm, tap the Network icon.
2. Select the Wi-Fi network you are currently connected to.
3. If it isn't already selected, tick Connect automatically.
4. Repeat as necessary.

When you are connected to Wi-Fi, nothing is counted against any metered data plan you may subscribe to.

HOT TIP: You want to be connected to Wi-Fi as often as possible, so that you'll have access to the Internet as often as possible.

DID YOU KNOW?

You can also forget a network. To see this option (and others), long tap the network to forget.

Know when you're on Wi-Fi and when on a metered data plan

It's okay to watch movies on Netflix, videos on YouTube, and other large online data when you are connected to a Wi-Fi network. But if you do this while connected to a mobile data network, one with a data limit, you'll use up your weekly or monthly data quota very quickly. It's important to be able to tell quickly what kind of network you're connected to.

1. From the Settings charm, tap the Network icon.
2. Select the network you are currently connected to.
3. If you notice that you are connected to a metered data connection, be careful how much data you use.
4. To make sure you always know when you connect to your mobile data plan or device, deselect Connect automatically.

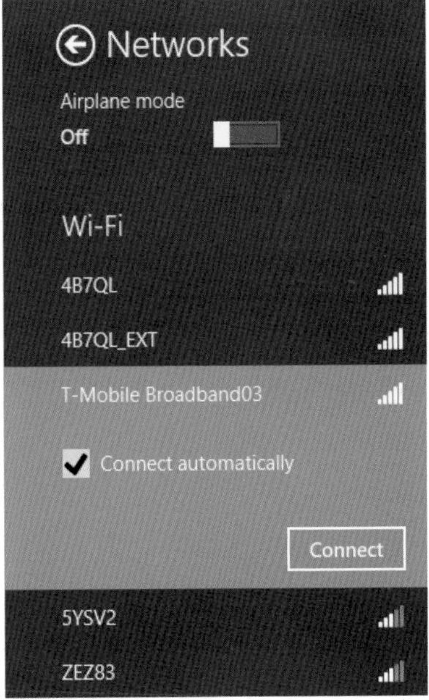

HOT TIP: The only way you'll have always-available Internet is to purchase a mobile data device and/or plan. Read on to learn how.

DID YOU KNOW?

Even if your device isn't supported by default by a mobile data provider, you can purchase an external USB device to connect with (provided your tablet offers this kind of port).

Purchase a mobile data device or plan

You learned in Chapter 5 how to obtain always-available Internet. The gist of that chapter is outlined here.

1. Know what to ask before committing to a plan.
2. Consider a mobile provider.
3. Consider an ISP.
4. Considera satellite provider.
5. Obtain the proper settings.
6. Make the connection.

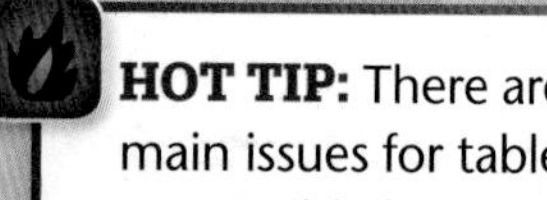

HOT TIP: There are three main issues for tablet users: compatible hardware, coverage areas and cost.

DID YOU KNOW?
If your tablet has a USB port and runs Windows 8, you should be able to obtain always-on Internet service.

Get touch-friendly apps

There are a lot of touch-friendly apps at the App Store. You can find out about an app from its Details page. There are a few really popular touch apps though, and we've listed them here. You can find the most popular apps from the Store by searching. Here we've searched for Top free from the Spotlight category.

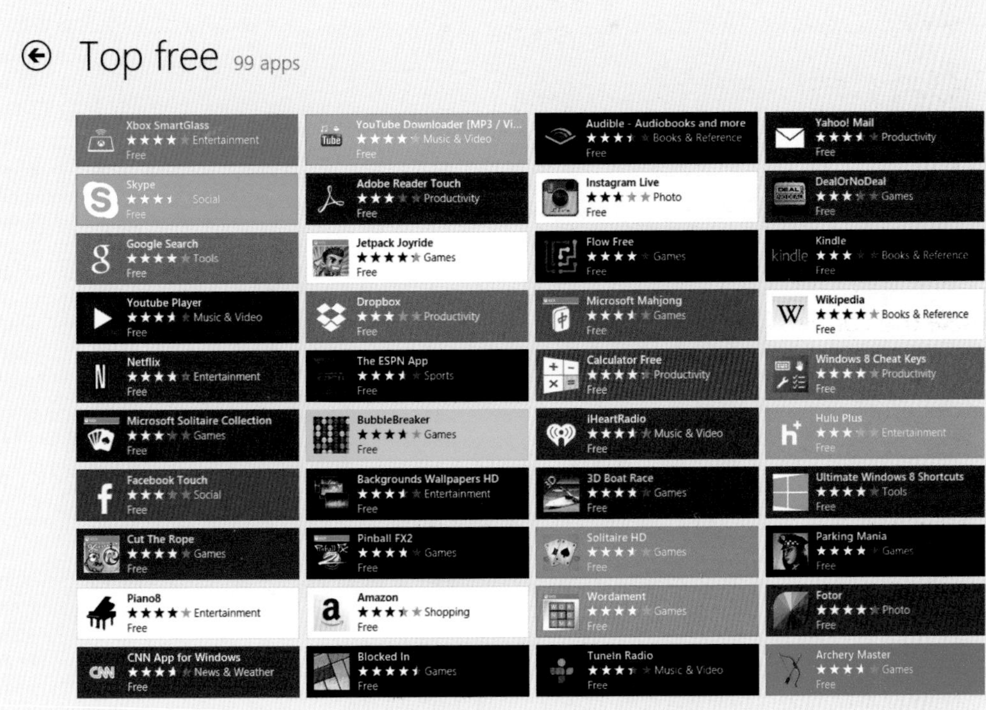

- Skype – for participating in video calls.
- Netflix – for watching Netflix media.
- Microsoft Solitaire collection – for playing variations of Solitaire.
- Adobe Reader Touch – for working with Adobe documents.
- Kindle – for reading Kindle books.

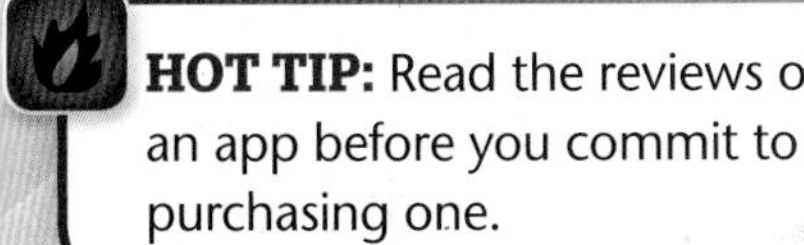

HOT TIP: Read the reviews of an app before you commit to purchasing one.

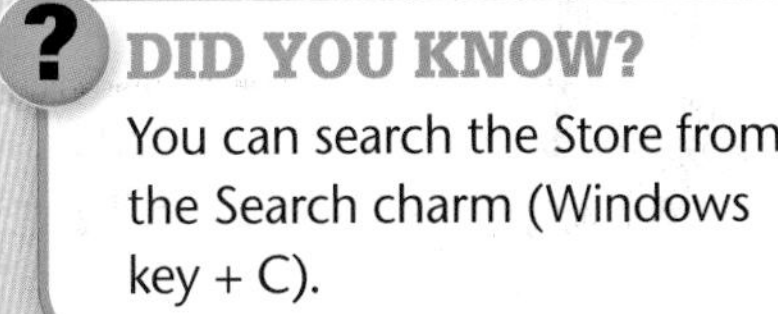

DID YOU KNOW?

You can search the Store from the Search charm (Windows key + C).

Top 10 Laptop & Tablet Problems Solved

Problem 1: I don't understand the difference between an app and a Desktop app

There are two kinds of apps available on your laptop or tablet. One is called a Start screen app, the other a Desktop app.

- Start Screen app – a simple program that enables you to do something quickly and easily, such as check email, send a message, check the weather or surf the Internet. *Apps*, as they are known, offer less functionality than fully fledged programs (*Desktop apps*) and are more like what you'd see on a smartphone than a traditional computer. Here is the Internet Explorer app.

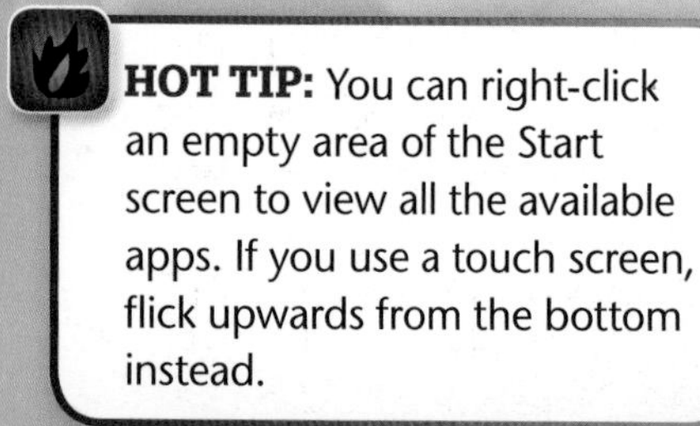

HOT TIP: You can right-click an empty area of the Start screen to view all the available apps. If you use a touch screen, flick upwards from the bottom instead.

- Desktop app – this type of app represents the traditional programs you may already be familiar with. Desktop apps are complete programs like Paint, Notepad, Windows Media Player, Internet Explorer, and similar third-party programs such as Adobe Reader. They open on the *Desktop*. Here is the Internet Explorer Desktop app.

DID YOU KNOW?

Some applications have two versions. As you can see here, there is an Internet Explorer *app* that is available from the Start screen, and an Internet Explorer *Desktop app* available from the Desktop.

Problem 2: My Start screen is cluttered with tiles for apps I'll never use

As you become more familiar with apps, you may find you use some quite often and others rarely, if ever. It's easy to move the tiles for the apps you use often to the left side of the Start screen for easier access and move others further away (or remove them completely).

1. At the Start screen, click and hold a tile to move.
2. Drag the tile to a new area of the screen and drop it there.
3. Repeat as desired.
4. To remove a tile from the Start screen:
   a. Right-click the tile. (Touch users tap, hold and drag a little downwards.)
   b. Click Unpin from Start.

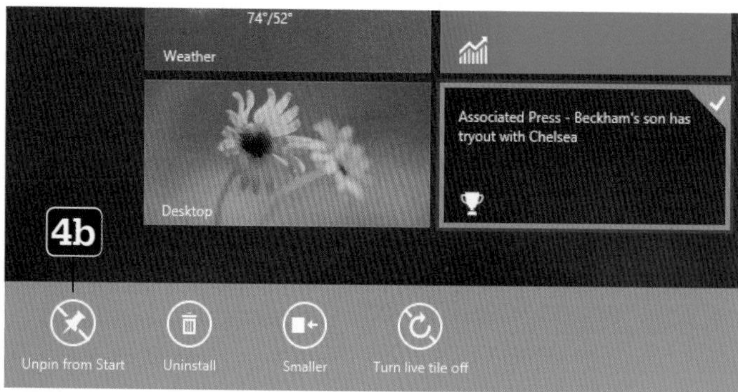

HOT TIP: If you have a touch device, you'll have to touch, hold and drag a little downwards to start to move the tile, then continue dragging until you have it at its new location. Remove your finger to drop it there.

HOT TIP: If you decide you want to put an app tile back on the Start screen after removing it, right-click the Start screen, click All apps, right-click the app to add and click Pin to Start.

Problem 3: The tiles on the Start screen keep flipping information. Can I turn this off?

Many of the tiles on the Start screen become 'live' after you use them. That means they show up-to-date information on the Start screen and that information flips. Here Weather, Sports and Finance are live. If this bothers you, you can disable the live feature.

1. Note the tiles that are currently live. (Three of the four tiles shown here are live.)

2. Right-click the live tile you want to turn off.
3. Click Turn live tile off.
4. Repeat these steps but click Turn live tile on to undo this.

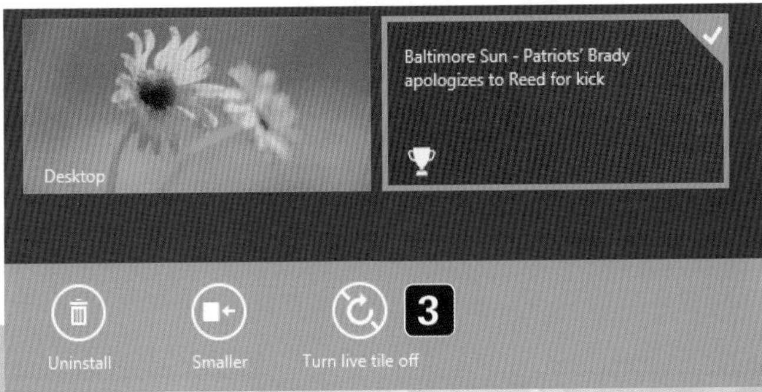

? DID YOU KNOW?
Not all tiles are live. Maps is not a live tile, for instance.

HOT TIP: To select a tile with touch only, tap, hold and drag downwards a little. You'll know a tile has been selected when a tick appears on it.

Problem 4: I can't get on the Internet when I'm not connected to a Wi-Fi network

In order to have always-available Internet you need to find a provider that offers it. Mobile providers are quite popular, but they all offer differing plans. Make sure you ask some important questions. You can use the answers to compare the various mobile plans you are considering.

- Do I have to sign a contract for a year or two years or do you have a pay-as-you-go plan?
- Is there a limit on how much data I can use each month? Is there a limit on how many hours I can be online? How much does it cost if I go over that limit?
- How much is the service per month? How much will taxes and fees add to that?
- Are there any set-up costs or activation fees?
- Am I required to purchase additional hardware? If so, what does it cost? Is it compatible with my device?

- Is there a 30-day return policy or grace period, in case the connection is not as good or as strong as I had hoped?

HOT TIP: Try to stay away from one- and two-year contracts; you may decide later you don't really need the service or you might find something cheaper.

ALERT: Whatever service you choose, make sure you know you'll be alerted via email when you are nearing your data limit.

Problem 5: I can't find anything. How do I find something, like a file?

After you create data, you save it to your hard drive. When you're ready to use the data again, you have to locate it and open it. There are several ways to locate a saved file. If you know the document is in the My Documents folder, you can open File Explorer and click Documents. Then you can double-click the file to open it. However, if you aren't sure where the file is, you can search for it from the Start screen.

1. Click the Windows key on the keyboard to return to the Start screen.
2. Start typing the name of the file or a unique word in the file.
3. Click Files in the Search pane.
4. Click the desired result.

? DID YOU KNOW?

You can search for a word in a file, such as a word in a document or presentation slide. You don't have to search using a word in the file name. The word will need to be unique though, so that the results don't offer too many files to browse through.

Problem 6: There is an application I use often, but there isn't a tile for it on the Start screen

There are more windows, apps, programs and applications available than those that appear on the Start screen by default. There's the Calculator, for instance, and Windows Media Player, Control Panel, Windows Explorer and Notepad, to name a few. You can add any item to the Start screen to have easier access to it.

1. Right-click an empty area of the Start screen. On a touch screen, flick upwards from the bottom of the screen.
2. Click All apps.
3. Right-click (or tap, hold and drag downwards) an item you'd like to add.
4. From the bar that appears at the bottom of the page, click Pin to Start.

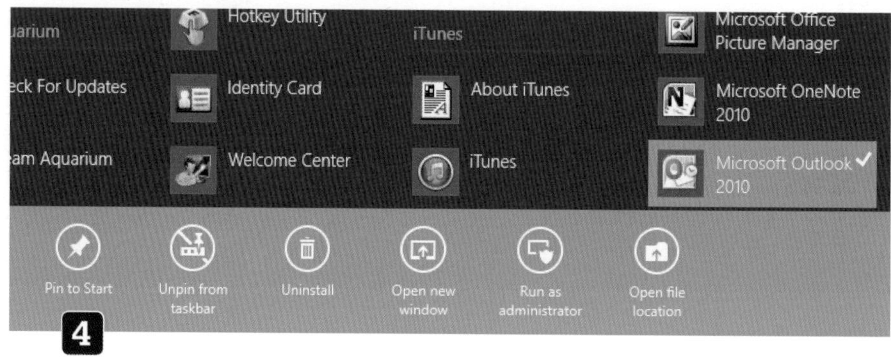

5. Return to the Start screen and locate the new tile. It will be placed on the far right. You may want to drag it left to reposition it.

DID YOU KNOW?
You can open an app from the All apps screen by clicking it once.

HOT TIP: Add tiles for apps, applications, system tools, windows and other items that you know you'll use often. You may want to add Control Panel if you're familiar with that feature, for instance.

Problem 7: I want to create a music CD but there isn't an option in the Music app

The Music app doesn't offer any options for working with music, for that you need to use Windows Media Player. You can copy the music to a portable device (music player, tablet or phone) or you can create your own CDs, choosing the songs to copy and placing them on the CD in the desired order. It's important to note that Windows RT doesn't include Windows Media Player.

1. Open Media Player.
2. Insert a blank CD and click the Burn tab.
3. Click any song or album to add and drag it to the List pane, shown here. You can drag any song to move it to a new position in the Burn list.
4. When you've added the songs you want, click Start burn.

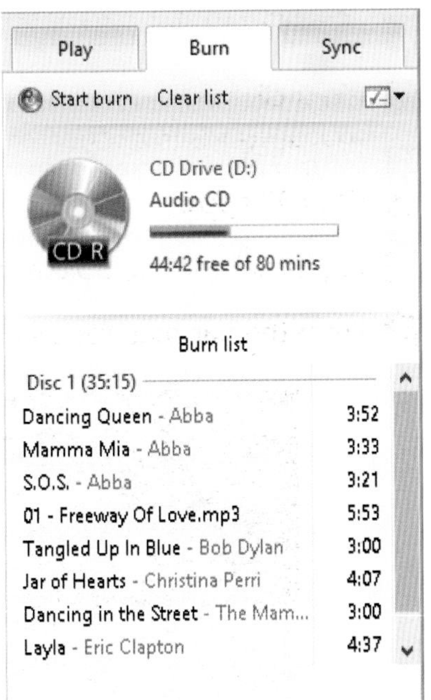

DID YOU KNOW?
Look at the slider in the List pane to see how much room is left on the CD. A typical CD can hold about 80 minutes of music.

HOT TIP: Click the arrow beside Organize and click Options to change the settings configured by default, including whether or not to use 'volume levelling' when burning CDs or if you want to burn the CD without any gaps between tracks.

WHAT DOES THIS MEAN?
Burn: a term used to describe the process of copying music from a computer to a CD.

Problem 8: How do I back up my files?

File History saves copies of your files regularly so you can get them back if they're lost or damaged. While most of the security features in Windows 8 are enabled by default (such as the Firewall and Windows Defender), File History is not: you must manually enable it. You'll need an external drive for File History for it to be effective so it's best to run backups when you have your laptop at home or at work.

1. Connect an external drive or make sure a network drive is available.
2. From the Start screen, type File History.
3. Click Settings, then click File History.
4. In the File History window, click Turn on.
5. Wait while File History copies your files for the first time.

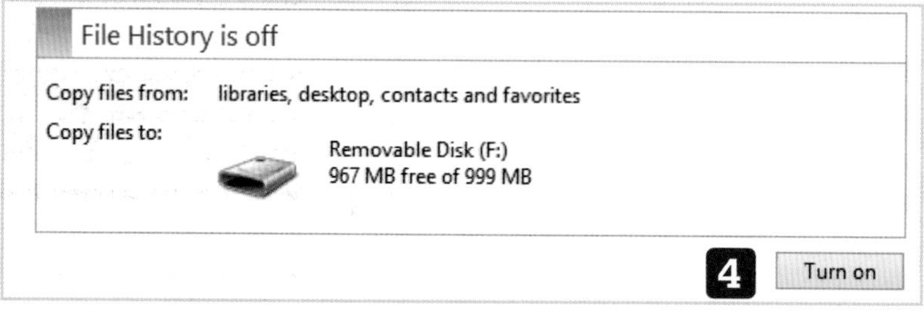

HOT TIP: Click Advanced Settings to change how often File History makes copies of files once the initial backup is created. Every hour is the default.

ALERT: If you ever need to restore files using File History, open the File History window and click Restore personal files.

Problem 9: I installed something from the Internet and now my laptop isn't working as it should

System Restore regularly creates and saves restore points that contain information about your laptop that Windows uses to work properly. If your laptop starts acting up, you can use System Restore to restore it to a time when the laptop was working properly. Before you start, connect your laptop to an electrical outlet.

1. At the Start screen, type System Restore.
2. Click Settings, then click Create a restore point.
3. Click System Restore.
4. Click Next to accept and apply the recommended restore point.
5. Click Finish.
6. Wait patiently while the process completes.

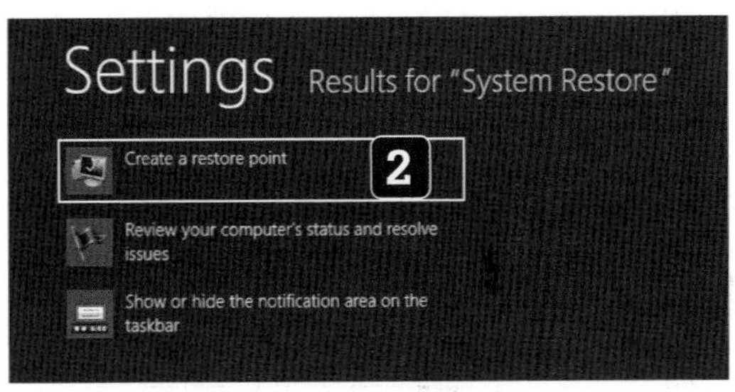

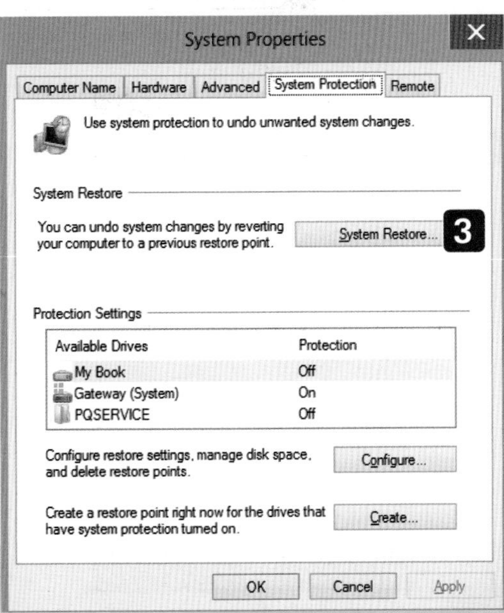

DID YOU KNOW?

System Restore works only with its own system files, so running System Restore will not affect any of your personal data. Your pictures, email, documents, music, etc. will not be deleted or changed.

ALERT: If running System Restore on a laptop or tablet, make sure it's plugged in. System Restore should never be interrupted.

WHAT DOES THIS MEAN?

Restore point: a snapshot of a computer's previous state that can be applied in place of the current state, to make an unstable computer stable again.

Problem 10: I can't tell when I'm connected to Wi-Fi and when I'm using my metered data plan

It's okay to watch movies on Netflix, videos on YouTube and other large online data when you are connected to a Wi-Fi network. But if you do this while connected to a mobile data network, one with a data limit, you'll use up your weekly or monthly data quota very quickly. It's important to be able to tell quickly what kind of network you're connected to.

1. From the Settings charm, tap the Network icon.
2. Select the network you are currently connected to.
3. If you notice that you are connected to a metered data connection, be careful how much data you use.
4. To make sure you always know when you connect to your mobile data plan or device, deselect Connect automatically.

HOT TIP: The only way you'll have always-available Internet is to purchase a mobile data device and/or plan.

? DID YOU KNOW?

Even if your device isn't supported by default by a mobile data provider, you can purchase an external USB device to connect with (provided your tablet offers this kind of port).